THE CULT OF THE

Was There A Bang?

EEK & MEEK® by Howie Schneider

*Albert Einstein's admission of error
may have been his greatest error.*

THE CULT OF THE

Was There A Bang?

William C. Mitchell

COSMIC SENSE BOOKS

Post Office Box 3472

Carson City, Nevada 89702

U. S. A.

To Holly

The Cult of the BIG BANG
Was There A Bang?

© Copyright, 1995 by William C. Mitchell. All Rights Reserved.

SECOND PRINTING

C O S M I C   S E N S E   B O O K S
Post Office Box 3472, Carson City, Nevada 89702, U. S. A.

Library of Congress Catalog Card Number: 94-78655

ISBN: 0-9643188-0-6

Book Design & Prepress
WHITE SAGE STUDIOS, VIRGINIA CITY, NEVADA

Printed by BOOKCRAFTERS, Chelsea, Michigan

— PRINTED   IN   THE   UNITED   STATES   OF   AMERICA —

Contents

Figures

Preface

Big Bang cosmology is so thoroughly entrenched that it is accepted as virtual truth throughout the scientific community and, as a result, throughout the general populace. Until a couple of years ago, despite some nagging concerns, I had also accepted the prevailing Big Bang Theory. If it was acceptable to the great minds of the cosmological world, it certainly must have a lot going for it.

But as my interest in the subject grew, and my retirement provided time for more study, problems multiplied and doubts increased. Cosmology articles and books would mention a problem here and there, but almost invariably they would be dismissed as of little consequence; insignificant aberrations to be cleared up after a little more effort was expended in support of the prevailing view.

Once aware of this pattern, it became clear that enormous effort had been spent, and continues to be spent, in support of the Big Bang. Obviously that is not the method of impartial research that is the hallmark of pure science. How could good and talented men in search of truth participate in these endeavors? Other forces must be at work to corrupt the process.

As will be discussed in the text, the answer to that question is not the intentional sins of individuals, but merely the way the system works, resulting in what I have facetiously called *The Cult of the Big Bang*.

Eventually it became apparent that, if all the problems of Big Bang Theory (including some newly discovered ones) were to be gathered together, they would provide overwhelming evidence against it. Despite the handicap of minimal literary skill, I decided to compile that evidence and present it here.

I also decided that it would be appropriate to propose an alternate theory that might have fewer faults. As I had struggled with a growing list of concerns about Big Bang Theory, some ideas for what I believe to be a simpler, less troubled cosmology came together. I decided to present those ideas as one possible alternative to the Big Bang.

Although I hope not, the quantity of evidence presented here against Big Bang Theory may seem excessive. However, Big Bang cosmologists are marvelously ingenious fellows. History has repeatedly demonstrated their ability to circumvent problems. Each time new evidence against the Big Bang has been presented in the past, it has been vigorously combatted by newly invented ideas. Because one might expect even greater efforts to counter a compilation of such evidence, perhaps some overkill is appropriate.

Although much of this work is devoted to debunking Big Bang Theory (and I will therefore undoubtedly be dismissed by many as just another heretical Big Bang basher) the intent is not malicious. It is presented in the hope that, by filling the need for a comprehensive compilation of the deficiencies of that theory and the presentation of some alternative ideas, I might make a positive contribution to the field of cosmology. Certainly no disrespect is intended for the great minds that have pioneered that field.

W.C.M.

Introduction

B ig Bang cosmological theory seems to be the natural outcome of Albert Einstein's General Theory of Relativity and
the later discovery of the expansion of the universe. In hindsight,
the idea of tracing back the rate of expansion of the universe
in accordance with solutions to Einstein's gravitational field
equations to a time of zero size, infinite density and infinite temperature seems inevitable.

This concept has immense appeal. Stories of the origin of the
universe abound in the various religions of the world, but none
of those are acceptable as literal truth to the modern scientific
mind. To those minds the Big Bang filled a void by providing a
reasonably credible evolution of the universe and at least a stop-
gap concept of its origin. Man's intense desire for knowledge of
the origin of his world and of himself, as evidenced by the myths
of all the tribes of the world, seems to have been at least partially
and tentatively answered. Big Bang Theory has been well received by the more liberal minded of the Judeo-Christian
community who have found it to be an acceptable interpretation
of the Bible's story of creation.

Following the discovery in the 1960s of microwave background radiation, that had been predicted earlier by BB theory,
it has been acclaimed as virtual positive proof, not only of the

Big Bang itself, but of the smoothness of the Big Bang that had been predicted as well.

In accordance with Einstein's work, and that of mathematicians who followed him, the concept of curved space was incorporated into Big Bang Theory. In keeping with that concept is the idea that the universe isn't expanding; space itself is expanding. Thus the site of the Big Bang cannot be found. It didn't occur at a particular location in the universe; it happened all over. These ideas have become important ingredients of Big Bang Theory.

As a result of the work of mathematicians who solved Einstein's equations, followers of Big Bang Theory came to believe that there are three possible cases of curvature; positive, negative and flat. Positive curvature exists if the average amount of matter distributed throughout space is greater than a critical amount, resulting in the slowing of the expansion of the universe, followed by its collapse (a closed universe); negative curvature of space exists if the average amount of matter is less than that critical amount, resulting in an ever expanding universe (an open universe); and uncurved space exists if the average amount of matter is at the borderline critical level, resulting in a gradual slowing of expansion (a flat universe).

As time progressed, questions regarding details of Big Bang Theory have arisen. Through the years many modifications to that theory have been proposed, and some have been incorporated. Most innovative among these is the relatively new idea of inflation; an enormously rapid expansion of the minutely tiny universe before the start of the traditional hot Big Bang that has gained acceptance over the past dozen years. Quantum theory, which had been developed and become accepted years after the original Big Bang Theory, was put to work by theorists to solve some Big Bang problems.

But none of those schemes have provided satisfactory solutions to the basic problems of Big Bang Theory and, despite the simplicity claimed for them, they have only served to complicate it and introduce additional problems. Major problems, such as the source of energy and matter for the Big Bang, and the smoothness of the explosion remain.

In the earlier years of Big Bang Theory a group of scientists who couldn't accept its flaws developed an alternate theory. That theory was the almost totally discredited Steady State Theory in which the configuration of the universe has remained essentially the same for unknown eons. In that theory new matter is continuously generated in space, thus providing new material for the evolution of new stars and galaxies as old ones die, and keeping the density of the universe constant throughout the ages. But that concept, due to flaws that were perceived as greater than those of the Big Bang, has lost all but very few adherents.

(Two of the basic problems that caused the rejection of the old Steady State Theory are its lack of an acceptable rationale for the generation of new matter in space and for a source of pressure for the expansion of the universe. Ironically these are also two of the major problems of the Big Bang, but on a grand scale for that event.)

Following the next three chapters of this book, that provide some background on relativity, particle physics and quantum theory, two chapters on Big Bang Theory are presented, then more background and a chapter on inflation are presented. In those chapters, and in several that follow them, many problems and inconsistencies of Big Bang Theory that have been glossed over for decades are discussed. All of those flaws, plus some new ones, are for the first time reviewed in a single document. It is hoped that the preponderance of evidence against it will open some minds regarding the validity of Big Bang Theory.

(Some relatively simple mathematics is utilized in these discussions. If the reader doesn't care to become involved in that, it can be skimmed over without much loss. It is important only that he or she follow the logic of the text.)

Following those chapters, so as not to tear down a popular theory without presenting some ideas to replace it, alternate theories are mentioned, and one of those is rather strongly suggested as a replacement for the Big Bang. Hopefully that alternative will be of some interest to the reader.

In this presentation the words smoothness or uniformity (of the universe) will usually be used in place of several other terms commonly, and somewhat redundantly, used by Big Bang cosmologists to convey a similar concept. The terms referred to are: isotropy, homogeneity, Copernican Principle and Cosmological Principal.

Isotropy is defined as indicating the universe to be the same in all directions, but not necessarily the same everywhere. Homogeneity is defined as indicating the universe to be the same everywhere, but not necessarily the same in all directions. The

Copernican Principle states that we occupy no special place in that universe, and the Cosmological Principle states, in addition, that is true for any other observers there might be elsewhere in the universe. (If the universe is isotropic everywhere it is also homogeneous.) For the sake of simplicity the words smoothness or uniformity will be used to represent these general meanings, and the words non-uniformity or irregularity will be used to represent the opposite.

For the purpose of economy, this presentation will usually use the letters BB to mean Big Bang, BBT to mean BB Theory, SS to mean Steady State, and SST to mean SS Theory. This usage might result in considerable savings in typing effort, time, ink and paper, with little loss in clarity. Also, MYRs is sometimes used for millions of years, BYRs for billions of years, MLYs for millions of light years, and BLYs for billions of light years. (One light year is about 5.88 trillion miles.)

The term "classical physics" herein is intended to mean classical physics as understood by Einstein; that is, as it was understood before his invention of relativity.

As we will see in Chapter 15, there has been considerable fraternization between physicists, mathematicians and astronomers on the subject of cosmology. Like one big happy family, the great majority of them agree with each other on all but a few minor points. Virtually every scientific and media article on the subject is presented with the assumption that the BB is all but a proven fact. Almost without exception the basic tenets of BBT are repeated: the exploding universe, its Hubble expansion, its smoothness, and proof of these by microwave background radiation. To a non-believer all of this could present the appearance of a BB cult.

Of course there really isn't a cult. However, as judged by outward appearances, BBT has all the earmarks of one. Except for a few heretics who have been excommunicated, those of the BB persuasion rarely deviate from its dogma. It appears to the outsider that the basic tenets of BBT are as sacred as divine revelation; to question them is not only irreverent, it borders on blasphemy.

So for all practical purposes there might as well be a cult. If it looks, sounds and feels like a cult, perhaps it can be thought of as a cult. So I have called this book *The Cult of the Big Bang*.

O N E

About
Relativity

The casual reader may find the background material of
Chapters 1 through 3 somewhat tedious. To avoid discour-
agement at the outset, it is suggested that those readers scan
these chapters only as thoroughly as necessary to obtain a gen-
eral familiarization with the topics presented.

Because much of cosmology in general, and BBT in particular, are based on the theories of relativity, some background
leading up to their development and a brief discussion of them
are presented here. Some implications of and fallacies regarding
relativity are also presented.

In 1851 French physicist Armand Hippolyte Fizeau, who had
devoted a good portion of his career to techniques for measuring the speed of light, conducted an experiment to determine
how the velocity of light is effected by the motion of the medium
in which it travels. By the use of full and half silvered mirrors, a
combination of tubes containing water flowing in opposite directions, a single source of monochromatic light, and the means
of observing interference patterns, he found that the difference
in light velocity was less than that which would be expected due
to the direct effect of the flow rate of the water. But he did observe a measurable effect that he attributed to the ether, a
hypothetical stationary "luminiferous medium" that was believed to fill the space of the universe and partially "drag" along
with the Earth's motion.

Fizeau developed an empirical expression for his experimental
results that the velocity of light in a moving fluid was $v=c/n$ plus
or minus $v(1- 1/n^2)$, where v is the velocity of the fluid, c the

velocity of light in vacuum, and n the index of refraction of water. This factor was later found to be significant.

In 1881 a sophisticated mechanism was used to measure the effect of the ether's relative velocity on the speed of light. To the amazement of all of science, the effect was found to be zero. Measurements were repeated many times in many ways and the results were always nil.

That experiment, which was developed and conducted by American physicists Albert A. Michelson and Edward W. Morley, was designed to compare the effect of the speed of the ether on the speed of light traveling with and traveling across the direction of the ether. In order to eliminate the possibility of systematic error the entire device could be rotated through 360 degrees.

It is of interest to note that the correction factor for light traveling to and fro in the direction of the ether would be $1/(1-v^2/c^2)$ and the correction factor for light traveling to and fro across the ether would be the square root of that amount. (Travel across would take longer.) The difference between these factors would provide for the determination of the effect of the velocity of the ether. This was done by observation of light interference patterns in a manner similar to the Fizeau experiment.

The expected results were flawlessly derived on the basis of the known velocity of light and the expected velocity of the ether, which was thought to be as much as the velocity of the Earth through space. But the effects of the ether were convincingly absent. No difference in the time of travel of light was found for any orientation of the apparatus. Ultimately, all concerned were forced to abandon the concept of the ether of space.

The implications of this discovery were profound. There was now no medium in which electromagnetic fields propagated and, even worse, there were no reference coordinates for the solar system, the galaxy or the universe. Physicists, previously convinced of and satisfied with the presence of ether as a medium for electromagnetism and as a static spatial reference, could make no sense of this.

As a possible solution to the mystery of the missing ether, British/Irish physicist George F. Fitzgerald suggested what is known as the Fitzgerald contraction. He proposed that matter moving through the ether shrinks by a factor of the square root of

$(1-v^2/c^2)$ in the direction of motion of the ether. This amount of physical shrinkage in the Michelson-Morley device in the direction of the ether would correct for its apparent absence. Although this rationalization proved to be incorrect, this shrinkage factor was also later found to be significant.

In 1895 Dutch physicist H. A. Lorentz, working on the solution to the mystery of the missing ether (independently of Fitzgerald) also proposed that the length of matter in the direction of its travel would be shortened by a factor of the square root of $(1-v^2/c^2)$ and he added that time would be slowed by a factor of the reciprocal of that expression. These conclusions resulted from his development of a set of empirically derived equations known as the Lorentz transformations, which were the result of the premise of a stationary ether and Newtonian physics. Unfortunately he ascribed no special physical significance to them, and merely considered them to be aids to calculations.

Albert Einstein published his work on the Special Theory of Relativity in 1905. (He was only 26 years old!). His results regarding length and time were the same as those of Lorentz. But his mathematics were based on the postulates that (1) the motion of a body traveling at uniform velocity cannot be detected by observation on that body (only motion relative to it can be detected), and (2) that light is propagated in empty space with a definite velocity c that is independent of the motion of the emitting body. In other words, except for the speed of light, all motion is relative. Neither the concept of ether nor an absolute space reference are necessary.

Based on those postulates he was able to provide mathematical derivations for the Lorentz transformations. Those equations, previously thought to have no real physical significance, now became extremely important. To the factors given by Lorentz, that is, time slows and length shortens, he added that mass increases as the speed of light is approached. He was later (in 1907) able to determine that energy is equal to mass times c squared, or $E=mc^2$.

Relative to the time of a stationary body, the time of a moving body appears to slow by a factor of one divided the square root of $(1-v^2/c^2)$, where v is the relative speed of the moving body and c is the speed of light, which equals 300,000 kilometers per second. (This phenomenon is known as "time dilation.") The length of a moving body appears to shrink (in the direction of its motion) by a factor of the square root of $(1-v^2/c^2)$; and the mass of a moving body appears to increase by a factor of one divided by the square root of $(1-v^2/c^2)$. In these equations c is the velocity of light in a vacuum. Its speed in any other material differs from c.

As an example of these of these effects, as an object reaches a velocity of 80 percent of the speed of light $(1-v^2/c^2 = 0.6)$, to a stationary observer its time would appear to slow by a factor of 1-2/3, its length would appear to shrink by a factor of 0.6, and its mass would appear to increase by a factor of 1-2/3.

It is important to note that, because there is no frame of spatial reference, the situations described are mutual. To a second observer, in what was referred to as the moving body (moving relative to the first observer), the time of the first observer slows by the same factor. This mutuality applies to all three expressions; those for time, length and mass.

At the low velocities normally encountered in our daily lives these equations of Special Relativity need not be considered. But when dealing with "relativistic" speeds such as those of distant galaxies, particle accelerators, or of future interplanetary rockets, for example, these effects become important.

It should also be noted that, for velocities greater than the speed of light (v greater than c), the square root of $(1-v^2/c^2)$ would equal some number multiplied by the square root of minus 1. The appearance of this "imaginary" number should make one uneasy about speeds greater than that of light, which in a subsequent paragraph are shown to be impossible.

In his explanation of Special Relativity Einstein provided an example of a large rotating disk in deep space (no gravitational field). By use of a measuring rod it will be found that, because of tangential velocity at the edge of the disk, the measuring rod will shrink in that direction. But it will retain its normal length in the radial direction. Thus, if it is used to measure the circumference and the diameter of the disk, the ratio of the two measurements will be larger than 2π (= 2 x 3.1416).

According to Einstein this situation will occur regardless of the type of measuring device in use. For example, if a person could drive an automobile around and across the disc, he would find that same result by means of odometer readings. If the auto had an accurate clock and an accurate speedometer he could obtain the same result by their use. The odometer would indicate a greater distance, the clock would indicate a longer time, and the speedometer would indicate a lower rate by a factor that is the square of that of the odometer.

(It has been suggested by some that the edge of the rotating disk would shrink by the same factor as the measuring rod, and in proportion to the reaction of the odometer and clock/speedometer combination, thus invalidating this result. Why the disk would not shrink in proportion to distance from its center in accordance with Special Relativity, and how it might survive that shrinkage without severe distortion, is not explained. But who is equipped to question the logic of Einstein and his disciples?)

In addition to Einstein becoming the world's most famous theoretical physicist, his expression for energy's equivalence to the product of mass times c squared became the world's most famous equation. Its development is briefly described in the following paragraphs. (In this equation energy is in ergs, mass is in grams, and c is 300 million meters per second.)

Upon rejection of the idea of the "ether of space" for its transport it was necessary to explain the propagation of light, and other electromagnetic radiation, through empty space. Light rays might now be thought of as the flow of oscillating matter through space in accordance with Maxwell's equations. In fact it was known that light exerts a pressure on a surface that intercepts it. The existence of this pressure was first proved by the Russian physicist P. N. Lebedev and was shown to be equal to twice the amount of reflected energy divided by the velocity of light. (The pressure of the sun's radiation has been proposed as a means of "sailing" a spacecraft between the planets of the solar system.)

The pressure of light on a mirror is analogous to that of a stream of water splashing off a wall. The rate of the mass of water (m) flowing at a velocity (v) results in a change in its momentum from +mv to -mv, or 2mv. For the mass of light reflecting from a mirror at velocity c its pressure must be 2mc. Because that is equal to the empirically derived value to the pressure of light, or $2E/c$, from the previous paragraph, $2mc=2E/c$ and $E=mc^2$.

Einstein's conviction of the validity of the postulates of Special Relativity, the absence of ether and the lack of a spatial reference, resulted in this famous equation which of course proved to be true, and became totally accepted throughout the world of science.

Because c is an extremely large number it only requires a minute amount of mass to produce a prodigious amount of energy. An ordinary flashlight that produces a few watts of electromagnetic energy looses only on the order of a trillionth of a gram of mass per minute. On the other hand, the radiated energy of the sun is enormous; its daily loss of mass is about 400 million tons.

This formula for the equivalence of mass and energy is universally true for all forms of mass and energy, including fire, explosion, and chemical and nuclear reactions. Even a glass of hot water weighs minutely more than when it losses some of its heat energy upon cooling. $E = mc^2$ also applies to kinetic energy, and accounts for the increase in mass of a body in motion in accordance with the Special Theory of Relativity; $M = M_0$ divided by the square root of $(1 - v^2/c^2)$.

It might also be mentioned here that the combination of two speeds in the same direction is no longer given by $v = v_1 + v_2$ but by $v = v_1 + v_2$ divided by $[1 + (v_1 + v_2)/c^2]$. For slow speeds this expression approaches the former equation, but at relativistic speeds it is important. If one of the speeds were c this equation becomes $v = c$. In fact, even if both of the speeds were equal to c the equation remains $v = c$. Thus Einstein's work showed that a velocity greater than c cannot be reached.

For the case of light passing through a medium other than vacuum, having an index of refraction n (water, for example), the expression for velocity becomes $v = (c/n + v)$ divided by $(1 + cv/nc^2)$. Multiplying the numerator and denominator by $(1 - v/nc)$ we get $v = (c/n + v - v/n^2 - v^2/nc)$ divided by $(1 - v^2/n^2c^2)$.

If, as it was in Fizeau's experiment, v/c is very small, v^2/c^2 and v^2/nc are also very smalll and thus can be ignored. Thus v is approximately equal to $c/n + v(1 - 1/n^2)$ which is the same as the empirical formula Fizeau derived from the results of his experiment, now explained by the work of Lorentz and Einstein.

One aspect of Special Relativity applicable to cosmology relates to red shift, the lengthening of the wavelength of electromagnetic radiation (decreased frequency) received from galaxies, quasars and other distant sources in the universe.

Redshift (z) of radiation, as determined by American astronomer Edwin Hubble for relatively close sources, is directly proportional to the velocity (and thus to the distance) of the source: $v=cz$ and $d=cz/H$, where H is an observationally determined quantity, the Hubble constant. However, these expressions are not valid for distant sources. As will be discussed in more detail in Chapter 12, for distant sources, which have high (relativistic) velocities, these simple relationships must be modified in accordance with the Lorentz transformations and the Special Theory of Relativity.

However, as will be discussed, the effects of General Relativity may add to the effects of Special Relativity. Because Special Relativity doesn't take into consideration the effect of extremely high gravitational force on radiation as it leaves a massive source (which is known as Einstein shift), the presently accepted interpretation of red shift as an indication of the velocity of distant bodies may prove to be inadequate.

So far the discussion of Special Relativity has been "relatively" simple, but when we get into General Relativity it gets somewhat more difficult.

The Theory of General Relativity is based on the postulates of Special Relativity. But Special Relativity had only to do with linear motion, that is, it was not concerned with acceleration or deceleration. Special Relativity is a special case of General Relativity in the same way that static electric and magnetic fields are special cases of Maxwell's equations for dynamic electromagnetic theory.

After publishing his work on Special Relativity, Einstein struggled for years to incorporate nonlinear motion into his ideas on relativity. He eventually accomplished his goal, producing a set of ten "field equations" that describe the four-dimensional space-time geometry of gravity. These equations, published in 1916, provided the basis for the General Theory of Relativity, a modern theory of gravity that goes far beyond of the work of Isaac Newton.

This theory treats time as a fourth "imaginary" dimension which, combined with the three dimensions of Euclidean space, produces a four-dimensional space-time construction or "continuum." Unfortunately, four-dimensional space-time (based on a non-Euclidean form of geometry invented decades earlier by

German mathematician Bernard Reimann) cannot be clearly visualized by the human mind. It can be treated only as a mathematical construction, whose four dimensions can, to a degree, be visualized as analogous to the surface of a three-dimensional sphere or other three-dimensional surface.

An important consequence of General Relativity is that space is no longer impassive emptiness; it is distorted by gravity. The curvature of space results in the curved path of matter as it travels through a gravitational field. Because electromagnetic radiation, including light, has an equivalent mass, its path is "bent" by the gravity of a massive body.

A second important consequence of General Relativity is that acceleration and gravity are equivalent.

In attempting to explain that aspect of his theory Albert Einstein and his followers, which includes virtually every scientist in the world today, have written, heard, or read about a person confined in an elevator-like box in outer space. If that box is somehow continuously accelerated upward by an external force, it would be impossible for its occupant to distinguish between the effects of that acceleration or of a gravitational force (or some combination of those). Even if he or she were aware that the box were suspended by a rope tied to its top, and could measure its tension, they would be unable to make that determination.

As further proof of this phenomenon (assuming that the box had been accelerated to a sufficiently high speed), if a ray of light were to travel through the box in such a way that its path could be observed (perhaps it grazes one of the walls), its path could be determined to be parabolic.

The path of that light beam would be "warped" equally by acceleration or gravitation and, because there is no spatial reference in the universe, the location of the box, whether it is influenced by the gravitational field of a large mass below it, or whether it is being accelerated by an external force, is as good as any other reference point. Einstein thus reached the conclusion that gravity and acceleration not only produce similar results, but that they are equivalent. Furthermore, he suggested that there is no force of gravity; only the geometry of curved space.

He went on to successfully predict the "warping" of the path of light rays from stars as they pass close to the sun. His calculations also provided a basis for the observed and previously unexplained small rotation of the axis of the elliptical orbit of the planet Mercury each time it passes close to the sun. The results of both of these were acclaimed, and Einstein thought they were fairly good, but there is room for some doubt as to accuracy in both cases.

(A number of questions can be raised regarding the validity of the results regarding the orbit of Mercury. Some of those relate to the following possibilities: There is some uncertainty regarding the orbit of Mercury, and solar wind might effect its orbit. The sun is not perfectly spherical; it has been shown to be an oblate spheroid. There may be tidal distortions of both bodies. There may be other nonuniformities and proximity effects; when bodies are close to each other their centers of gravitational attraction are shifted toward each other.)

Another question that has been raised regarding General Relativity concerns its neglect of Mach's principle. Nineteenth century Austrian mathematician, physicist and philosopher Ernst Mach (in 1893) suggested that the inertial properties of matter are in some manner related to the rest of the matter of the universe. As a brief illustration of this idea, if your body is rotated (even if you are in outer space) you can sense centrifugal forces; but if there were no other matter in the universe would you still have those sensations?

Einstein explains these effects as the result of the properties of empty space; it is not really empty but has a physical content. That, of course, hasn't been fully proven and some have suggested that there remain inertial interactions of the matter of the universe that are not fully explained by relativity.

Regardless of various questions it appears that space is positively curved within a gravitational field. This is supported by consideration of three observers each on a different planet of the solar system (that is, within the gravitational field of the sun). If they were each to accurately measure the angles of sighting to each other they would discover that the observed angles would add to more than 180 degrees; slightly more than they would for a flat surface.

This is explained by the fact that the effect of the sun's gravity on light is to bend its path between the observers. The effect is similar to measuring the angle between three points on the surface of a sphere (such as the Earth), which is considered to have positive curvature. (The lines connecting the three points are called geodesics.)

Our definition of a straight line has traditionally been the path of light. But now we find that path to be different than we thought. What we had previously considered to be the standard for a straight line may have failed us.

However, it should be remembered that, in causing the path of light to bend, it is quite possible that gravitational effects merely create the illusion of curved space. (To those who believe that "space" means "nothing," "curved space" is an oxymoron; how can "nothing" be curved?) It should also be remembered that, although gravitation and acceleration can be described by the same mathematics, their identicality is not proven. In fact, as we will see, quantum theory questions that sameness.

It should be emphasized that Einstein's interpretation of curved space included only positive curvature. His concept of curved space-time was analogous to a three-dimensional spherical (or elliptical) surface. The absence of mass would result in zero curvature, the presence of some mass would result in some positive curvature, and greater mass would result in a greater degree of positive curvature. As will be discussed, the idea of a negatively curved universe was introduced by others who subsequently produced solutions to Einstein's equations.

In Einstein's book, *Relativity The Special and General Theories*, there is no mention of negatively curved space, and there is no mention of it in other serious books on Einstein's work, such as the *Biography of Physics* by George Gamow, or *Understanding Relativity* by professor of science history Stanley Goldberg. In all of these works there is only discussion of positively curved space as a result of either gravitational attraction or an equivalent accelerative force.

Regarding the curvature of space, a tale is sometimes told, even by those who believe in a universe of negative curvature, that creates confusion. It is said that, due to the curvature of space, a high speed spacecraft, flying outward in any single direction, might eventually return home from the opposite direction.

Another version of this tale is that the shining of a powerful laser beam into the sky might be expected to someday illuminate a spot on the opposite side of the Earth. But for these stories to have any plausibility the curvature of space-time would have to be positive and of a proper closed configuration to provide those results. That is, the curvature must be the four-dimensional analog of a sphere or ellipsoid. Negatively curved space, that is said not to close on itself, could not result in such occurrences.

Regarding another commonly misunderstood phenomenon, the reader will probably recall reading or hearing stories about a space traveler who left the Earth in a high speed (relativistic) spaceship for a number of years. According to the story, due to the speed of the ship, time runs slower for the spaceman as compared to the ground crew's time, when he returns he will not have aged as much as they.

For example, if he and one of the ground crew were 30 years old at launch time and the spaceship had traveled at about 3/4 of the speed of light for 30 years, according to the Lorentz transformations, time dilation would be such that the spaceman's time in space was only about 20 years. Upon his return his age would be only about 50 instead of the 60 years of the ground crewman. (His age would be 30 times one plus the square root of $(1- v^2/c^2)$ or $30 \times (1+.66)=49.8$ years.) If the spaceship traveled at 90% of the speed of light for 30 years the spaceman would return at age 43 as compared to the 60 years of the ground crewman.

Such a phenomenon, which has been called the "time paradox" or the "twin paradox," is of course, not only counter-intuitive, but incorrectly interpreted. If it were merely the result of the time dilation of Special Relativity, the mutuality of time dilation would deny this effect. The relative speeds of two bodies would be the same. The slowing of the clocks of one (as observed from the other) would be the same as the slowing of the clocks of the other (as observed from the first).

Time dilation of Special Relativity is concerned only with linear motion. In relativistic round-trip space-travel nonlinear motion, that is, acceleration and deceleration, necessarily occurs. Therefore General Relativity, which provides the basis for the twin paradox, must be taken into consideration. The age of a space traveler would be less than the age of his twin who remained at home, but that would not be the result of linear velocity in accordance with Special Relativity, but a consequence of nonlinear velocity in accordance with General Relativity. Thus the twin clock paradox is not a paradox at all. It should instead be called the "twin clock effect."

Tests have been performed that have provided some degree of verification of this phenomenon. For example, an atomic clock has been flown around the Earth (obviously at speeds far lower than "relativistic") that, upon its return, showed an earlier time than that of an identical clock that remained at home. The time differential, although minute, showed good agreement with theoretical calculations. Other experiments, including particle accelerator tests regarding time dilation and altitude tests regarding gravitational effects on elapsed time, have provided support for other aspects of both Special and General Relativity.

This discussion has been presented, not only to provide some background on Relativity in order to enable the reader to make his own judgements regarding the validity of various cosmological schemes, but to illustrate that discrimination is required regarding what is presented in the media regarding scientific theory.

Relativity is not totally proven and is still subject to some question. Although it is still theory, there is vast convincing evidence in support of it. However, cosmological theory is quite a different case. It is still in its infancy and, unlike relativity, there are few proven facts in support of any cosmology; all the evidence regarding the ancient history of the universe is purely circumstantial. Great care should be exercised regarding the acceptance of ideas concerning theory that is on such shaky ground.

TWO

The Standard Model of Particle Physics

B ecause cosmology in general and BBT in particular are based not only on the theories of relativity but on modern particle physics and quantum theory, it might be of value to the reader to have at least a rudimentary understanding of these subjects. In this chapter the so-called standard model of the fundamental particles and forces of nature will be introduced. In the next chapter the relationship of this model to quantum theory will be discussed and some of its history presented.

The standard model is based on what is called "gauge theory," a unified theory of the electromagnetic, strong, and weak interactions of the elementary particles of nature. Consideration of the hypothetical unit of gravitational force, the graviton, and the hypothetical unifying Higgs boson is also included. Although these particles have not been observed they are included to provide a more complete picture of particle theory as envisioned by modern theorists.

Much of the details of the standard model are dependent upon what is called gauge symmetry, a theory concerned with mathematical transformations in space and time, and with the symmetries of the laws of nature and of the quantum particles of the standard model. Gauge theory is based on a complex branch of mathematics known as group theory (invented more than a century ago by Evariste Galois), that has to do with the effect of various sequences of transformations on an object or groups of objects in time and space.

It should be understood that the particles of nature are called particles only as a matter of convenience. They are actually forms of energy that exhibit the characteristics of both particles and waves. For example, photons appear as discrete increments of energy when causing a light sensing device such as a photomultiplier tube to emit single detectable electrons, but they also possess wave transmission characteristics over the entire electromagnetic spectrum that includes radio, heat, light, ultraviolet, X-ray and gamma ray wavelengths. This duality of characteristics provides a simple and well known example of the attributes of quantum theory which is believed to apply to all the elementary particles of nature.

Although this duality of quantum phenomena is inconsistent with normal human experience and intuitive understanding, it has been demonstrated to apply to natural phenomena, and is therefore accepted. Perhaps some future theory will be advanced that will reconcile quantum duality with everyday experience, but in the meantime it must be taken as correct.

There are at least five "layers" of the structure of the matter of the universe. These are molecules, atoms, nuclei, hadrons (protons and neutrons) and fermions (leptons and quarks). It is possible that a sixth, or even more, layers exist. Fermions may be made up of even smaller particles, but evidence of their existence has not been discovered. The standard model is concerned with the structure of the atoms of the elements, but hasn't much to do with the molecules of compounds (molecular structure), which would take us into the field of chemistry. It is primarily concerned with the three lower layers of matter; especially the lowest two levels, fermions and hadrons, and with the forces that "mediate" the interactions between them.

The elementary particles called fermions, which are listed in Figure 1, are considered to be the building blocks of nature. Fermions are named after famous Italian-American physicist Enrico Fermi. They are divided into two general groups; leptons and quarks. All fermions are spin 1/2 particles that have four possible polarizations (X, Y, Z or T), of which only two are available to electrons. (Spin 1/2 means that they have an intrinsic angular momentum of 1/2 h, where h is Planck's constant, 10^{-27} erg-second.)

There are twelve fermions, six leptons and six quarks, each of which has a different rest mass. These occur in pairs, and each of them has its antiparticle (not listed in Figure 1) of opposite charge, but otherwise of identical properties. Leptons have electric charges of either one or zero, and quarks have electric charges of either plus 2/3 or minus 1/3.

The name "lepton" is the Greek word for light or small, and the name "hadron" is from the Greek word *hadros*, for robust. The word "quark" had no real meaning. It was adopted (from a passage in *Finnegans Wake* by James Joyce that goes "three quarks for Muster Mark") for the name of particles first proposed (in 1963) by Murray Gell-Mann and independently by George Zweig (both of the California Institute of Technology) for the structure of hadrons.

As indicated in the Figure 1, fermions are further divided into three families or generations. Family one consists of the electron, its neutrino, and up and down quarks; family two of the muon, its neutrino, and charm and strange quarks; and family three of the tau, its neutrino, and top and bottom quarks (also called truth and beauty). To date the top quark has not been found.

The ordinary matter of the universe is made up of the particles of family one. Second and third family particles (with the possible exception of neutrinos) are unstable, meaning that they are very short lived; they rapidly decay into more stable particles of lower mass. Their lifetimes are within the range of 10^{-25} to 10^{-6} seconds.

With the possible exception of the proton which has been shown to have a lifetime of at least 10^{31} seconds, far longer than the age of the universe as reckoned by BBT, all the fundamental particle have limited lifetimes. Unless a neutron is in a stable nucleus, it decays (to a proton, electron and a neutrino) in about ten minutes, but more exotic particles have lifetimes between one millionth and one ten-trillionth of a second. As examples of short lived particles, muons (mu mesons) decay in about one millionth of a second to an electron, neutrino and an antineutrino; and pions (pi mesons), of which there are three kinds having plus, minus or no charge, decay much faster. Charged pions decay in 10^{-8} second and neutral pions decay in 10^{-16} second. These particles can only be observed as the result of high-velocity collisions in particle accelerators.

Scientists have for many years considered the possibility of the existence of more than three families of fundamental particles, but recent experiments at the Large Electron-Positron (LEP) collider at the European Laboratory for Particle Physics (known as CERN) have fairly conclusively demonstrated that the families are limited to three.

Each family of leptons and quarks is about one to two orders of magnitude more massive than the previous family. The more massive the particle, the more energy is required to produce it, and the minimum required energy is equal to its rest mass. This means that higher and higher accelerator energies are required to produce the more massive particles. For example, the Fermilab (for Fermi National Accelerator Laboratory) Tevatron near Chicago can produce proton-antiproton collisions as great as 1.8 trillion electron volts (TeV), sufficient to produce tau particles having a rest mass of 1,784 million electron volts (1,784 MeV or 1.784 TeV).

It should be noted that, although these numbers are very large, one electron volt is only the energy needed to move an electron through a potential of one volt. Thus to move one electron, that has a rest mass of 9.11 times 10^{-28} grams, through a trillion volts (1 TeV) - or a trillion electrons through one volt - is only 1.6 ergs of work, about enough to lift a feather a few inches. (An erg is the amount of work done by a force of one dyne moving through one centimeter, and a dyne is a force of only one gram-centimeter per second squared.)

Of the particles of the standard model, electrons, protons, neutrons and photons are the most familiar. Electrons of course account for the flow of electricity in conductors, through the atmosphere as lightning, and as the beam of the cathode ray tubes of radar and television displays. They are spin 1/2 leptons having a rest mass of 0.511 MeV and an electrical charge of minus one. Except for their greater mass and short life, muons (mu mesons) and taus (tau mesons) are similar to electrons. The antiparticle of the electron is the positron which has the same characteristics as the electron except for its unit positive charge.

Neutrinos are spin 1/2, zero electrical charge partners of the corresponding leptons of their family. They have very low mass as compared to their partners, or perhaps none at all. They are not involved in electromagnetic or strong interactions of the fundamental particles. Because of their low mass and lack of interactions neutrinos can travel through other matter, including the entire diameter of the Earth. The tau neutrino has not been detected.

There are six types or "flavors" of quarks; up, down, charm, strange, top and bottom. Up, charm and top quarks, one of each family, have electrical charges of plus 2/3 and rest masses of 4 MeV, 1300 MeV and about 89 GeV (89 billion electron volts) respectively. Down, strange and bottom quarks, the second of each family, have an electrical charge of minus 1/3 and rest masses of 7 MeV, 150 MeV and 5.5 GeV respectively.

In addition to their electrical charge, each quark can be of three different "colors"; usually called red, green and blue. Quark's flavors and colors are purely artificial; they are arbitrarily chosen names for previously unknown characteristics of newly discovered particles. Color is to the strong force what charge is to the electric force. Electric charge has only two states (positive and negative), whereas color has three states. The six corresponding antiquark colors (charges) are anti-red, anti-green, and anti-blue.

Quarks are thought to be truly fundamental, having neither structure or spatial dimensions, but individual quarks have not been observed, that is, they have not been isolated. Accelerator experiments seem to verify that sets of three quarks exist within protons. These particles, and their antiparticles, may still be considered hypothetical, but there is considerable evidence in support of their existence. Because of its importance to verification of theory, the quest for the undetected top quark is of major interest to physicists.

All particles made up of quarks are called hadrons, of which there are two classes: baryons (meaning "heavy ones"), made up of three quarks (also antibaryons made up of three antiquarks) that have 1/2 integer spin; and mesons, made up of a quark and an antiquark that have integer spin, i.e., they have a spin of zero or one. Of the baryons, protons are made up of two up quarks and one down quark giving them an electrical charge of plus one, and neutrons are made up of one up quark and two down quarks giving them an electrical charge of zero. Neutrons and protons in turn adhere to form atomic nuclei. (Neutrons and protons are called nucleons.)

There are other hadrons called "strange" particles that result from accelerator collisions. These include, for example, a relatively stable strange baryon called a "lamda" in which one of the up quarks is replaced by a strange quark. The proton, neutron and the lamda, among the lowest energy level hadrons, are relatively stable and readily observable. Others, of higher energy configurations, are very short lived, and rapidly decay into lower level hadrons.

Mesons, the second category of hadrons, are made up of a quark and an antiquark. They have integer spin and a charge of zero. As an example, B mesons are made up of a bottom quark and an antidown or an antistrange quark. Pi mesons or pions, that have also been observed in accelerators, are short lived, light mass hadrons that are thought to be necessary to the structure of atomic nuclei, i.e., the force that binds proton and neutrons within atomic nuclei is thought to be due to the exchange of pions and other hadrons of this second type.

There are believed to be only four basic forces in our universe. These are electromagnetism, the strong nuclear force, the weak nuclear force and gravity. Standard model gauge bosons (named after Indian physicist S. N. Bose) are believed to provide the four corresponding coupling forces that generate attraction and repulsion among the different types of fermions. The force between particles arises from the exchange of these "mediators" at finite speed, i.e., at speed less than that of light. The mediator of electromagnetism is the photon, of the strong force is the gluon, and of the weak force is the Z zero, the W minus and the W plus bosons. These coupling forces have vector fields, meaning they have directional orientation and magnitude, and their carriers are spin 1. (Spin one bosons are "vector bosons.") The hypothetical graviton (spin 2) is the thought to be the mediator of gravitation, and the hypothetical Higgs boson (spin 0) is thought to be necessary for mathematical consistency of the entire standard model.

Photons (electromagnetic force vector bosons), the particles or quanta of electromagnetism, have zero rest mass, zero electric charge and infinite range, but a strength of only one one-hundredth of that of the strong nuclear force. They interact with all particles having electromagnetic charge. They bind electrons to nuclei to form atoms and thus play a major role in determining the chemistry of the universe. Quantum electromagnetic relationships are described by the mathematical theory called quantum electrodynamics or QED.

Gluons (strong force vector bosons), the mediators of the strong nuclear force, also have zero rest mass and zero electric charge, but their range is limited to about 10^{-13} centimeters. The strong force is responsible for the large amount of energy released by nuclear fusion. Gluons act within atomic nuclei to bind quarks together and to bind protons and neutrons. There are eight types of gluons corresponding to eight combinations of the three colors of quarks, i.e., red-antigreen, red-antiblue, etc. In addition to binding quarks to form protons and neutrons, gluons can bind to each other. For example, a red-antigreen gluon and a green-antiblue gluon can bind to form a red-antiblue gluon. Quantum strong force interactions with quarks are described by the mathematical theory known as quantum chromodynamics or QCD (chromo for "color").

The weak nuclear force has a strength of about 10^{-13} times that of the strong nuclear force and a range of about 10^{-16} centimeters. The weak force acts on both leptons and hadrons and is responsible for radioactive decay of one particle to another of lesser mass. It is also responsible for nuclear reactions in the stars. Of its three related mediators, called intermediate vector bosons, Z zero has a rest mass of 91.2 GeV and an electrical charge of zero, W minus has a rest mass of 90 GeV and a charge of minus 1, and W plus has the same rest mass but the opposite electrical charge of plus one.

Intermediate vector bosons have lifetimes of only on the order of 10^{-25} seconds. Z zero, the most massive particle observed, weighs about 100 times as much as a proton. Individual Z zero particles differ slightly in mass; the spread of their mass is known as mass width. They decay in about 10^{-25} second to produce a pair of elementary particles such as an electron and a positron.

Theoretical physicists Steven Weinberg and Abdus Salam (in 1968) developed a unified quantum theory concerning the electromagnetic and the weak field phenomena that is known as electroweak theory. In addition, attempts have been made by many others to extend this unification to include strong field theory into what is known as grand unified field theories or GUTs. Some variations of these theories appear to have some degree of merit. The standard model is the integration of the quantum theory of quarks interacting with gluon strong force mediators and the weak and electromagnetic interactions which, except for gravity, explain much of the physical world.

Gravitons, the hypothetical mediating quanta of gravitation, are said to have a rest mass of zero, a spin of two, and no electrical charge. Gravitational force, which is a tensor field, has a strength of 10^{-38} times that of the strong force, but its range is infinite. (The definition of a tensor field, which involves the modulus—the parameters—of a quaternium, a set of four vectors, is well beyond the scope of this book.)

Because of its extreme weakness, gravity has negligible impact on experimental verification of gauge theory. However, even though it is the weakest of the forces, because it is not canceled out over large distances, as in the case of electromagnetic force, it has the greatest impact at great distances. A major quest of theoretical physicists is to incorporate the force of gravity into an all-encompassing unified theory, which, although nonexistent, has been named the theory of everything or TOE. To date no satisfactory TOE has been developed.

The hypothetical Higgs boson has zero spin and zero electrical charge. Its mass is thought to be at least 5 GeV, probably about 90 GeV, and possibly as much as one TeV (trillion electron volts). It is the mediator of the hypothetical Higgs force, which is a scalar field, i.e., it has only magnitude; no directional orientation. Gauge theory predicts a Higgs field of infinite range that is needed for mathematical consistency of the standard model. It is thought to be necessary for the generation of the mass of other particles. The Higgs boson is not considered to be a full fledged member of the standard model but it is well accepted by physicists as essential to modern theory. Even if the Higgs field turns out to an erroneous concept, they believe there must be an alternate source for the mass of the universe.

FERMIONS (All fermions are spin 1/2 particles)

LEPTONS

Family	Particle Name	Symbol	Rest Mass	Electrical Charge
1 {	Electron	e	0.511 MeV	- 1
	Electron Neutrino	ν_e	< 10 eV	0
2 {	Muon	$\mu-$	106.6 MeV	- 1
	Muon Neutrino	ν_μ	< .25 eV	0
3 {	Tau (or Tauon)	$\tau-$	1,784 MeV	- 1
	Tau Teutrino	ν_τ	< 65 MeV	0

QUARKS

Particle Name	Symbol	Mass at Rest	Electrical Charge
UP	u	4 MeV	+ 2 / 3
DOWN	d	7 MeV	- 1 / 3
CHARM	c	1300 MeV	+ 2 / 3
STRANGE	s	150 MeV	- 1 / 3
TOP or Truth	t	About 150 GeV	+ 2 / 3
BOTTOM or Beauty	b	5.5 GeV	- 1 / 3

BOSONS

Force	Range	Strength*	Carrier	Rest Mass (Gev)	Spin	Electrical Charge
Electromagnetism (vector field)	Infinite	10^{-2}	Photon	0	1	0
Strong (vector field)	10^{-13} cm	1	Gluon	0	1	0
Weak (vector field)	10^{-15} cm	10^{-13}	Z°	91.2	1	0
			W-	90	1	-1
			W+	90	1	+1
Gravity (tensor field)	Infinite	10^{-38}	Graviton	0	2	0
Higgs (scaler field)	Infinite	?	Higgs Boson	>25	0	0

* Strength at 10^{-12} cm in comparison with the strong force

Various sources disagree on the values of ranges and strengths of some bosons.
The values given here cannot be considered to be exact.

FIGURE 1. STANDARD MODEL OF ELEMENTARY PARTICLES

List of Characteristics

THREE

About
Quantum Theory

As we have seen, the standard model of modern physics is based to a large extent on quantum theory. Various attempts to overcome faults that were found in standard BBT have also been based on quantum theory. It may therefore be useful to review some ideas from quantum theory and some of its history.

It was all started by German physics professor Max Planck in about 1900. His initial quantum ideas came out of his studies of black-body radiation from which his radiation law developed. (A black-body radiator is simply a material that has a very black rough surface that allows it to readily absorb or radiate heat energy.) He found that he could derive the correct law of distribution of radiated energy if he made some assumptions, one of which was that energy is produced in discrete amounts and another is that the amount of energy is equal to an integer (a whole number) multiplied by the frequency (the Greek letter nu) of the radiated energy and by a constant which is the famous Planck constant called h ($E = n \times \nu \times h$).

It had been known for some time that light can cause electrons to be ejected from metals and that their velocity is not dependent on light intensity but on its frequency, and that the number ejected is not dependent on the frequency but on the intensity of the light. Based on that phenomenon, with knowledge of Planck's work, in 1905 Albert Einstein proposed that light acts as though it is transmitted in quanta, or units of energy, equal to hv, Planck's constant times frequency. (The constant n can be omitted if the proper units of v and h are used.)

In 1911 British physics professor Ernest Rutherford (born in New Zealand) proposed an atomic structure having electrons in orbit about the atomic nucleus, a brilliant idea, but according to classical physics it couldn't exist. Energy would be continuously radiated and electrons would spiral into the nucleus. Danish physicist Niels Bohr in 1913 modified Rutherford's model to incorporate the quantum ideas of Planck and Einstein. In his model electrons occupied only orbits of permitted energy levels. A quantum of energy is emitted when an electron "jumps" from one energy level to a lower one. This theory provided an explanation for discrete spectral emission lines from various elements.

However great the logic of quantum theory, until about 1920, it was still only an unverified theory. At that time American theoretical physicist Arthur Compton, while studying the behavior of X-rays, found that when they were directed at matter they would be scattered, but the scattered radiation would be of longer wavelength. In 1923 he was able to explain this effect as the result of the X-ray quantums on electrons. The X-ray quantum continues on its way but with lower energy, i.e., longer wavelength, and the electron absorbs the lost energy. Laboratory confirmation of this phenomenon, called the Compton effect, was a major factor in subsequent general acceptance of early quantum ideas and its further rapid development.

In 1925 Austrian physicist Wolfgang Pauli discovered his exclusion principle that further clarified atomic structure. According to this principle, electrons in orbit about the atomic nucleus cannot be adjacent to each other due to their mutual repulsion; a kind of a quantum version of Archimedes' principle that no two bodies can occupy the same space at the same time.

This repulsion is in addition to that of like negative charges. It was a newly discovered effect called exchange force based on quantum theory that keeps electrons apart and prevents them from falling into the nucleus. It applies only to spin 1/2 particles, i.e., fermions (leptons and quarks); not to integer spin particles, the mediators of the fundamental forces. The Pauli exclusion principle showed, among other things, that in an atom there can be only a small number of energy states for an electron, and only a small number of electrons can occupy each state.

Also in 1925 German theoretical physicist Werner Heisenberg, with his colleagues at the Copenhagen institute, using the mathematics of matrices, developed a mathematical description of the relationships of the frequency, the intensity and the polarization of atomic spectral emission lines. His mathematical method, called matrix mechanics, avoided the use of a mechanical model of the atom, and provided quantum theory with a sound mathematical basis. In 1926 British theoretical physicist Paul Dirac presented an equivalent mathematical basis called noncommunicative algebra, and Austrian theoretical physicist Erwin Schrodinger presented his work on wave mechanics in which the state of a mechanical system is given by a "wave function."

Later, in collaboration with theoretical physicist Max Born (who was a teacher of Fermi, Heisenberg and J. Robert Oppenheimer) and Pascual Jordan, Heisenberg developed a more complete version of quantum theory, called quantum mechanics, that could be used to calculate the properties of atoms. The simple picture of electrons as solid particles in orbit around a nucleus, like planets around the sun, was no longer acceptable. The particles of physics appeared to have a dual nature, sometimes seeming to behave like particles and sometimes like waves. This new theory was able to explain their behavior in detail. It also applied to electromagnetism, i.e., it showed how Einstein's idea of particles of light (photons) could be mathematically described.

Much of this early work on the development of quantum theory was done at the Institute for Theoretical Physics at Copenhagen, where Niels Bohr was the undisputed leader and mentor of his disciples, who included Born, Heisenberg, Jordan and Pauli. That is where the Copenhagen or standard interpretation of quantum theory, which included the dual nature of quantum particle behavior and the concept of observer participation, originated. Bohr himself played a major role in these developments.

Basing his work on relativity, and the new quantum ideas, British astronomer Sir Arthur Eddington in 1926 published his work in which he described the processes within the stars. He suggested that nuclear reactions provided their energy. Although these processes were not fully understood until years later, his general concept and many of its details were later proven correct.

In 1927 Heisenberg presented his famous uncertainty principle. According to this principle the position and the momentum (mass times velocity) of a particle cannot be measured simultaneously. If these measurements of a single particle are repeated they will be found to fluctuate around an average value. Unlike measurements of classical mechanics, in quantum mechanics only a probability distribution of measurements can be determined. Classical physics becomes a special case of quantum physics that applies to large-scale matter, but is not valid for fundamental microscopic particle behavior. A new way of thinking about particle physics had to be adopted.

In 1928 theoretical physicists Pascual Jordan, Eugene Wigner and subsequently Heisenberg and Pauli showed that each of the force fields of nature has an associated particle that is the quantized form of the field. This was an entirely new idea. Fields have quantum attributes. Their particles, photons, gluons, Ws and Zs are included in the standard model. In modern field theory gravitation is thought to have its particle, the graviton, and even the hypothetical Higgs field is thought to have a Higgs particle.

By 1928 Paul Dirac had formulated what is known as the Dirac equation governing the behavior of electrons, but only for the very simplest system, that of the hydrogen atom, having only one proton and one electron. He found, however, that his equation also described a new particle having the same characteristics as the electron except that it had an opposite (positive) electrical charge. The existence of this antielectron, now known as the positron, was detected in 1932 by Carl Anderson, who was then a graduate student of physics at the California Institute of Technology. Since that time antiparticles of many of the particles of the standard model have been observed in particle accelerators.

Dirac's work also showed that if a particle and its antiparticle should collide they would be annihilated, producing a shower of gamma rays, and, on the other hand, if enough energy is provided, a particle and its antiparticle could be created. The energy required would be equivalent to the rest masses of the particles, in accordance with Einstein's $E=mc^2$.

Dirac's development of quantum electrodynamics (QED) in 1928, that utilized only one arbitrary constant, Planck's constant, provided the basis for many highly accurate predictions of elementary particle behavior. The discovery of antiparticles drastically changed all of particle physics. Matter was previously thought to be permanent and unchangeable. Because it was demonstrated that particles and antiparticles can be created in the vacuum of high energy accelerators, it became possible to believe that might happen under natural circumstances.

Following that, several new particles were predicted and subsequently found. Based on his previous work, and that of others, Wolfgang Pauli was able to predict the existence of an extremely low mass, chargeless particle that would therefore be difficult to detect. Another of the architects of quantum theory, Enrico Fermi, named Pauli's particle the neutrino from the Italian word *bambino*. The existence of this baby particle was confirmed in an accelerator in the 1950s.

The neutrino was discovered by James Chadwick in 1932, and in 1934 a massive hadron, the pi meson, or pion, (200 times heavier than an electron) was predicted by Japanese physicist Hiedki Yukawa and detected in 1938 in atomic nuclei. Most of the new particles are extremely short lived—as short as 10^{-24} second—making them very difficult to detect.

In the 1940s several large particle accelerators were built to aid in the quest for more knowledge of particle physics. It was known that the nucleus of atoms was made up of electrically neutral neutrons and positively charged protons. Much was known about the properties of electrons and photons, but little was known about the structure of neutrons and protons or other particles of the modern standard model. In the late 1940s pi mesons were observed in accelerator laboratories. In the early 1950s many more such highly reactive particles were discovered. Those particles, called hadrons, created quite a problem. There was no understanding as to how they fit into the structure of matter.

It turned out that all hadrons, which includes protons and neutrons, are composed of a new variety of particles called quarks, held together by gluons as has been described. This elaborate theory (QCD) regarding the structure of hadrons is a truly remarkable result of the conceptual genius of its originators, physicists Murray Gell-Mann and George Zweig in 1963. Since its discovery this structure has been confirmed beyond any doubt. Gell-Mann/Zweig theory provided an immense simplification to the understanding of the structure of the universe. Instead of the possibility of different neutrons and protons for each element, all of them are composed of combinations of a relatively small number of quarks; six "flavors" each of eight possible "colors" for a total of 48 possible varieties of quarks.

Individual quarks have not been observed, and this work wasn't taken very seriously until accelerator experiments in 1967 provided evidence of these point particles orbiting each other within protons and neutrons. Although there is no evidence of it as yet, quarks may someday be found to in turn consist of even smaller components, but there is little doubt about the quark composition of hadrons.

Electrons, photons and quarks are said to be point particles, meaning they have no size, and therefore they are symmetrical. Like a perfectly symmetrical sphere they have no orientation. An analogy to this may be water in the center of a tank whose molecules of H_2O are unaligned; they are oriented in random directions. But if that water should freeze its molecules become aligned, at least in local areas, and the symmetry is gone; symmetry has been "broken."

Prior to the 19th century a branch of mathematics called group theory was developed that had to do with "symmetrical operations." As a simple example, when a sphere is subjected to two different series of rotations its appearance is unchanged. But when these operations are applied to nonsymmetrical objects the result of each series may be quite different. Group theory, which describes symmetrical operations by a form of algebra that can be applied not only to three-dimensional space but to higher dimensional systems, including four-dimensional space-time, and to transformations of many kinds.

Hungarian-American physicist Eugene Wigner in 1939 was the first to consider group theory implications of the Lorentz transformations as related to quantum theory. From this he discovered that the mathematics of group theory can be used to classify each quantum particle according its rest mass and its spin. If rest mass is zero, as it is for a photon, a particle can travel at the speed of light, and if greater than zero it can only travel at a lesser speed. Quantum particles have spins of only zero and 1/2 increments. If a particle has a spin of zero or a full integer it is a boson. If it has a spin of 1/2, 3/2, 5/2, etc. it is a fermion.

Wigner also showed that Heisenberg's uncertainty principle did not apply to the measurement of these characteristics of particles. Rest mass and spin can be precisely measured, thus providing a convenient means of classifying particles; especially so because it also applies to multiple particle configurations such as atomic nuclei. Much of the standard model of fundamental particles is dependent upon gauge theory, or gauge symmetry, which relates geometrical transformations in space and time to particle symmetries in accordance with group theory and within the confines of the Special Theory of Relativity. Wigner was thus able to reconcile quantum theory with the Special Theory of Relativity.

Some serious difficulties with quantum theory were encountered in the 1930s and 1940s. Some calculations persistently resulted in infinite masses, for which there is no place in the real world. These problems could be overcome by a mathematical trick called renormalization in which the infinite numbers were replaced by observed masses.

Renormalization has to do with the fact that calculations regarding a point particle such as an electron can result in an infinite mass at that point. But of course the electron doesn't have infinite mass, so the actual mass is substituted for the infinity that arises, thus correcting the problem. This procedure provided correct solutions but was still considered a trick.

In the late 1940s several theoretical physicists, including Freeman Dyson, Richard Feynman, Julian Schwinger and Sin-itiro Tomonaga working on quantum electrodynamics (QED), the study of the interactions of electrons and photons, showed that renormalization resulted in predictions of exactly the results of laboratory experiments regarding these particles. Renormalization was no longer considered an "ad hoc" mathematical trick, but a necessary procedure of quantum theory.

In the late 1960s mathematician Kenneth Wilson found a physical basis for the renormalization process in the strange scaling behavior of what are called "fractals" wherein the length of a crooked line (such as a coastline) may appear to vary greatly as the distance from which it is viewed is changed. This situation is analogous to that of quantum particles who's mass and coupling strength changes according to the distance scale at which they are examined.

According to current quantum thinking, all of the particles are manifestations of various fields. But the definition of a field is very difficult. Before Einstein's paper on Special Relativity of 1905 showed it to be false, the prevailing belief was that fields consisted of unknown matter that flowed through the ether of space, a concept that has been totally discredited. The many fields of various kinds, that might best be visualized as forces that can occupy and travel through space, require no medium through which to travel.

Quantum theorist believe that space is not empty, but filled with these fields. Their energy fills the vacuum of space. Vacuum is not "nothing"; it is the lowest possible level of energy. However, fluctuations of this energy can cause particles to appear.

Some physicists believe that fields are all there are in the universe and that they are the simplest irreducible fundamental entities of physics. Perhaps all the particles of nature are fully defined by field equations that describe their properties and their interactions. According to quantum theorist Steven Weinberg, author in 1977 of the well known book on BBT, *The First Three Minutes*, all of reality is a set of fields. Everything else can be derived from the dynamics of quantum fields.

Every field can be defined by its field equations and, if fields obey Einstein's Special Relativity and can be classified by Wigner's method, every field has as rest mass and a spin. Fields are further classified according to other characteristics such as electrical charge or "color." For example, if a field has a rest mass of 0.511 MeV, a spin of 1/2 and a charge of -1, it must be that of and electron field. Some fields that correspond to massless quantum particles, such as electromagnetism and gravitation, have infinite range. Others correspond to the interactions of more massive particles, such as weak bosons, that have very limited range.

Fields of the same classification can of course combine to add or subtract in space in a straightforward manner to produce instantaneous net fields. If the field should vary with time, for example, it is a function of time and space, then four dimensions are involved in its field equations. But because fields are quantized, that is, they obey the laws of quantum theory, the intensity of a field at each point in space is a matter of probability. Just as the path and location of a quantum particle is subject to Heisenberg's uncertainty principle, that principle also applies to the fields of the quantum physics.

Fields are thus probability waves for their quantum particles. The universe is said by some theoretical physicists to be extremely simple; it consists only of space that is filled with nothing but quantum fields that can appear as quantum particles speeding in all directions as they interact with each other according to the rules of Special Relativity and quantum theory. The mathematics of quantum theory is said to overcome the duality of the fundamental particles and accurately describe their properties and their interactions in all respects throughout the entire universe and for all time.

As has been mentioned, the standard model of particle physics is based on gauge theory, which in turn is based on group theory. This application of gauge theory is due to the work of physicists C. N. Yang and Robert Mills in 1968 which has become known as Yang-Mills field theory. The work of recent theoretical physicists has shown that Yang-Mills field quantities are not apparent until the symmetry of those fields are broken. (All particles were symmetrical until their symmetry was broken.) Thus all the matter of the universe is present because its original total symmetry once was broken.

Like supercooled water that suddenly freezes, symmetry was unstable, but broken symmetry, like the ice that forms, is stable. Apparently this symmetry breaking can be spontaneous. This was first suggested by Edinburgh physicist Peter Higgs in 1965. Following that Steven Weinberg, Pakistani physicist Abdus Salam, Sheldon Glashow and other physicists used Higgs' idea in a Yang-Mills gauge theory model to unite the electromagnetic and the weak forces, thus developing the electroweak theory. This work was neglected until 1971 when it was shown that the Yang-Mills theories were renormalizable and could be used to calculate electromagnetic interactions in agreement with the results of quantum electrodynamics. The Higgs boson was needed to make the electroweak theory renormalizable.

Higgs' idea of a symmetry breaking field has tentatively been incorporated into the standard model. This hypothetical spinless but massive Higgs boson is used to mathematically investigate the symmetry breaking process. According to Yang-Mills theory all fields are massless and hidden, but when gauge symmetry breaks, some of them acquire mass. The validity of electroweak theory, which was based on the Yang-Mills model and Higgs symmetry breaking was demonstrated by its prediction of the intermediate vector bosons, Z zero, W- and W+ particles. When they were experimentally discovered, Ws in 1982 and Zs in 1983, they had masses of almost the exact amounts predicted.

(The detection of these extremely short lived particles—the Zs have a life of 10^{-25} second—took until those late dates because of their great mass; about 90 MeV. The creation of detectable quantities of these particles required powerful accelerators that were not previously available. The Higgs boson, which may be considerably more massive than these particles, may require the use of even more powerful accelerators that are presently proposed or under construction.)

Electromagnetic and weak field theories were thus unified to produce electroweak theory. The quest by theoretical physicists to add the strong field theory to that to produce what has been named grand unified theory, or GUT, has since continued but with only minor success. Many physicists seem to feel confident that this will be accomplished relatively soon—perhaps within a few years.

That will leave the greatest quest of all, one that Einstein and many other theorists have struggled with for decades, for a single unified theory of all the laws of the universe; the theory of everything, or TOE. In GUT Einstein's Special Relativity is united with quantum theory by Wigner's work. If TOE is someday developed, as hoped, it will unite his General Relativity with all of quantum theory.

In the meantime, the standard model is the result of the work of a number of geniuses over almost a century. There are some missing pieces and perhaps some errors, and some theories that require modification but, as proven by experimental results, the current gauge theory standard model represents the best information available on the fundamental particles of physics. With the possible exception of the work of a single individual, Albert Einstein himself, the gradual development of quantum theory to its present state, and its merger with Special Relativity by the efforts of those mentioned, and by a number of others who deserve to be mentioned, is undoubtedly the greatest scientific accomplishment of the 20th century.

FOUR

Big Bang
Theory

Now that some introduction to relativity, the elementary particles and quantum theory has been presented we can proceed to introduce standard (pre-inflation) BBT. As this review of BBT and its history are read it should be remembered that what is presented is an unproven theory; not proven fact. (A major change has been made to standard BBT during the past dozen years by the incorporation of "inflation." That will be discussed in a later chapter.)

In the mid-1920s Belgian cleric and theoretical astronomer Georges Lemaitre, who is considered the Father of the Big Bang, originated the idea that the universe started from a highly compressed and extremely hot state which he called the "primeval atom." As this matter expanded it thinned out, cooled down and aggregated into stars and galaxies.

Some 20 years later, Russian-American physicist George Gamow expanded on that idea, basing his work on Russian meteorologist and mathematician Alexander A. Friedmann's solutions to Albert Einstein's General Relativity field equations in 1922, and on the work of Edwin Hubble and Milton Humason in the late 1920s that provided observational data supporting the expansion of the universe. Friedmann's work, although known to Einstein, was unknown to Hubble and Humason. It had gone essentially unnoticed until it was independently duplicated by Lemaitre in 1927. In 1948 Gamow presented the basic BBT that provided the basis for all the BB cosmology that has followed. (The term Big Bang was coined in 1950 by British astronomer Fred Hoyle, one of the originators of the rival Steady State cosmology.)

Prior to Hubble and Humason's work that showed it to be expanding, the universe was thought to be static, that is, except for the planets of the solar system, all the heavenly bodies were fixed in space. Einstein's equations contained a term of undetermined magnitude, now known as the cosmological constant, that he assumed represented a "cosmic repulsion" force that opposed the force of gravity and provided the balancing force required for a static universe. But following Friedmann's work, later supported by the work of mathematicians Howard B. Robertson and Arthur Walker, and after the universe was known to be expanding in accordance with Hubble's law, most physicists, including Einstein, accepted the standard BBT, that is also called the "FRW cosmology" after Friedmann, Robertson and Walker.

At that point Einstein abandoned his cosmic repulsion term (by merely setting it equal to zero), calling it the greatest mistake of his career. If he had not interpreted it as representing a gravity balancing force, he might very well have crowned his achievements by showing his equations to predict the expansion of the universe. Instead that prediction was made by Friedmann.

Over the intervening years, Gamow's basic theory has evolved. BB scenarios based on General Relativity have been elaborated, and Gamow's date of the BB of less than two billion years ago, has increased to 10 to 15 billion years ago. (The age of the universe will be discussed in chapter 13.) Three alternate scenarios for closed, open or flat universes, resulted from the FRW solutions. The space of the closed universe has positive curvature, that of the open universe has negative curvature, and that of the flat universe is uncurved.

In FRW cosmology the closed universe case would result in the eventual cessation of expansion followed by the collapse of the universe. That would occur if the average density of the universe exceeds a critical value. It might result in continuing cycles of explosion, expansion and collapse. The open case would cause the expansion of the universe to forever increase. In the borderline flat case, in which Euclidean geometry and classical physics would apply, the expansion of the universe would slowly diminish and eventually cease. This flat universe case is known as the Einstein-de Sitter model in which both the cosmological constant and the curvature of space are negligibly small.

Many present day BB cosmologists believe that the flat case is the most likely. Although the observed density of the universe falls far short of that required for a flat universe, enough "missing mass" is believed by them to exist in space to approach the critical amount, which is estimated to be an average of about three atoms per cubic meter. Although there seems to be considerable agreement on flatness among very modern cosmologists, the open universe case, requiring somewhat less density, and the closed universe case, requiring somewhat greater density, have some support among BBT advocates. These three BB cases will be discussed in more detail in the next chapter.

All of the early BBT options suffer from some real or perceived concerns. The greatest of these, and one that effects them all, may be the "singularity problem." The human mind has a difficult time handling the concept of infinite mass/energy density at infinitely high temperature in an infinitely small space for an infinitely short time. According to standard BBT, at the instant of creation all of the mass of the universe exploded at or very near the speed-of-light. However, if that were so, each minute particle of matter would require infinite or near infinite energy to propel it from the infinite gravity of infinite density (infinite curvature of space). The total energy required for the BB might approach an infinity times an infinity!

The lack of large-scale smoothness of the universe has also presented a major problem to BBT. BB cosmologists have insisted from the beginning that beyond some boundary the universe is smooth. It is isotropic and homogeneous, and the Copernican and Cosmological Principles apply. Through the years, as larger nonuniformities have been discovered, BBers have pushed that boundary further into space. Despite the recent discovery of enormous irregularities, many of them believe that, on a still larger scale, the universe will yet prove to be smooth.

This belief in smoothness, which apparently started as a result of a misunderstanding about the application of Einstein's field equations, has become an important element of BBT. It seems that BB cosmologists have gotten themselves "wrapped around the axle" on this topic. Despite contradictory evidence, some of them go to great lengths to explain how smoothness might have occurred following a chaotic or even mildly irregular BB explosion.

If the initial BB wasn't extremely smooth, there may be another serious problem related to the smoothness of the universe. Once the matter of the early universe had been blasted away from the hot BB at "relativistic" velocity and beyond gravitational attraction, there would be no possibility of interactions to cause its smoothing. On the other hand, if there was perfect initial smoothness, there would be no possibility of interactions to cause galaxies or clusters of galaxies to form; according to Special Relativity "faster-than-light signaling" is not possible. This problem, that is called the "horizon problem," also causes concern among BB theorists.

The belief of BB proponents in uniformity is consistent with the idea that we are no more in the center of the universe than any other "observer" in another part of the universe might be. This is said to be consistent with the idea (attributed to General Relativity) that, rather than the matter of the universe expanding in space, space itself is expanding. As BB cosmologist W. B. Bonnor said, "This is not merely a difference of words, the active role of space in dynamics is one of the main ideas which Einstein brought to physics when he created general relativity."

The idea of expanding curved space-time incorporates the concept that the hot BB didn't happen at a single point within the present universe; it happened at a single point that has now expanded to be everywhere within the curved space-time continuum of the universe. American astronomers Gott, Gunn, Schramm and Tinsley (formerly Australian) tell us, "it is not sensible to ask where the big bang took place. The point-universe was not an object isolated in space; it was the entire universe, and so the only answer is that the big bang happened everywhere." To them this means that "our galaxy is indeed at the center of the universe, but so is every other galaxy;" all points within the BB universe are at its center.

Of course the expansion of space doesn't apply to local areas. For example, gravitational fields hold galaxies together, and the other three force fields hold pieces of matter, such as humans and their measuring devices, together. If these were also expanding we wouldn't be able to gauge the expansion of the universe. Even the mutual gravitational attraction between the galaxies of our local group, such as the Andromeda galaxy that is 2.5 million light years distant, draws them together.

BB cosmologists believe that there is considerable physical evidence in support of BBT. Hubble expansion of the universe is mentioned by some as a major piece of evidence in support of BBT. In a 1991 article that was designed to put to rest once and for all any doubt about the credibility of BBT, cosmologists Peebles, Schramm, Turner and Kron stated that, "improvements in the tests of homogeneity and Hubble's law...must be counted as impressive successes for the standard model," meaning standard BBT. However, that expansion is consistent with a SS universe and other possible cosmologies as well as BBT. In the old SST of continual creation of matter throughout space, for example, all galaxies might be departing from each other exactly as they are observed to do. As a result, other evidence is normally cited as being most significant in support of BBT.

In that same article, in all seriousness, Peebles et al. stated that equations describing the temperature and the density (the average density of baryons) of the universe "have been tested back to Z (redshift) equal to 10^{10}." A red shift of that amount is equivalent to a minute fraction of a second after the BB. That statement is of course an obvious untruth. Not only have such tests not been performed, it is utterly impossible to perform them. (To some modern theorists "tested" has come to mean "conformed to favored theory.")

Some BB cosmologists, including American astrophysicists David N. Schramm and Gary Steigman, feel that the strongest evidence for BBT comes from the need for the extremely high temperatures of the BB for "primeval nucleosynthesis" (nuclear fusion) to "forge" some of the light elements of the universe from neutrons and protons. (See Chapter 10.) But the presence of uniform microwave background radiation, is usually presented as the most important physical evidence, not only for a BB, but for a smooth BB. However, as we will see (in Chapter 10), the extreme uniformity of that radiation, which is believed to originate early in the history of the BB universe, is difficult to reconcile with the presently observed nonuniformity of the universe.

BB cosmologists have worked out a time line for the the evolution of the universe. A series of events based on quantum theory have been placed at various points in time in the history of the BB universe. A general summary of this chronology is described here and illustrated in Figure 2. Not all BB cosmologists agree on the details of this chronology, but it is representative of what exists in the literature.

Prior to the invention of inflation theory, other than the singularity that occurred at zero time, BBers had no consistent proposal for what might have happened before Planck time. At that time, 10^{-43} second after the BB, the temperature of the minutely small and unbelievably dense universe had cooled from infinity to about 10^{32} degrees K. (K is for degrees Kelvin, the absolute temperature scale.) But now, with the advent of the theory of everything (TOE), some of them think that this is when quantum theory symmetry breaking resulted in the freeing of the hypothetical particles of gravity—the gravitons.

(It should be noted that TOE & GUTs are relatively recent developments that were not incorporated in early standard BBT. TOE is highly speculative, but one or another form of GUT is now considered plausible by a number of theoretical physicists and BB cosmologists.)

At about that energy level, equivalent to about 10^{19} GeV (billions of electron volts), a Higgs-type scalar field caused gravitons to acquire mass, loose their symmetry and form the "quantum soup" of the early universe. Until then, during the first tiny instant of its existence, the universe contained no particles with mass; just a "symmetrical gas" of energetic stuff that had no recognizable form, that is said to have been in perfect equilibrium.

Following that, as the universe cooled and expanded, symmetry would be broken again and again to produce all the other particles of the universe, that is, they would acquire mass from the Higgs field (or fields—there may be more than one) and come into existence as unique particles.

According the current BBT, the next postulated symmetry breaking occurred at about 10^{-33} second, when the temperature cooled to about 10^{27} K, equivalent to about 10^{15} GeV. According to presently popular hypothetical grand unified theories the symmetry of the still minute, dense universe was broken, this time to produce quarks and qluons, the mediators of the strong force that bind quarks to form hadrons.

However, because the energy level of the universe was too great, hadrons couldn't be held together. Quarks, antiquarks and gluons that "fell out of equilibrium" remained uncombined until the temperature dropped to about 10^{14} K, at about 10^{-8} second.

(Quantum theory requires the generation of particle pairs, i.e., for every particle produced an antiparticle must be produced. However, it is said that some electrically neutral particles, such as photons, gluons, and gravitons, are their own antiparticles. They are said to be self-conjugate.)

Notice in Figure 2 that the energy level of an accelerator now proposed is about 2,000 GeV (or 2 TeV), equivalent to a temperature of about 10^{16} K. That accelerator is the giant Fermilab Tevatron located near Chicago, which might be be able to provide for the discovery of other hypothesized particles but it will not be nearly large enough to verify either GUT or TOE. The size and power for an accelerator that would be capable of verifying GUTs puts it totally out of the range of human capability. An accelerator of that power, about 10 billion times the power of the Tevatron, would have to be light years is size and, for TOE, an accelerator would have to be tens of light-years in size.

At 10^{-10} second, when the temperature of the universe was about 10^{15} degrees K, which corresponds to about 100 GeV, weak force bosons (W minus, W plus and Z zero), and leptons (electrons, muons, neutrinos and photons—no antiphotos) started to form. Symmetry breaking was responsible for creating these particles. Until then they were just part of the massless and formless energy of the symmetrical gas of the universe. Now they were given mass by the Higgs scalar field, and they too "fell out of the quantum soup." The energy levels needed to generate these particles is well within the capabilities of existing accelerators, and their existence has been verified many times.

By 10^{-8} second after the BB, at a temperature of about 10^{14} K, electroweak symmetry breaking was complete and the hot dense gas of the universe included leptons, quarks, gluons, antiparticles and photons.

At that time the energy level of the universe became low

enough to allow the coupling strength of gluons to bind quarks together. Hadrons (and, of course, antihadrons) started to form. That continued until about 10^{-4} second (one ten-thousandth second), at a temperature of 10^{12} K, at which time no individual quarks remained. Prior to that period continual quark/antiquark and gluon creation and annihilation had occurred. Until then quarks were "free" but ever since then the coupling strength of the strong force bosons is so great that quarks have never existed singly. Scientists have seen evidence of their presence in hadrons, but never as individual particles.

At the end of the period of hadron formation, at one ten-thousandth of a second after the BB, the temperature of the universe had cooled to about 10^{12} K, and the density of the universe is said to have decreased to the still enormous value of about 1,000 tons per cubic centimeter. The universe then consisted of the leptons, their antiparticles, mesons, their antiparticles, some neutrons and protons. It has been proposed that GUT processes had resulted in the elimination of antineutrons and antiprotons from the universe.

As the temperature dropped from 10^{12} K to 10^{10} K (at one second after the BB) tau neutrinos, mu neutrinos and electron neutrinos were formed due to symmetry breaking. Neutrons decayed into protons and antielectron neutrinos, and muons and antimuons annihilated into electrons, positrons, muon neutrinos and electron neutrinos. At one second after the BB some tau neutrinos also remained, but tau particles had been similarly annihilated. Due to the initial excess of electrons (apparently also explained by GUTs), all positrons had been annihilated.

Photons (electromagnetic radiation) dominated the universe, as it did until about 300,000 years after the BB. The ratio of electrons and protons to photons was only about one in hundreds of millions, and there was only about one neutron for each five protons. Neutrinos, like photons, are believed to have survived to this day, and they "flood" the universe; perhaps as many as hundreds per cubic centimeter of space. Neutrinos, that might possess a minute amount of mass, and thus, because of their prevalence, might contribute significantly to the missing matter of the universe. However due to their extremely weak interactions with other matter, they are difficult to detect.

At one second after the BB the temperature of the universe had dropped to about 10^{10} K (10 billion degrees absolute), and its density to a couple of hundred pounds per cubic centimeter, but it was still a hot, dense, opaque fluid. If the universe had expanded at a constant rate its size would then have been on the order of 300,000 kilometers, as compared to its present size (according to BBT) of about 10^{23} kilometers. (Expansion is linear; temperature and density are inversely proportional to time but size is directly proportional.)

At that time quarks became bound into neutrons and protons, and electrons joined with protons to form nuclei of the first and the simplest of atoms, those of hydrogen. It is supposed that at that time thermonuclear reactions started. In the period of one second to a few minutes after the BB, this process is said to be responsible for the production of the nuclei of a number of light elements which includes helium (about 25 percent of much as hydrogen) and small amounts of deuterium and lithium. Because of the high energy level of photons their reactions with electrons wouldn't allow the formation of complete stable atoms.

At about 200 seconds BB nucleosynthesis ended. Expansion and cooling then continued until about 300,000 years (estimates vary between 100,000 and 1,000,000 years) after the BB when the temperature dropped to about 3,000 K. (Some say as high as 4,500 K.) In the meantime nothing else of great significance occurred. Radiation continued to dominate the universe, i.e., photons continued to react with electrons which were absorbed and reradiated at a furious pace throughout the universe.

At about 300,000 years, "decoupling" occurred, when, as professors of astronomy Rees (of Cambridge) and Silk (of Berkeley) said, "the fireball ceased to be a plasma of electrons and particles." The temperature had cooled and the density decreased to the point where photon interactions with electrons essentially ceased. Electrons then combined with nuclei to form complete atoms of the light elements. Photons were freed to travel through the universe. The universe, which until that time was opaque, now became transparent.

After the decoupling it is thought that small irregularities of distribution of matter in the expanding universe resulted in the eventual accumulation of matter into galaxies and clusters of galaxies. This process is thought to have started in earnest at about one billion years after the BB and the evolution of the universe has proceeded since then, producing the universe as we see it today, about three times 10^{17} seconds (10 billion years) after the BB.

It should be noted that the more-or-less standard chronology described here is based on a constant rate of expansion since the BB occurred about 10 billion years ago. That timing is equivalent to a Hubble constant (H) of 30 km per sec per million light years (about 98 km per sec per megaparsec). That constant rate, e.i., negligible deceleration of expansion since the BB, may be fairly consistent with the low average density that is observed, but it is inconsistent with the beliefs of the majority of BB cosmologists who believe in a near flat, flat or a closed universe.

For those BBers who believe in a flat universe having that Hubble constant, the BB would have happened only 2/3 as long ago as in a fixed-rate universe, or about 6.67 billion years ago. For those who believe in an open universe, the BB would have happened somewhat earlier and, for those who believe in a closed universe, it would have happened somewhat later. Although a linear chronology similar to that of Figure 2 has been repeatedly used in presentations on BBT, it is far from a correct representation of the decelerating expansion that is accepted by the majority of BBers. Somehow this discrepancy continues to be overlooked by BBers.

The integrity of this elaborate story, generated by a host of theoretical physicists, might at first appear to be on fairly firm ground. But there is another fallacy, beyond the inconsistency noted above, evident in the BBT time scale. BBT is a scheme that was developed out of General Relativity and the discovery of the expansion of the universe resulting in the concept of higher temperature in a younger, denser universe. The postulated higher temperature, and thus higher energy level, that increases toward infinity as we go back in time can accommodate the creation of particles requiring any conceivable degree of energy.

Thus the generation of any particle that is postulated or experimentally produced in an accelerator at any level of energy can be assigned a point in time on the BB time scale. Regardless of how great that energy level might be, it necessarily corresponds to some time following the BB. Thus the events of the time line might merely be contrived relationships, and quantum particle theory need not be tied to BBT or burdened with its problems.

BB theorists Schramm and Steigman tell us that "predictions based on the evolution of the universe" in accordance with a time line like that of Figure 2, "are consistent with observations made 10 billion years later." But the events of that chronology are not predictions at all. That chronology was created in recent years, about 10 billion years after those events are said to have occurred. It took years of effort by teams of geniuses to synthesize that amazing chronology, but there is no compelling reason to believe a word of it!

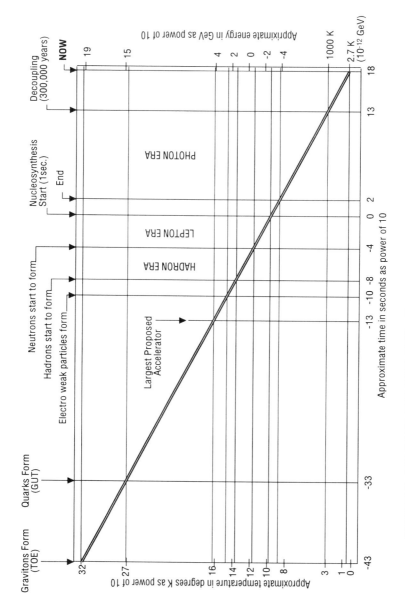

FIGURE 2. BIG BANG CHRONOLOGY – Temperature/Energy/Time Relationships

– 56 –

FIVE

The
Big Bang Cases

It would be of great interest to BB cosmologists to determine whether their universe is open, closed or flat. There is con siderable disagreement among them on this topic. Some favor the open case, some the closed case and some the flat case. Among those who favor the closed case, some believe in a repeating BB, and some believe the universe will not explode again. Some aspects of these various cases of BB cosmology are illustrated in Figure 3.

The closed universe case (represented by the area below Curve 2 in Figure 3) that in BBT corresponds to positively curved space, has a rate of expansion that is lower than escape velocity, which will eventually result in the cessation of expansion, followed by the collapse of the universe (as represented by Curve 1 of Figure 3). In this case, advocated by Princeton astronomer James E. Peebles, Princeton astrophysicist Jeremiah Ostriker and others, the average density of the universe exceeds a critical value and, the greater the density is beyond critical, the sooner that collapse will occur.

Some BB cosmologists believe that, upon its collapse, the universe will re-explode, re-expand, and re-collapse in continuing cycles (as represented by Curve 1a). Some believe that these cycles have occurred in the past (not shown in Figure 3), and will continue in the future; among them are astronomer Joseph Silk and physicist John Wheeler, who is now emeritus professor at Princeton University. George Gamow thought there was at least one previous collapse of the universe but that it wouldn't happen again; it would disperse toward rarefaction. Silk calculated that the number of past cycles of the universe is limited to less than 100. Some BB cosmologists have suggested that BB cycles lose energy and diminish with each cycle. Others have suggested that the universe might gain energy with each cycle.

Although the observed mass of the universe is estimated to be only about one or two percent of the amount needed to cause collapse, closed universe advocates believe that the necessary missing mass, possibly the "cold dark matter" (CDM) of space, will eventually be found. However, it would seem that the possibility of a density very much greater than that critical amount is out of the question. If density were that great (and the age of the universe more than just a few billion years) the expansion of the BB universe might have peaked, and it would by now be contracting rather than expanding as observed.

In the BB open universe case, represented by the area between Curves 2 and 3 of Figure 3 (actually all the area above Curve 2 is "open"), corresponding to negatively curved space, the average density would be less than the critical amount, and the rate of expansion would be greater than escape velocity, causing the expansion of the universe to forever increase, but at a diminishing rate. Expansion would be decelerating due to gravity, but would be less than in the closed case. Proponents of the BB open universe case include astrophysicist Richard Gott, astronomer James E. Gunn and physicist George Gamow.

There is a borderline case between the BB open and the closed cases, wherein expansion is opposed by the equal and opposite force of gravity, the average density of the universe is at the critical value, and the velocity of matter of the universe is just at escape velocity. In this case the expansion will eventually cease and the universe will become static (as represented by Curve 2 of Figure 3). This case is said to correspond to flat space, in which Euclidean geometry and classical physics apply. It is called the flat case but, if Einstein was correct, and there is no negative curvature of space, it might more correctly be called the balanced or critical case.

For that situation to exist there would have to be a very special reason; some special theory would be needed to explain how nature might have provided the necessary precise balance of forces. Some theorists have said that, for a universe that may now be less than perfectly flat, in order for the universe to be as flat as it now is, in earlier times it would have had to have been very much flatter. It has been calculated that, at 10^{-43} seconds after the BB, it would have had to be flat within one trillionth of one percent. The mystery as to how such flatness might have occurred has been called the "flatness problem."

Several prominent BB cosmologists, including B. J. Carr, Paul Davies and Andrei Linde, support the flat universe case. Although formerly indicating a preference for the closed cycling universe, Stephen Hawking, Cambridge professor of theoretical physics, famous for his work in quantum cosmology and theory of black holes, has been quoted as saying that his "best guess" is that the universe is flat. British cosmologist and quantum physicist Davies has said that one of the "remarkable coincidences" of the BBT primeval explosion "is the way in which the strength of the explosion was exactly matched to the gravitational power of the cosmos such that the expansion rate lies today very close to the borderline between re-collapse and rapid dispersal."

Flat BB universe proponents believe sufficient missing mass exists in space for it to be at critical density, which has been estimated to be an average of about three atoms per cubic meter (or five times 10^{-24} grams per cubic meter). They believe the missing mass, and thus the average density, to be somewhat less than that believed by closed universe BBers and somewhat greater than that believed by open universe BBers.

If the rate of expansion of the universe has been constant since the BB, its size has been proportional to its age. When plotted on a graph of expansion versus time (Curve 3 of Figure 3, that corresponds to the linear expansion of Figure 2) this case appears as a straight line out to the edge of time. In this fixed-rate case the BB would have occurred at Hubble time, the time that is indicated by the extension of the presently observed rate of Hubble expansion, which puts it at about 12 billion years ago.

(The most recent estimate of the rate of expansion of the universe, the Hubble constant (H) is estimated to be about 80 km per second per megaparsec (Mpc) or about 25 km per second per million years. Hubble time (T_H), the time of the BB if expansion were constant since then, equals $1/H$. For an H of 25 km/sec/MLYs, T_H is 12 billion years.)

Data presented in 1970 by astronomers Rees and Silk, based on a study by Hale Observatory astronomer Allan Sandage, who has continued Hubble's work, indicates that the recessional velocity of galaxies is very close to a linear function out to distances of over 3 billion light years. Data of a few years later (presented by Gott, Gunn, Schramm and Tinsley) show evidence of a somewhat greater rate of expansion beyond about 3 billion light years. These observations tend to support a universe of decelerating expansion, i.e., the rate of expansion is not fixed, and it doesn't appear to be increasing. But, because these observations were based on bolometric magnitude, i.e., energy received by light sensing devices, they cannot be considered conclusive.

(Celestial brightness or star magnitude is measured in a system that gives higher numbers to dimmer objects. The "first magnitude" is equivalent to the brightness of a candle at 1,300 feet. Each increase in bolometric magnitude of one is equal to a decrease of brightness by a factor of about 2.5 and each increase of 5 is equal to a decrease in brightness of 100. Human eyes can see out to about magnitude 6. The most powerful land based telescopes with modern sensing devices can "see" to about magnitude 24.)

Bolometer measurements don't compensate for differing source luminosities. If, for example, galaxies were more brilliant in the remote past, their distance, and thus their recessional speed, as judged by brilliance, would be less than that as judged by their red shift. But, as we will see, doubts about the accuracy of measurements of massive bodies by means of red shift add to the uncertainties regarding the distance of remote massive bodies, their relative velocities, and thus the rate of expansion of the ancient universe.

However, if the above mentioned observations are to be trusted, and because there obviously is considerable matter in the universe (and in the absence of cosmic repulsion), it might seem reasonable to expect that the rate of expansion of a BB universe is decelerating. Also, in the absence of some very special theory, the universe should not be expected to be expanding at a fixed rate. That reasoning constituted one of the flaws attributed to

SST that postulated a universe that had been expanding at a fixed rate for innumerable billions of years.

As represented by Curve 4 of Figure 3, there are conceivable cases in which the expansion of the universe would be increasing. There were some early cosmological schemes that offered accelerating expansion, including a model that "bounces" due to cosmic repulsion, and the Eddington-Lemaitre model, that started out steady state after which there was exponentially increasing expansion.

Recently it has been suggested by University of Chicago physicist Michael Turner that, if there were a small cosmological constant, it could add to the expansion rate resulting from the BB, and cause an increasing rate of expansion of the universe. Even more recently, ardent BBers Peebles, Schramm, Turner and Kron stated that if objects of the universe prove to be older than 17 billion years, "it would drive us to a cosmological constant." A lower rate of expansion in the past would allow for an older BB universe. However, in standard BBT (the FWR model), there is no rationale for a fixed rate universe or one of increasing expansion.

As apparent from the preceding, there are a number of problems related to the various BBT cosmological scenarios. Among those the singularity problem would seem to be the greatest.

Unlike the BBT closed cycling case (or SST), that defer the question of the origin of the universe, the open, the flat and the noncycling closed cases of BBT have the immediate problem of a source of energy and matter for their "one-shot" singularity. In the early days of BBT, in the excitement of this new intriguing theory, the lack of explanation for a universe out-of-nothing seemed to go unnoticed or unquestioned but, as time passed, there was increasing awareness that the law of the conservation of mass/energy should not have been ignored, and that BB proponents had a serious problem on their hands.

The closed cycling universe case requires an initial BB and subsequent BBs that repeat at intervals of perhaps on the order of 20 to 50 billion years. Because they (all but the first) are not "ex nihilo," but depend on the collapsed matter and energy of the previous cycle of the universe to fuel them, these repeating singularities may not be as difficult to accept as the one-shot singularity. But even a collapsed universe could not explain its re-explosion. All singularities are anomalous. They are the greatest problem of BBT.

British astrophysicist W. B. Bonnor in 1960 said that "a singularity in mathematics is an indication of the breakdown of a theory" and that it must be done away with. Oxford professor of astrophysics Dennis Sciama in 1967 said that the singularity is "one of the botches" of the universe. B. J. Carr in 1982 said that "all known physics breaks down" in a singularity. Sciama, a former SST advocate, reported that the problem of the "unpleasant singularity" helped motivate British mathematicians Herman Bondi and Thomas Gold and British astronomer Fred Hoyle to develop the old SST.

An example of the problems associated with a BB singularity, repeated here for emphasis, is that every particle of matter that was blasted from the infinite gravity of the BB might require as much as an infinite force to propel it, which, of course, seems quite improbable. The incorporation of inflation into BBT theory in recent years is claimed to have solved the singularity problem, but a partial revision of theory doesn't seem sufficient to circumvent the law of conservation of mass/energy. Even Andrei Linde, the originator of new inflation, admitted (in 1985) that a final solution to the singularity problem "will be possible only after the development of a complete quantum theory," meaning TOE.

Two other major problems that have plagued all of the BBT cases, the smoothness problem and the related horizon problem, were introduced in Chapter 4. For those BB cosmologists who prefer the BB flat or balanced universe case, there is the additional serious problem of explaining the special situation of a universe having an average density exactly equal to its critical level; the flatness problem. Inflation theorists claim to have solved these additional problems, but that is also subject to considerable question.

In a near-balanced, balanced or closed case there is the problem of missing mass. The directly observed density of the universe is estimated to be one or two percent of the critical amount. The density inferred from studies of the rotation of galaxies might raise the total density to about 10 times that amount in the vicinity of galaxies. But, because there is no evidence that the density is equally high in vast intergalactic space, greater mass within the galaxies might result in only a small increase in the average mass of the universe.

Even if the average density of missing matter were of that same magnitude throughout space, the flat universe case would require a density about 10 times again as great (somewhat more for the closed case, and somewhat less for the open case). Up to 99 percent of the mass of matter distributed throughout the universe would have to consist of mysterious stuff, perhaps non-baryonic CDM, having no known characteristic other than gravitational attraction.

Considerable effort has been made to explain theoretically, and to find observationally, sufficient additional matter in space to justify these cases, but it hasn't been found. Rees and Silk suggest that some missing mass might exist in the form of burnt-out galaxies and black holes within them. Others have suggested that some of this dark matter might exist of gas, dust grains, neutrinos (if they are found to have mass), low mass stars, large planets, small black holes, magnetic monopoles, cosmic strings or sheets, or gravitational waves. In recent years exotic particles called photinos, axions, gravatinos, neutralinos, MACHOS (massive astrophysical halo objects—a new name for brown dwarfs), WIMPS (weakly interacting massive particles), and CHAMPS (charged massive particles) have been added to the list. Most of these have either been ruled out or are purely speculative. A lack of sufficient density continues to deny a closed or nearly closed BB universe.

A cycling universe that repeatedly collapses and rebounds would have the additional problem of the bounce. Although John Archibald Wheeler (in 1970) suggested a means by which a rebound might occur in accordance with quantum theory, no generally acceptable explanation has been advanced for a rebound. Regarding such a bounce, Edward Tryon (in 1973) said, "No satisfactory mechanism has ever been proposed," while B. J. Carr (in 1981) said that, "physics cannot yet explain what could cause this bounce."

In fact, theories for the formation and the life of black holes—in which many theorists, including Wheeler (also in 1970), indicate that black holes are "laboratory models" for processes of a collapsing universe—are not predicted to explode, but only to gradually dissipate by quantum evaporation, a process called

Hawking radiation after its originator in 1974. Furthermore, European astronomers Courvoisier and Robson tell us (1991) that, "According to the theory of general relativity, a black hole is the ultimate stable configuration for a very massive object."

If the black hole is a model for a collapsing BB universe, why wouldn't it spin like a black hole? Because virtually all stellar matter, including satellites, planets, stars, galaxies and clusters spin or orbit or both (not to mention all the particles of modern physics), shouldn't we also expect the universe as a whole to be rotating? Why wouldn't it, upon its collapse, spiral into an enormous black hole, rather than become an exploding singularity?

American physicist Heintz Pagels has suggested, although he thought the evidence is against it, that, "the entire universe and all the galaxies in it could be rotating. The universe would then have an axis of rotation, a preferred direction, and would not be isotropic." Cambridge radio astronomer Adrian Webster disagreed (in 1976), saying that, if the universe were rotating, it would be detectable by differential Doppler effects.

But that is not necessarily so. The universe could be rotation at a presently undetectable rate, or the lack of observation of rotation could be due to the thermalization of the matter of surrounding space (as will be discussed in Chapter 9), whether by energy from the BB or from other possible sources.

An additional problem of the cycling closed case may be that observed irregularities in the distribution of matter in space indicate that there is a significant lack of proportionality of velocity to distance. The discovery of formations of galaxies spread over many millions of light-years that are held together in their own gravitational environment, provides evidence of this lack of proportionality. Therefore, unless there is a spinning collapse, à la black hole, the matter of the universe might not converge.

Some matter of the collapsing universe might arrive at the anticipated site of the next BB somewhat earlier than other matter, and thus proceed to shoot out at relativistic speeds into space in the opposite direction from whence it came. Later arriving matter, having nothing to impact, would also shoot out in the opposite direction. One might expect that a horizon problem, similar to that of the expanding BB universe, would apply to a collapsing universe, preventing the re-aggregation of collapsing matter. At the time of the next proposed collapse, instead of the envisioned BB, chaos might result.

(This convergence problem might tend to discourage acceptance of the cycling BB universe. But, on the other hand, it might suggest an alternate scheme for the bounce of a cycling universe, this one without an explosion.)

As an examination of Figure 3 will verify, if the flat universe BB happened 8 billion years ago (H=25 km per sec per million light-years; Hubble time T_H=12 billion years), and recent geological and astrophysical studies are correct in estimating the age of some stars and galaxies to be as old as 15 billion years, the flat and closed universe cases are impossible. The universe is far too old to allow them. Furthermore, if the ages of stars and galaxies are greater than 12 billion years, as they very likely are, the BB open case is also impossible.

The only possible variation of BBT that would allow a sufficiently old universe would be one having a slower expansion in the past (as represented by Curve 4 of Figure 3). The only known postulated cause for that situation of increasing expansion would be a relatively large cosmological constant. Although that may be possible under some cosmologies, it is not normally accepted by BBers. The physical evidence for the ages of stars and galaxies therefore causes serious doubts about standard BBT.

Even if the Hubble constant were found to have a value as low as 15 km per second per million light years, and the flat case BB would therefore have occurred about $13^1/_3$ billion years ago, because some stars and galaxies are estimated to be considerably older than that, there would be little likelihood for a flat or closed universe; especially for a closed universe that might collapse within 100 billion years.

In addition to logical considerations based on older information, several very recent astronomical studies related to the density of the universe have been conducted. One of these had to do with the distribution of galaxies in surrounding space, one with the speed of surrounding galaxies versus their distance, and one with the relative velocity of our nearest neighboring galaxy, the Large Magellanic Cloud. All of these investigations have provided evidence denying the possibility of a flat or closed universe.

Famed astronomer Vera Rubin has been quoted as saying, "We are being driven to the conclusion from dynamics, that we live in a low density, ever-expanding universe." Marc Postman of the

Space Telescope Science Institute, reporting on the results of a recent study of the density of clusters of galaxies in the universe, has stated that, "These numbers imply that...the best theories are wrong, and the universe will keep on blowing up fast and forever."

Discoveries of very large-scale irregularities in the universe, such as gigantic voids and sheets of galaxies, and the fairly recently discovered "Great Wall" of galaxies, have not only discredited the BBT concept of smoothness but, because it is estimated that their formation would have taken as long as 100 billion years, they also provide compelling evidence of the impossibility of a closed, flat or even slightly open BB universe. In fact, if large galactic structures required only 15 billion years for their formation, all cases of standard BBT would be out of the question.

BB theorists tell us that the negatively curved space of an open universe is saddle-shaped. Thus it doesn't close upon itself and it has no edge. They also tell us that the space of the balanced universe is neither positively or negatively curved but flat, and that universe has no edge. However, those same cosmologist tell us that space is expanding and that the BB happened everywhere. But BBers should be aware that those characteristics are incompatible with open or flat space; they require a closed universe. In addition to the impossibility of a closed or a flat universe, and probably also a somewhat open universe, due to age and other considerations, the illogicality of ascribing the space expansion and BB everywhere characteristics of a closed universe to a BB flat or open universe should be clearly apparent, and should cause further doubts about the possibility of any of these cases.

Also, if possible implications of his abandoned cosmic repulsion are ignored, Albert Einstein's presentation of General Relativity does not include negative curvature of space. Positive curvature of space is a function of the density of matter. According to Einstein, if there were no matter present, space would be uncurved but, because the universe isn't empty, all of space has some degree of positive curvature. The greater the density, the greater the positive curvature. If there had been a BB having infinite density, it would at that time have had infinite positive curvature.

However, if the space of the universe has negative curvature, as postulated by BBers for the open universe case, there would have to be a negative force that causes that negative curvature and opposes and exceeds the positive gravitational force of the matter of the universe. And of course the BB flat case could only be the result of a negative force that cancels the effect of the positive gravity of the matter of the universe.

In other words, the BBers acceptance of a flat or negatively curved space thereby implicitly acknowledges the existence of something akin to Einstein's cosmic repulsion. Their mathematics, if valid, provides that inevitable conclusion. There must be more than an equation to explain negative curvature; the mathematics must represent some physical phenomenon, something like a cosmic repulsion or a positive cosmological constant.

It is clear that most, if not all, BBers believe that the expansion of the universe is slowing due to gravitation. But it is not clear how that deceleration might occur. Because they believe that the space of the universe is expanding, one might conclude that they believe it is the expansion of space that is slowing, rather than merely the expansion of the matter of the universe.

General Relativity indicates that space is "warped" by gravitational force, but it is not clear to what extent, if at all, gravity might cause the deceleration of expanding space. Quantum theory postulates certain physical attributes for empty space but it has not been shown how gravity might interact with those. Thus it is not known how gravity might cause the deceleration of expanding space.

Perhaps due to that uncertainty, although it again is not clear, BBers might believe that it is the matter of the universe, rather than the space of the universe, that is decelerating due to gravity. But in that case it would seem that the matter of the universe must have an "inward" velocity relative to expanding space; perhaps an awkward situation. It is not clear whether matter or space is decelerating; or perhaps both are decelerating, possibly doubling the effect of gravity—an even more akward situation.

Because it has not been found in previous literature, this deceleration quandary may present a new problem to BBers. How they might respond to it is not known.

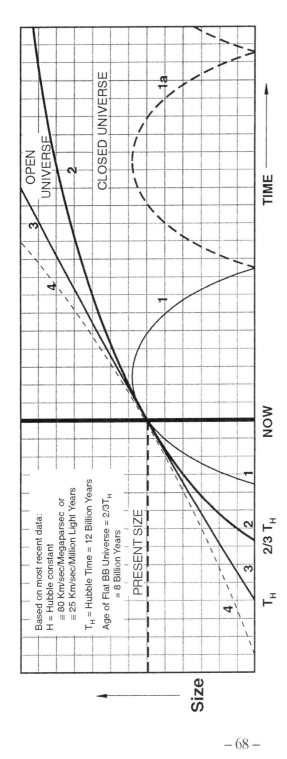

Based on most recent data:

H = Hubble constant
≡ 80 Km/sec/Megaparsec or
≡ 25 Km/sec/Million Light Years

T_H = Hubble Time = 12 Billion Years

Age of Flat BB Universe = $2/3 T_H$
= 8 Billion Years

OPEN UNIVERSE

CLOSED UNIVERSE

PRESENT SIZE

Size

T_H $2/3 T_H$ NOW

TIME

1.   Closed Universe. All cases below curve 2 will close.
1a. Additional cycles of closed cycling universe.

2.   Flat Universe, border between open and closed universe.
     All cases above curve 2 are open.

3.   Fixed Rate Universe. (Constant expansion)

4.   Universe of Increasing Expansion. Not a standard BB case.

FIGURE 3: BIG BANG COSMOLOGICAL CASES (Size of the Big Bang Universe vs. Time)

- 68 -

SIX

Flights
of Fantasy

A few examples of the flights of fantasy of theoretical physicists during the past couple of decades are presented in this chapter. They are included in order to illustrate some of the wild ideas that been have proposed and to provide some additional background for the next chapter. Some of these ideas are the direct result of attempts to rationalize and support BBT. All are related to BBT, and have been applied to it.

Vacuum Fluctuations

The concept that the universe might consist of nothing but empty space filled with fields grew out of early quantum theory. From this came the idea that vacuum is not "nothing," but in "a state of least energy density." Fluctuations of energy in vacuum can result in "false vacuum," in which it is said that gravity becomes a repulsive rather than an attractive force, and in which particles of matter can be spontaneously generated.

In 1973 Edward Tryon suggested that the entire universe originated as a vacuum fluctuation that "ran away with itself" generating highly curved space and producing an avalanche of particles that resulted in the BB. This was proposed as a means of circumventing the violation of the law of conservation of mass/energy of previous BBT, thus solving the singularity problem.

Tryon wrote that although they are "utterly commonplace in quantum field theory...vacuum fluctuations on the scale of our Universe are probably quite rare." This flight of fantasy didn't make much impact until the 1980s when it provided the basis for inflation theories. A variation of that, suggested by Martin Rees in 1976, was that when the curvature of space had the extreme value of the early BB universe, particle pairs could have been created out of gravitational fields in a manner similar to the creation of electron-positron pairs in strong electromagnetic fields. Thus Rees suggested that the space somehow became extremely curved—perhaps infinitely curved—before any matter came into existence.

Grand Unified Theories

As mentioned, some quantum theorists have come to believe that all that exists in the universe are force fields. If that is so, when the equations for those fields have been completely formulated all that needs to be known about physics, and probably metaphysics as well, will be known. Einstein was able to produce his great work without ever conducting an experiment. These theorists apparently have concluded that in like manner they might complete Einstein's quest for unified theory by sitting and manipulating mathematical abstractions. (They shouldn't be misled by Einstein's lack of experimentation. He believed, as did Mach, that measurements are essential for the validation of theory.)

Following the successes of theoretical physicists during the late 1970s and early 1980s in unifying electromagnetic theory (QED) with weak field theory to produce electroweak theory, many theorists have turned to the task of expanding that unification process to incorporate strong field theory (QCD) and thus developing a grand unified theory, or GUT. Because it doesn't include gravity, this theory is not intended be a complete unification, but only the next giant step in that direction. Some theorists feel that they are closing in on a credible GUT, but the extreme difficulty of incorporating gravity to produce the theory of everything, or TOE, may require many years of additional effort.

The simplest of the GUT theories, known as the SU(5) theory, indicates that the strong, weak and electromagnetic forces were indistinguishable before 10^{-33} second after the BB, which, according to BBT, is equivalent to an energy level of 10^{15} GeV (billion electron volts) and a temperature of 10^{27} degrees K. As the universe, whose size at that time was only about 10^{-29} cm, cooled to about that temperature, symmetry was broken, producing quarks and gluons. (It wasn't until about 10^{-10} second that the symmetry of the electroweak forces were broken.) In this theory leptons might be thought of as quarks of a fourth color.

The SU(5) GUT has encountered several problems. One of these is that it predicts that protons decay in about 10^{30} years, which according to BBT is about 10^{20} (100 billion billion) times the age of the universe. One would therefore expect it to be rather difficult to measure this decay. But, by isolating many times more than 10^{20} protons (2 million gallons of water) and using detectors of the predicted products of proton decay (a positron and a neutral pion), it has been determined that, if protons do decay (they had previously been thought to be "immortal"), it takes considerably longer than 10^{30} years; at least 100 times longer. Several proton decay experiments have been conducted (deep in salt and iron mines in the United States, in lead mines in Japan and in a tunnel between France and Italy), but no proton decays have been detected.

Another problem is that an SU(5) GUT appears to require an additional set of vector bosons which would in turn require an additional scalar field similar to the hypothetical Higgs field. The new bosons might have masses of hundreds of GeVs, many times greater than the weak vector bosons. Neither these bosons or the new Higgs-like field may ever be detectable.

A third problem encountered is that, if the new Higgs-type field exists, they require the existence of large amounts of isolated north and south magnetic poles, or monopoles and antimonopoles. GUT indicates that there may be as many magnetic monopoles in the universe as there are protons, which BBers estimate to be about 10^{80}. Although their abundance, their huge mass and their strong field should make them readily detectable (and of course they might prove to be the missing matter of the universe), attempts to find them have been unsuccessful.

Another area of doubt has arisen due to Brandeis University physics professor Larry Abbott's warning regarding an error in the estimated value of what he called the cosmological constant of quantum physics, which happens to be the same as the infamous cosmic repulsion term of Einstein's field equations.

Abbot reports that, according to quantum theory, this constant would be about 10^{46} times larger than measurements indicate. He tells us this difference reflects a deep misunderstanding of unified theory. The standard model of gauge theory, with its large number of fluctuating fields, including the well-known but hypothetical Higgs boson, is therefore "dumping too much into the vacuum," and it "may be based on a conception of vacuum or of spacetime that is flawed" and "The vanishingly small value of the cosmological constant indicates that important discoveries remain to be made." One might expect this news to dampen the enthusiasm for vacuum fluctuations of a magnitude sufficient to generate the mass of the universe and to blast it out to 10 billion light years.

The chance for acceptance of an unmodified SU(5) GUT is obviously quite poor. As a result, a number of variations have been proposed. One variation involves additional sets of particles of greater mass called technicolor quarks (techniquarks) mediated by technicolor gluons and reacting in technicolor fields. Theorists may be looking for these in the products of more powerful accelerators of the future.

Magnetic Monopoles

The idea of magnetic monopoles goes all the way back to 1931 when Dirac, while working on electromagnetic field theory, found that the mathematics indicated the possibility of their existence. If so, they would have a magnetic charge analogous to the electrical charge of an electron. The idea of magnetic monopoles was brought up to date by Dutch physicist Gerard t'Hooft and Russian physicist A.M. Polyakof in 1974 when they showed (theoretically) that when symmetries of some of the gauge field theories are broken, magnetic monopoles would be produced, and that their properties could be calculated.

More recently it has been proposed that magnetic monopoles are "solitrons" of energy in space. Solitrons were first discovered as surges of channel water; solitary waves of energy that travel at relatively high speed. The mathematics of the soliton has been known for a century. It has been applied in other fields such as plasma physics, and more recently to magnetic monopoles that are said to remain intact and propagate in a manner similar to water solitrons. Of course, as with other quantum particle pairs, if a monopole and an antimonopole were to meet they would annihilate with an enormous release of energy.

According to GUT theories magnetic monopoles are estimated to be about 10^{-14} cm in diameter and to be extremely massive, about 10^{16} times more massive than a proton. Assuming BBT were correct, they were created in the first 10^{-35} second after the BB, traveled ever since, and now roam the universe. They are extremely abundant, absolutely stable, and are said to possess some additional exotic characteristics. Because of their powerful magnetic field they should be easy to detect; immense accelerators are not required for that purpose. In fact, devices have been designed to detect GUT monoples by electromagnetic induction. However, except for one presumably false indication that has never been repeated, none have been detected.

Multiple Worlds and Domains

One of the first to relate quantum theory to cosmology was renowned American physicist John Archibald Wheeler. In regard to the cycling BB case, which he apparently accepted at that time, he suggested in 1970 that the probability amplitude concept of quantum theory as applied to the collapse of the universe might provide some answers about the outcome of that event. According to Wheeler the universe is "squeezed through a knot hole" and what comes out is anybody's guess. Each collapse could result in a whole new set of properties but, as in quantum electrodynamics, the outcome is subject to the participation of the observer.

Wheeler introduced to BB cosmology a many-worlds concept that was proposed in 1957 by his student Hugh Everett in his theoretical physics Ph.D. thesis. In this many-worlds interpretation of quantum mechanics a system is not well defined until it has been measured or "observed" in some manner. A measurement can not be made with certainty, only the probability of the outcome of a measurement can be predicted. This concept is especially strange when applied on the macroscopic level. Everett decided that the universe splits into parallel branches when observed, each branch corresponding to a different possible outcome.

This many-worlds concept sounds rather bizarre but, as we will see, Russian physicist Andrei Linde apparently thought enough of it to integrate it into his theory of chaotic new inflation. In his version of BBT, as the early universe cooled, separate domains developed in various regions of the universe that had totally different sets of physical laws. They were separated by massive domain walls, and observers in one domain, such as ourselves, have no means of establishing contact with other domains. Because of vast inflation of the universe, the domain walls are beyond the range of telescopes, and for the same reason the problematic magnetic monopoles are so far away that they don't disturb the evolution of our domain.

The generation of domain walls has also been described in another manner. It has been suggested that, as the extremely early BB universe cooled, the Higgs field came into being. If the cooling was not uniform the Higgs field would have different properties in different regions of space. This would result in some strong interactions at the boundaries of regions, generating massive domain walls.

The Theory of Everything

As with their previous attempts to produce lesser unifications, when physicists have attempted to integrate gravity with quantum theory to produce a TOE, infinities show up. But in this case equations for the graviton's interactions were found to be nonrenormalizable; infinities appeared that could not be disposed of. But an even more fundamental problem is perceived that has to do with the equivalence principle of General Relativity, in which a gravitation and acceleration are considered identical phenomena.

As we have seen in the discussion of General Relativity, a man in a box in space can't differentiate between a constant acceleration and a gravitational force due to the proximity of a large mass (or a combination of those). According to quantum theory, however, gravity is the result of the exchange of gravitons (the "mediators of gravity"). If that is so, how it is possible for their presence to depend on the acceleration of an object presents a serious dilemma for the TOE theorist.

(It is timidly suggested here that, just because the physical effects of gravity and acceleration result in identical mathematical treatment, it doesn't necessarily follow that gravity and acceleration are identical phenomenon. Mathematical expressions happen to be the same or very similar for many physical phenomena without leading to the conclusion that they are identical. If it were possible for Einstein to have made a second error, at least one TOE problem might be solved.)

Although theoretical physicists have worked for years to reconcile gravity and quantum theory, the above mentioned problems, and a number of others, have prevented any real progress. Some degree of success might be claimed for GUT theories in unifying electromagnetic, weak and strong forces, but until gravity is integrated with quantum theory (that is used by BBers to describe matters at BB scales smaller than about 10^{-33} cm) there can be no single integrated TOE.

Supersymmetry and Beyond

The flights of fantasy of theoretical physicists seem almost limitless. Perhaps just a few more should be mentioned as examples of their extreme ideas. Among these are the reportedly renormalizable supersymmetry grand unified theory (SUSY-GUT) that involves the proposal of five dimensions and in which the spin of particles can change. The desirable result of this is that all particles can be viewed as of a single Yang-Mills superfield. This theory results in the proposal of new particles that are mirror images of the particles of the standard model. Newly proposed particles necessary to supersymmetry theory are hypothetical light supersymmetric particles or LSPs.

Further modifications of supersymmetry have resulted in a theory called supergravity that incorporates gravity as a gauge field. Einstein's theory of gravity can in this theory be considered as a description of the hypothetical spin 2 boson called the graviton, as discussed in Chapter 3. This variation is alleged to be at least partially renormalizable.

Superstring theory, which was developed in the 1980s, holds that all the matter and forces of nature, including the weak, the strong, electromagnetism, and gravity, are the result of vibrations of minutely small strings of extremely high energy that form loops throughout space.

In what appears to be an attempt to exceed Einstein in the count of dimensions of the universe, more advanced theories have been presented that incorporate as many as 10 or 11 dimensions (and one with as many as 26 dimensions). It is of some comfort to note that those dimensions beyond the fourth, as in the case of the fifth dimension of supersymmetry, are all "small dimensions" that do not conflict with our everyday experience.

Some physicists have advanced the idea of "worm holes" of space. Perhaps when the matter of one domain (or universe) collapses into a black hole it can leave that domain by means of a four-dimensional tunnel. Its mass/energy can reappear in another domain at another time and space. Conversely, new energy, perhaps in the form of massive brilliant quasars (quasistellar radio sources), can arrive in our domain by squeezing through worm holes from other domains.

Some say whole new universes can be generated by worm holes in space-time. Perhaps the energy for the BB at the start of our own space-time arrived through a worm hole, thus solving the mass/energy conservation problem of BBT. It has been suggested that worm holes provide a rationale for the vast expansion of the early universe as postulated under inflation theory.

Based on what has gone on in the past there will undoubtedly be more flights of fantasy as time goes on. If the same pattern is followed each of these will be more grand and complex, and make greater claims in support of BBT. Paul Dirac once said, "It is more important to have beauty in one's equations than to have them fit experiment." Theoretical physicists seem to have taken these words to heart and are carrying them to extremes in their quest for support of BBT.

Regarding scientists working on TOE, Murray Gell-Mann, a Nobel Prize winner for his work in quantum chromodynamics, is quoted as saying, "Most of them don't know what they are doing. They're just using various mathematical tricks." Hopefully the direction of cosmological endeavor will soon change toward a broader goal than merely to provide more and more elaborate theoretical schemes in support of BBT.

Black Holes

Because the possibility of the existence of black holes is almost universally known it may seem that they shouldn't be included here as a flight of fantasy. But there is a lot more to black hole lore than commonly known. For example, contrary to popular belief, energy may be able to escape their enormous gravitational force, and some who believe there was a BB also believe that a large number of relatively small black holes may exist throughout the universe.

As with the BB itself, Einstein's General Relativity provided a mathematical basis for black holes. When stars the size of the sun die, i.e., use up their nuclear fuel, gravitation causes them to collapse into what is called white dwarfs about the size of the earth that have very high density. Stars that are about one half again as large, but less than about 3-1/2 times as large as the sun, collapse into neutron stars that are on the order of 10 miles in diameter and have enormous densities. Stars that are more than about 3-1/2 times the size of the sun are believed to collapse into black holes that are so compact that their escape velocity is greater than the speed of light. That means, regardless of how hot and luminous they might be, no light, heat or other radiation or matter can escape from them. Thus they cannot be seen or directly sensed by any type of radiation detector.

Black holes, that were given that name by John Wheeler, are enclosed within an area that is called their event horizon, also called the Schwarzchild radius after German astronomer Karl Schwarzchild who originated the idea in 1915. External matter or radiation that nears the event horizon is more and more subject to the attraction of the gravitational force of the black hole. But when it falls within the invisible event horizon it is gone. It cannot escape, and its energy equivalent becomes part of the black hole. If another star should be nearby its matter might gradually be pulled into the black hole. This can happen if the black hole and a star are members of a binary pair, which, because of the abundance of binary stars in the universe, may not be a rare occurrence. The abundance of binary stars also results in the rather common occurrence of star-neutron star binaries.

The observation of star-hole binaries also appears to provide the best evidence of the existence of black holes. Because the pair orbit about their common center of gravity, the wobbling motion of the normal star of the pair can be analyzed to detect the presence of its invisible partner. It turns out that this kind of observation provides convincing evidence of the existence of black holes, without one ever having been directly observed. Cal Tech astronomer-theorist Kip Thorne is 80% certain that Cygnus X-1 is a binary pair in which the invisible member of the pair is a black hole. Most astronomers would agree with him.

Even though neither matter nor radiation can directly escape black holes it is believed that they can loose mass by a process that is explained by quantum theory. At the very edge of the event horizon, where gravitational field energy levels may be sufficiently high, particle pairs might form. Instead of rejoining in mutual annihilation, before that can happen, one particle of a pair might fall through the event horizon. Either a particle or an antiparticle might then be free to escape the clutches of the black hole. Thus matter, or its energy equivalent, effectively leaves the area and the black hole slowly looses mass. This process is named Hawking radiation after its originator, who is responsible for development of much of current theory regarding black holes.

Hawking, who is a proponent of BBT, also tells us that at the time of the BB conditions (within the first ten 10^{-20} second) were right for the birth of a very large number of much smaller black holes. Huge forces occurring an instant after the start of the BB could produce sufficient pressure to compress irregular areas of matter into billions of small black holes that now populate the universe. Because they cannot be seen, they may provide the dark matter of the universe that is sought by cosmologists who are attempting to determine whether the universe is open, flat or closed.

In contrast to large black holes resulting from collapsing stars, that might take far longer than the age of the universe (as estimated by BBT theorists) to evaporate by Hawking radiation, these small black holes might have lives short enough to regularly meet their death in violent explosions; perhaps as many as two per century per cubic light year in our neighborhood. (Because one light-year is about 6 trillion miles, this might not present too serious a threat to our safety.)

Hawking theorized that when small black holes, which may be about the size of a proton and may weigh about a billion tons, are near the end of their existence their gravitational field can no longer hold them together and they explode in a powerful burst of gamma rays. Undoubtedly it will be suggested that these are the source of at least some of the gamma ray bursts recently detected by NASA's Compton Gamma Ray Observatory satellite.

SEVEN

Inflation

Sometime after 1970 BBT cosmologists began to recognize the possibilities presented by quantum mechanics with its concepts of probability amplitude and vacuum fluctuations to solve some of the problems of the BBT. Now two major achievements of the century in physics, General Relativity and quantum theory, might be combined to describe the origin and evolution of the universe. One result of this marriage of quantum theory and BB cosmology was a new development called inflation, perhaps the ultimate flight of fantasy.

As might be expected after reading the previous chapter, under quantum theory BB cosmologist decided that almost any conceivable event might have some degree of probability. Accordingly, each cycle of the rebounding universe can be a whole new ball game, and multiple worlds, domains or even universes can result from each BB, and each of these can have different sets of physical laws, numerical constants, sizes and life cycles. These worlds or domains don't have to be sequential. They can occur at any time or place, be far apart in time or space, occupy the same time and space, or overlay each other, with no interference, communication or knowledge of each other. They can be few or in great abundance. Each of them can be created out-of-nothing, now allowed by quantum vacuum energy. A BB could happen anywhere at any time.

These are just some of the extreme ideas that have resulted from the quest to utilize quantum theory for the elimination of problems of the previous BB model. Although much of standard BBT was based on his ideas, Einstein's reluctance to accept quantum theory was ignored in this frenzy.

As mentioned, one of the early leaders in this race was John Wheeler, who believed in a cycling universe. In 1970 he suggested that the probability amplitude concept of quantum theory might be applied to the collapse of the universe. The universe is "squeezed through a knot hole" meaning Planck length (1.6×10^{-33}cm), and the world that results from the rebound could have a whole new set of physical laws.

Somewhat later physicist Edward P. Tryon proposed that the universe resulted from a giant quantum vacuum fluctuation. He tells us that quantum fluctuations are commonplace in quantum field theory and, although probably quite rare on the scale of our universe, "Our universe is simply one of those things that happen from time to time."

According to the probabilities of quantum field theory these things arise on various scales and, although they come from nowhere, they do not violate the law of conservation of mass/energy. That is because, according to Tryon, the universe has zero net energy; gravitational force is negative and equal and opposite to all the other energy of the universe.

That makes some sense. As an analogy, when you blow up a balloon you might conclude it has zero net energy because the energy put in is saved in the compressed breath and is opposed by the negative force of the stretched rubber. When the breath is released the input energy (except for some heat losses) can be retrieved. The energy you put into the balloon might be thought of as being temporarily borrowed. But borrowing enough energy to blow up the world for a period of some 50 billion years (until its collapse?) doesn't seem to meet the test of energy conservation.

In 1976 astronomer Martin Rees suggested that quantum mechanics may have caused the smoothness of the universe. But, for an understanding of that, we must await the development of the theory of quantum gravity to explain the events of the first 10^{-23} second of the BB. During that period of extreme space curvature and quantum gravitation large-scale smoothness developed, but small amplitude fluctuations resulted in the formation of the galaxies. He suggested that the Theory of Everything (TOE), yet to be developed, might solve both the conservation of mass/energy and the smoothness problems. But he wasn't too sure of any of that.

Cosmologist B. J. Carr in 1982 mentioned quantum mechanics and the many-worlds concept as they related to his discussion of the Anthropic Principle (which will be discussed further on). But, perhaps in his preoccupation with that topic, he failed to appreciate their potential to provide an explanation for energy to fuel the BB. If fact, he expressed his uneasiness regarding the probability amplitude aspect of quantum theory when he wrote, "This concept is very strange, especially when applied to situations where the quantum uncertainty on a microscopic level can manifest itself on a macroscopic level."

However, MIT physics professor Alan Guth did not miss the implications of quantum theory. His concept of the inflationary universe, published in 1981, marked a radical change in the direction of BBT. The BB was no longer thought of simply as an explosion. It started as an expansion of energy out of false vacuum (vacuum can become excited and adopt various levels of energy), which behaved like the cosmic repulsion force once proposed by Albert Einstein, but was of enormous magnitude. It had negative energy that fed on itself to expand exponentially. After vast expansion, because false vacuum is unstable, like the sudden freezing of supercooled water, it decayed into true vacuum in an enormous flash of radiation that turned into matter and antimatter.

The repulsion force then disappeared and inflation ceased. The universe continued to expand due to the initial impetus, after which it was slowed by gravitation, as in standard BBT. Although the cosmological constant had to have been enormous at the time of the BB, it would now have to be very small or zero in order to be consistent with the present flat universe as postulated by inflation theorists.

Guth's inflationary theory, which was developed in 1980 and published in 1981, describes an expansion by a factor of 10^{50} that occurred between 10^{-35} and 10^{-32} second after the BB. The speed of this inflation was orders of magnitude greater than the speed of light. (Although other figures have been given, Guth's expansion of the universe might have been from 10^{-25} cm to 10^{25} cm, which is about 10^7 light-years, or about 100 times the present size of our galaxy.)

Guth's idea for inflation may have come from Dutch astronomer Wilhelm de Sitter who in 1916 had suggested a cosmology in which there had been a runaway expansion of the universe, presumable due to Einstein's cosmic repulsion. It's of interest to note that cosmic repulsion was now resurrected in support of inflation theory. Davies proclaimed (in 1984) that, "The way now lies open for an explanation of the big bang…The universe would be subject to a cosmic repulsion force of such magnitude that it would cause headlong expansion at a high rate." However, instead of the minute force that Einstein had proposed as necessary to balance the force of gravity in space, it now took on the enormity required to blow up the entire universe.

(Because it isn't prominent in the literature, it may not have occurred to some inflationary theorists that if the cosmological constant had been larger in the early BB universe the rate of expansion might have been correspondingly greater. That could result in a BB universe much older than as presently calculated based on Hubble's constant, thus solving the BB age problem.)

The energy for the inflationary process is explained by the idea that cosmic repulsion is negative pressure that gains energy as it expands. Guth said that inflation provides a "free lunch;" in this case it is a giant feast that is based on the tiny bites of quantum electrodynamic electrons and positrons generated in intense electric fields. The problem of the singularity was now solved by the repulsive power of quantum vacuum that caused the explosion of space itself. (Davies referred to Guth's "free lunch" as "cosmic bootstrap." Both of these expressions might merely be euphemisms for "violation of the conservation of mass/energy.")

The strange series of events of the inflationary process also provided the remarkable situation that the force of expansion exactly matches the opposing force of gravity, and thus also solves the flatness problem. In addition, during the inflationary process, any initial irregularities in the early universe are stretched out sufficiently to provide for large-scale uniformity but not enough to prevent the formation of galaxies and clusters, thus solving the smoothness and the horizon problems.

Guth's inspiration for inflation theory came as he studied the problem of the absence of magnetic monopoles that were predicted by SU(5) GUT to fill the universe. These strange entities had never been observed, creating a serious problem for GUT. Guth's inflation was intended only to solve that problem but he later fortuitously found that it also might solve the BB flatness, smoothness and horizon problems. The advertised ability of inflation to provide solutions to some major problems of BBT is undoubtedly the reason it has gained considerable acceptance.

However, it was found that, because the phase change from false vacuum to true vacuum would not occur all at once, Guth's inflation would result in a number of "bubbles" in the universe. Because the boundaries of those are not observed in our universe, a new problem was created. In the mid-1980s Russian physicist Andrei Linde, while working on this problem, invented a modified inflation theory—chaotic hyper-expansion inflation—that would solve the bubble problem.

Linde's new inflation takes advantage of the unproven concept of scalar fields, like that of the hypothetical Higgs boson of gauge theory, that fill the universe. These fields, that are without direction, polarity or spin, and have only scalar magnitude, are responsible in modern field theory for "breaking the symmetry" to release nature's basic forces, the weak, the strong, the electromagnetic, and possibly the gravitational force, depending on the development of a totally unified theory (TOE).

Before these forces were separated in this manner they were indistinguishable. In the instant following the creation of the universe the scaler fields were weak, and thus the fundamental forces were unified and the universe was symmetrical. But, as the universe expanded and cooled, symmetry breaking proceeded. The result of the scalar fields in the early universe was a chaotic, $10^{1,000,000}$ inflation that occurred before the hot BB started. (That expansion is so great that upon its completion only an instant after the BB—and even now—the universe would be on the order of $10^{1,000,000}$ times the size of the present observable universe.)

The speed of expansion of new inflation was orders of magnitude greater than that of Guth's inflation. Apparently speeds many times greater than that of light are assumed to be permissible because no matter is involved. But it would seem that energy must certainly be involved and, if there is an Einstein mass/energy equivalence, these inflation theories are invalid. Einstein tells us that not even information can be transmitted faster than the speed of light.

During the new inflation period, lasting less than 10^{-30} second, oscillations of scalar fields caused the generation of not only our domain but many others (mini-universes) of a wide variety of characteristics about which, being confined in our own domain, we can learn nothing. Our domain just happened to develop three-dimensionality (or 4-dimensional space-time) and the physical laws that we observe, while other domains may have more or fewer dimensions and different sets of physical laws. Because of their different characteristics it would be impossible for inhabitants of different domains to communicate or obtain information about each other.

Linde tells us, although it's not obvious how, that his new chaotic inflationary scenario provides simple solutions to most of the problems of the standard BB model. The singularity problem is solved (because of zero net energy); it merely awaits the development of a complete quantum theory of gravity. The tremendous expansion during the inflationary period solved the flatness problem and, although its start was chaotic, it also solved the smoothness and horizon problems. During inflation the quantum fluctuations grew "in just the right way" to produce the relatively small inhomogeneities that we call galaxies and clusters, but not larger nonuniformities.

(If the latest estimated values of the Hubble constant and of the ages of galaxies prove to be as great as latest observations indicate, a flat BB universe is impossible. Because flatness is believed to be an inherent feature of the inflationary BB universe, the impossibility of a flat universe would seem to deny that theory.)

Linde, who invented several versions of new inflation, frequently changed his mind. He claimed that inflation solved the singularity problem but later contradicted himself by saying that, "A final solution will only be possible after the development of a complete quantum theory of gravity," meaning TOE.

Linde has claimed that vast inflationary expansion also solves an additional problem; that of the magnetic monopoles. Guth's original reason for inventing inflation was to address the problem of the generation of large amounts of these anomolies. In our present domain they are not a problem; magnetic poles invariably occur in pairs. But troublesome hypothetical single magnetic poles, as predicted by GUTs, occurred in profusion in the early BB universe. Guth's inflation failed to satisfactorily solve that problem and also that of bubble walls (which under new inflation became massive domain walls). Linde claims that new inflation theory solves these problems by dispersing the magnetic monopoles so thinly that they become insignificant, and domain walls are sent far beyond any observable distance.

Davies tells us that in addition to magnetic monopoles, GUTs would produce their one- and two-dimensional analogs, massive cosmic strings and sheets. These problematic flights of fantasy (neglected in Chapter 6) would also be dispersed to insignificance by new inflation. These vibrating strings and sheets of enormous density, like magnetic monopoles, are hypothetical quantum constructions in space. They should not be confused with actual galactic formations that have been discovered in recent years.

The preceding discussion necessarily presents only an abbreviated review of modern BBT trends. Although the previous chapters on quantum theory and flights of fantasy should help, the above can't possibly provide a thorough understanding of these ideas. But it is hoped that this review will indicate to the reader that these elaborate schemes do not provide solid solutions to the problems of the BBT. Instead, because of their esoteric complexities, they add to BB problems.

For example, it would seem that inflation theory, as currently accepted by mainstream BB cosmologists, introduces a some new problems. Those theorists postulate a universe that has expanded to unimaginable size, and thus we can observe only a tiny portion of it. But they continue to tell us that quasars can be seen to within a small percentage of the distance to the BB. They also continue to describe BB events essentially in accordance with the typical BB chronology of Figure 2 without consideration of the changes required to accomodate inflation. Certainly BB cosmologists must be aware of these discrepancies, but they are ignored. As in the cases of BB problems in the past, it apparently is assumed that some future theoretical innovation will solve them.

Linde's claim of simple solutions is an obvious distortion of the facts. The truth is that inflation theories are enormous complications. The past history of science has repeatedly demonstrated that as the mysteries of nature have gradually been solved the truth has always been beautifully simple and understandable, even by persons with limited background in the science of their time.

Since the beginning of BBT each new innovation of theory has been an attempt to eliminate one or more of the shortcomings of previous versions, but none have succeeded. Complexities have proliferated but the old problems of the singularity, of smoothness, horizon, flatness, missing mass, excess matter over antimatter, and several others remain to plague the BB cosmologist.

EIGHT

The Smoothness
of the Universe

The subject of smoothness was introduced in the previous discussion of BBT. As mentioned in the introduction, the word smoothness is here intended to be synonymous with large-scale uniformity, and both of those terms are intended to roughly denote the combined meaning of isotropy, homogeneity, the Copernican Principle and the Cosmological Principle.

BB cosmologists insist that, on a very large scale, the universe will be found to be smooth. However, questions arise as to how the initial explosion might have been sufficiently irregular to result in the formation of galaxies and clusters of galaxies without developing even larger irregularities as claimed by BB theory, or how the galaxies and clusters of galaxies could have formed as a result of gravitational attraction if there weren't relatively large irregularities in the density of the early BB universe. This smoothness problem has plagued cosmologists since BB was introduced by Gamow in 1954. Over the years BB theorists have developed a variety of scenarios to overcome this difficulty.

Carr in 1982 struggled with the problem of the "remarkable large-scale homogeneity" of the universe that could be solved by postulating that it started out very smooth, which is the idea most BB cosmologists seem to prefer, or that it started off chaotic and was smoothed as a result of various "dissipative effects" such as "little-understood quantum gravity" very soon after the BB. Whatever the cause, the degree of irregularity was "just right" (fine-tuned) to result in galaxies and clusters, while retaining large-scale uniformity. In 1985 Paul Davies said that, "The large scale uniformity of the universe is all the more mysterious on account of the fact that, on a somewhat smaller scale, the universe is *not* uniform."

The strong belief in large-scale uniformity originated as a result of some simplifications that were made in the process of solving the General Theory of Relativity field equations. Gamow reported in 1956 that, because it appeared that galaxies were spread fairly uniformly in space, matter could justifiably be considered smooth enough to make the assumption that the universe as a whole has a smooth general curvature. Alexander Friedmann had quite reasonably assumed uniformity as a simplification, without which it would have been very much more difficult, and perhaps impossible, to solve Einstein's equations.

This dependence on the uniformity of the universe as a simplifying assumption for the solution of a difficult mathematical problem became distorted in the minds of early BB cosmologists. In 1981 cosmological philosopher Ernan McMullin said that isotropy "is no longer the simplification for the sake of a first calculation that it once was." Smoothness became a requirement rather than a mathematical expedient. Through the years, despite the fact that it may not be essential to the BBT, the idea of large-scale uniformity became firm BBT dogma. As a result, some cosmologists have gone to great lengths to invent theories as to why there is sufficient small-scale nonuniformity to cause the formation of galaxies and clusters of galaxies, without significant large-scale irregularities. Even Heinz Pagels, very much a believer in smoothness, admitted (in 1985), "Really it is we— the model builders—who artificially put in the uniformity to begin with."

In recent years there have been increasing reports regarding very- large scale nonuniformity of the universe; first clusters of galaxies, then superclusters, later voids, relative empty regions estimated at 150 to 300 million light-years across and several billion light-years from us, surrounded by sheets of galaxies, and recently the 500 million light-year "Great Wall', a structure that spreads 20 degrees across the sky. It seems the more and the further the search, the more irregularities are found, suggesting that even more may be found in the future. (Very recently a galactic structure similar to the Great Wall has been reported in the southern sky that has been dubbed the Southern Wall.)

In an article on the Great Attractor, a mysterious point in space toward which our galaxy appears to be drifting, Carnegie Institute astronomer Alan Dressler tells us that the matter of the universe is "clumped together on unimaginably large scale, reflecting poorly understood events in the early universe" and, "If our results are verified, they will point to structures many times larger than the largest features that have been mapped recently, such as the cells of the "bubble universe" described in 1986 by astronomers John Huchra, Valerie de Lapparent and Margret Geller of the Harvard-Smithsonian Center for Astrophysics." (These are not the bubbles of Guth's inflation.)

If that wasn't enough bad news for BBT, recent satellite borne X-ray detectors have provided evidence of clusters of quasars that are ten or more billions of years old (within a few percent of the age of the BB universe). The nonuniform distribution of quasars so soon after the BB also seems to discredit the postulated smoothness of the early BB universe. But BBers still cling to the tenets of isotropy and homogeneity. In article after article, many of them, apparently with full knowledge of these developments, continue to repeat the words of their predecessors.

(As in other estimates of the age of distant massive bodies, estimates of the age of these clusters have been made using the current interpretation of red shift data and by application of BBT methods that are based on a preconceived age of the universe. The actual ages of quasars and their distribution in space could be quite different than indicated above.)

In 1985 Pagels insisted on smoothness "as revealed by the observed even distribution of galaxies and quasars in the sky" and, even after the recent discovery of the Great Wall of galaxies that extends across 500 million light years of space, some BBers haven't given up on large-scale smoothness. Astronomer Andrew Chaikin, in an article on the Great Wall, reported that famous Princeton BB astronomer James E. Peebles still believes that, "if you stand back far enough, the universe will turn out to be smooth."

This is all the more strange when it has never been made clear, other than for tradition, why large-scale uniformity is so important to BBT. Except that it interferes with the BBT basis for the smoothness of microwave background radiation, it's not clear that the observed lack of uniformity per se is harmful to the basic BB theory; shouldn't a universe that started by an explosion be expected to be quite nonuniform?

The uniformity of observed microwave background radiation of the universe, which is discussed in the next chapter, is seen by many, including Davies, Gott, Gunn, Schramm, as near positive proof of the smoothness of the universe. Davies wrote in 1984 that this radiation should "carry the imprint of any departures from uniformity." Some astronomers question whether the smoothness of background radiation originating a few hundred thousand years after the BB can be reconciled with the observed large-scale nonuniformity of the universe. But BB adherents continue to cite this radiation as the most important evidence of both the BB and its large-scale smoothness.

Regarding this tie between background radiation and smoothness, Davies provided us with the following imaginative statement: "If the universe were to expand faster in one direction than in others, it would depress the temperature of the background heat radiation coming from that direction, and also distort the pattern of motion of galaxies as viewed from the Earth. So not only did the universe commence with a bang of quite precise magnitude, it was a highly orchestrated explosion as well, a simultaneous outburst of exactly uniform vigor in every direction."

In recent years, as larger and larger irregularities have been found in the distribution of matter throughout space, and as the microwave background radiation has been found to be increasingly smooth, it has become increasingly difficult for BBers to support their belief in the large-scale smoothness of the universe. Their reluctance to admit that the smoothness of microwave background radiation is inconsistent with the observed large-scale nonuniformity of the universe has required them to periodically move the boundaries of what they consider small-scale irregularities out to greater and greater distances.

Attempts have been made to utilize quantum mechanics to reconcile small-scale irregularities with large-scale smoothness. As mentioned in previous discussion, both Rees and Carr have suggested that quantum gravitational effects might solve the smoothness problem; Guth's 1981 inflation might stretch out irregularities enough to solve the problem; and Linde's 1985 new inflation, that started out chaotic, was so enormous that it also solved the smoothness problem. Davies in 1982 agreed that inflation "stretched to death" any initial irregularities, but didn't produce complete uniformity, because a small degree of "clumping" was needed in the early universe to account for the present existence of galaxies and clusters.

None of these ideas offer a real solution to the smoothness problem. They sound more like wild speculation than scientific theories for what might have caused small-scale irregularities yet allowed large-scale uniformity.

Carr's mention of smoothing by "various dissipative effects" calls attention to an additional related problem; the horizon problem. As mentioned earlier, if an explosion caused the expansion of the universe, one might expect a rather high degree of irregularity. As a result, matter that blasted from the BB at relativistic speed would rapidly reach the point where mutual gravitational attraction was ineffective. That force, which is the only known force that might be effective, could no longer cause any smoothing of matter in space. That premise presents an additional problem to some BB scenarios.

Astronomical data, as determined by the conventional interpretation of red shift measurements, seem to indicate that quasar and radio galaxy formation was much more common in the distant past than at present. If that holds true for all directions into space, it might seem reasonable to conclude that our galaxy is at the center of a non-smooth (possibly isotropic, but not homogeneous) universe. Copernicus may have led BB cosmologists down the garden path. There may be a new BB problem; the Copernican Problem.

That may be good news for BBT advocates of the Anthropic Principle who, as we will see, suggest the same thing, but for different reasons. Consideration of a number of perceived coincidences among various physical constants and other factors caused them to ponder the possibility of a "fined-tuned' universe. That may have led some of them to consider that divine intervention had a hand in shaping things for the benefit of the human race, and that in turn led them to question the Copernican Principle (that we occupy no special place in the universe). Brandon Carter, an English cosmologist and strong proponent of the Anthropic Principle, suggests that this might be "a reaction against exaggerated subservience" to the Copernican Principle, which is "a most questionable dogma."

Astronomer and cosmologist G. F. R. Ellis, an advocate of the open universe case of BB theory, in 1975 suggested that, although microwave background radiation supports the isotropy of the universe (it looks the same in all directions), the distribution of radio sources may deny the homogeneity of the universe (it does not look the same in all parts of the universe), and we may therefore be at the center of the universe. If so, he suggested, the unproven cosmological assumption of the Copernican Principle may not be valid. (In 1989 Silk said that, "If the universe possesses a center, we must be very close to it, within less that 0.1 percent of the radius; otherwise, excessive anistropy in the radiation intensity would be produced, and we would detect more radiation from one direction than from the opposite direction.")

But a universe that is not homogeneous is heresy in the opinion of many BB proponents. If we are at the center of a nonuniform universe, much of the BB house of cards might crumble. BBers deny that the observation of a greater number of quasars and radio sources in the distant past (as determined by large red shifts) is evidence of nonuniformity. Rather they believe it is the result of evolution of the universe. That is, when looking back billions of years at these sources of radiation they are seen when the universe was young, when much more violent things were going on.

However, the BBer's interpretation of this "clumping' of quasars at great distances from us may be erroneous. Distant quasars, believed to be seen as they were a dozen or so billion years ago, may not provide valid evidence of an evolving universe. New questions are presented here for which BBT provides no answers: Why aren't quasars scattered throughout the universe from a BB that happened throughout the universe? Why aren't quasars of various ages more evenly distributed throughout an isotropic and homogeneous BB universe as are photons from the decoupling and other matter of that universe? There is no more reason for greater percentages of them to departing from us at relativistic speeds than there is for nearby galaxies that may also be many billions of years old.

As will be discussed in Chapter 11, it is quite likely that the current interpretation of red shift is incorrect, and quasars are not distributed as presently perceived by BBers. If that is so, the formation of quasars may have occurred more evenly throughout the past billions of years, as the previous discussion suggests. BBers have interpreted red shift measurements as indicative of a greater abundance of quasars in the past, thus providing evidence of an evolving universe. If that evidence is determined to be false, one of their favorite arguments in support of BB (and opposing old SST) would become invalid.

NINE

Background Radiation

Edward Tryon said in 1973, "Recent observations confirm that the 2.7 K background radiation …establishes beyond reasonable doubt that some version of the big bang theory is correct." Virtually every writer on cosmology since 1965 has made statements similar to that. Yet there remain many unanswered questions regarding that matter, some of which are presented in the following paragraphs.

The reception of microwave radio energy from surrounding space, originating at about 250 million years after the BB, was predicted by George Gamow in 1954 when he said that the "great event" occurred; when matter took over from radiation, i.e., "surpassed it in mass density."

That great event, now called the decoupling, is explained (according to standard BBT) as follows: The extremely hot and dense plasma of the early universe caused nuclear reactions that converted protons, electrons and neutrons into deuterium and helium nuclei. After only a few minutes of expansion following that, the BB temperature and density dropped and reactions ceased, leaving the ratio of helium to hydrogen as it is today. For a quarter million years the plasma emitted and absorbed electromagnetic radiation which would be scattered and rescattered by free electrons. By the end of that time the temperature and density dropped to where electrically neutral atoms were formed. That period, that lasted for thousands of years, is called the "decoupling era" because reactions between radiation and matter virtually ceased after that. According to standard BBT, at that point the previously opaque universe became clear, and radiation traveled unscattered through space to become the background radiation we receive today.

Gamow estimated that at the time of the decoupling the temperature of the universe was about 6,000 K (degrees Kelvin) and that it would now be at 50 K. Using his published method (of 1954) and his estimated age of the universe of five billion years, radiation from the great event would now be at about 38 K. Correcting this for the presently accepted age of the BB universe of 10 to 15 billion years would give an estimated temperature of about 27 degrees.

Based on Gamow's work, his students, Ralph Alpher and Robert Herman, in 1948 predicted that the present temperature would be about five degrees K. That prediction is repeatedly quoted as providing virtual proof of BBT, but Gamow's calculations of six years later, that resulted in considerably higher temperatures, contradict that number. Princeton Physicist Robert H. Dicke predicted less than 20 K in 1946. He apparently had forgotten about that and re-estimated the present temperature at 45 K in the 1960s. Dicke's estimate was later modified to about 10 K by his colleague James Peebles. Following the measurement of about three degrees by Arno Penzias and Robert Wilson of Bell Labs in 1965, Peebles readjusted his calculations to agree with that number.

This kind of "prediction," that is made after the facts are known, has occurred frequently in the history of cosmology; sufficiently often that a new word, "retrodiction," has been used by BB detractors.

The 5 K prediction of Alpher and Herman is invariably quoted by BBers when they report on the remarkably accurate prediction based on BBT. They fail to mention that the work by Alpher and Herman was based on some seriously erroneous assumptions. Those included the idea that all of the elements of the universe were generated in BB nuclear reactions prior to the decoupling; and they fail to mention that a number of other incorrect predictions were made by other prominent BB theorists.

As with the prophecies of Nostradamus and other seers, if enough predictions are made, some are sure to come to pass, and those that do not are often ignored.

Radio astronomer Adrian Webster in 1974 said the decoupling occurred about 300,000 years after the BB, producing black-body radiation at a temperature of about 5,000 degrees K. Those photons, which were "undisturbed from that time on," are the source of the microwave background radiation, at 2.7 degrees K, that was first detected by Penzias and Wilson (who's measurements were made at a wavelength of 7.35 cm; a frequency of 4 GHz). Webster's estimates of 10^{13} seconds, or about 300,000 years, and of 5,000 Degrees K, agree well with Gamow's estimates.

Webster explained that the 10-to-1 difference between Gamow's predicted present temperature and that derived from current observations is due to changes in the "large-scale dynamics of the universe … the temperature drops off a little faster than before" the great event. Dennis Sciama in 1967 wrote, without providing further explanation, that "a temperature as high as 30 degrees can be ruled out" because "cosmic ray protons and electrons interacting with such radiation" would produce effects that haven't been observed and "three degrees is about the highest permitted temperature from this point of view." These statements also appear to be retrodictions.

Referring back to Figure 2, the BB time line, if the lower right portion of this figure were carefully redrawn on an expanded scale, it would become apparent that the time line passes close to 1,000 degrees at the time of the decoupling. If the red shift from the decoupling to the present is a factor of 1,000, and the presently observed temperature is about three degrees K, the temperature at the decoupling should have been about 3,000 K. According to BBT the time line should therefore pass through 3,000 instead of 1,000. The comments of the preceding paragraph apparently were intended as an explanation for a slightly different time line, one that passes through 3,000 K at 300,000 years and then turn downward to pass through 2.7 k at the present time.

(It should be noted that if Figure 2 were changed to draw the time line for a present age of the universe of 15 billion years, as currently preferred by some BB cosmologists, the effect on Figure 2 would be negligible. That change would not compensate for the temperature discrepancy mentioned above.)

Rees and Silk in 1970 said that, working backward from an observed temperature of about three degrees K, because red shift since the event was about 1,000, the source temperature had to have been about 3,000 degrees K. But they also said that the time of the event was 100,000 years after the BB, when the temperature, according to Gamow's formula, would have been about 8,400 K. (According to Figure 2 that time would have been about 30,000 years after the BB.)

Also, for some unspecified reason, Carr (in 1982) decided that the decoupling took place one million years after the BB when the temperature of the universe was about 4,000 K. At that time, working backward with Gamow's formula, the temperature would be about 2,700 K. Later on (in 1980 and 1989) Silk said the decoupling started at 300,000 years and ended at 1,000,000 years after the BB. Berkeley physicist Richard A. Muller (in 1978) said that the temperature at the time of the decoupling was 4,500 K and the red shift of its radiation is 1,500. These disagreements among various theorists add to the confusion about the hypothetical decoupling.

According to data from American astronomer Carl Sagan and University of California at Santa Cruz physicist and SETI (Search for Extraterrestrial Intelligence) veteran Frank Drake in 1975, the frequency of detectable microwave background radiation is centered on about a 100-to-one range of one to 100 GHz, corresponding to wave lengths from 30 cm to 3 mm. (The full frequency range is somewhat wider.) A red shift of about 1,000 puts the source wavelength in the range of 3/10,000 cm to 3/100 cm, or about 3 to 300 microns, which falls within the infrared range.

Despite rather large discrepancies between actual predicted temperature and the observed temperature, and despite the time line discrepancy mentioned above, because the amplitude distribution (spectrum) of the received frequency closely resembles that of a black-body radiator, and because it is received very equally from all directions of space, its presence has been accepted as virtual positive verification of a BB about 10 billion years ago and of the uniformity of the early universe. Because so much stock is put in this radiation having originated at the time of the decoupling, perhaps these discrepancies should not be ignored.

Another disturbing factor regarding microwave background radiation (MBR) is the disagreement among BBers regarding the propagation of black-body photons. Some of them insist that this radiation comes directly from the decoupling (Webster's "undisturbed photons") but others indicate it might have bounced around the universe for the past 10 billion years. Rees and Silk wrote (in 1970) that, although prior to the decoupling these photons "attained thermal equilibrium with its surroundings as a result of repeated absorption and remission," they "would not all have been red shifted by exactly the same amount; in some directions they might have been scattered off material with a random velocity toward us, whereas in other directions the last-scattering surface may have been receding from us. As a consequence the microwave temperature would be slightly non-uniform over the sky."

If that statement is logical, as it seems to be, the vast irregularities in the distribution of matter throughout the universe that have been discovered in recent years tend to discredit the BB decoupling as the source of the MBR. How can radiation from the decoupling possibly be smooth to better than one part in 10,000 in a universe having such great irregularities? Paul Davies wrote, this radiation "would carry the imprint of any departures from uniformity encountered on the way." The imprints of those departures haven't been found.

Some BB cosmologists have made efforts to present mathematical proof that, because the universe is "optically thin," it is impossible for the temperature of space surrounding us to be equalized ("thermalized") and thus impossible for that to be the source of the black body spectrum of MBR that is observed. However, proof of a negative idea is difficult to support. Other cosmologists have found rationale in support of thermalization. For example, there is theoretical support, and both laboratory and astronomical evidence, for the presence of metallic "whiskers" that formed by the crystallization of atoms from supernovae and have become distributed throughout the space within and around our galaxy. Those particles could be of a size that would absorb energy in the band of wavelengths necessary to produce thermalization.

Additional evidence for the presence of whiskers in interstellar space may be provided by metallic flakes that are found, along with bits of silicon, in meteorites that are believed to have formed during the birth of the solar system. If BBers can postulate that as much as 99 percent of the mass of the universe is of unknown matter, perhaps it is reasonable to suggest that material in the space surrounding our galaxy has characteristics that provide for thermalization.

Some BB theorist have referred to the decoupling as a "flash." But others have indicated that it went on for close to a million years. During that time the radiated spectrum might have been distorted by changing temperature and changing red shift due to elapsed time. Later radiation would have lower source temperature and less red shift. BBers may have assumed that these effects would tend to cancel, but that may be erroneous. Unless the universe has the linear characteristics of Figure 2 (or Curve 3 of Figure 3), that is, it is of the fixed-rate variety, rather than closed, flat or somewhat open (having a decelerating expansion that is quite nonlinear) as they believe, that cancellation could not be perfect. Also, if the universe were less than perfectly spherical, cancellation would certainly have been less than perfect. If the decoupling occurred over an extended period, differences of time, temperature and travel should be expected to "smear" the radiated spectrum.

If BB black-body photons have been bouncing around the universe for 10 to 15 billion years, as mentioned by Rees, Silk, Davies and others, one might expect that random differences in path lengths would result in a further confused spectrum. With all the possibilities for smearing of BBT black-body radiation due to time and temperature differences, scattering, non-uniformity of its source and of the universe since then, it is unlikely that a black-body spectrum could have been preserved. Rather than supporting the postulated BB decoupling as the source of the MBR, its almost perfect black-body spectrum and its almost perfect smoothness tend to deny that position.

On the other hand, if black-body photons from the decoupling had traveled undisturbed as Webster said, because they travel at the speed of light, they must have outpaced any matter that was ejected from the exploding universe, and there would have been nothing ahead of them to absorb and reradiate them.

If the BB universe is flat and Euclid prevails, or if the universe is open, and space is negatively curved, how can space curvature be the cause of BB photons raining on us from all directions? Under BBT only a universe of closed, positively curved space might account for the arrival of BB black-body photons. But time constraints alone clearly show the closed universe case to be impossible. If there had been a BB, and if there had been a decoupling, any resulting photons would be at the edge of the universe, far beyond any other matter of the universe.

BB cosmologists accept that telescopically observed quasars on the order of 10 billion light-years distant and departing from us at relativistic speeds are seen as they were on the order of 10 billion years ago, perhaps within a few hundred million years after the decoupling. That situation poses some big questions for BBT. If black-body photons departed the BB only a relatively short time before the matter that made up quasars, and at only slightly greater velocity, why aren't some of the millions of quasars in space traveling toward us are black-body photons? If the characteristics of closed curved space explain the motion of photons, why don't they apply to other matter from the BB including galaxies, clusters of galaxies, quasars and other stuff in space?

Referring to the BB chronology of Figure 2, in the period between one ten thousandth of a second and one second, called the lepton era, enormous amounts of neutrinos were freed to travel the universe similarly to the freeing of photons at the decoupling some 300,000 years later.

Some years ago, in an experiment that was designed to detect neutrinos that are believed to come from the sun, a large neutrino detector was built. (Neutrinos are produced when protons are turned into neutrons in the nuclear reactions that occur in the sun's core.) This detector utilized a tank containing one hundred thousand gallons of a chemical (tetrachlorethylene) that would react with neutrinos to produce radio active argon-37 that could in turn be sensed. After years of operation, that experiment was able to detect less than a third of the expected number of neutrinos. More recently an experimental laboratory in Italy called GALLEX, that utilizes gallium-71 to capture neutrinos to produce radioactive germanium-71, reported a detection rate of only about two-thirds of that expected from the sun.

Because neutrinos can penetrate other matter (they can travel completely through the Earth), it is not possible to restrict their direction of arrival, and it is not possible to determine whether those that are detected come from the sun or some other source. If vast quantities of neutrinos from the BB fly through the universe from all directions in a similar manner to photons, one would expect the total number detected would be considerably greater than those expected from the sun. But that hasn't happened.

The reason for their absence is, of course, is that they aren't there. If BBT were valid, and if neutrinos had escaped from the BB, they wouldn't be here. They would have escaped to the edge of the universe; and, if neutrinos from the BB had escaped to the edge of the universe, it would seem reasonable to believe that the photons from the BB had done the same. By that line of reasoning it is inconsistent and illogical to believe that the MBR can provide evidence in support of BBT.

It is of interest to note that neutrinos from supernova S1987A have been detected, and that their detection has provided evidence of their high speed and low mass; not very different than that of photons. If neutrinos from S1987A were detected, why haven't vast amounts of them from the postulated BB decoupling also been detected?

There seems to be little doubt that the spectrum of the MBR is that of black-body radiation. However, some BB cosmologists believe that the MBR didn't come to us directly from the decoupling, but that it has been repeatedly absorbed and reradiated by matter in space for 10 billion years or more. As a result of that process the temperature of the matter of space has reached thermal equilibrium. Surrounding space has been thermalized and thus produces radiation having a black-body spectrum; the MBR consists of photons that have been re-emitted from relatively nearby space matter.

It would seem that the thermalization of surrounding space as an intermediate source of the MBR we receive is an acceptable concept. If it is correct, there are many cosmic sources of energy other than a BB decoupling that might have produced that thermalization, and presence of MBR provides no real proof that it originated in the BB.

In a paper that was prepared before any reliable data was found in the literature regarding received MBR signal strength, the following estimate was presented regarding the total energy of the BB decoupling. Although rough approximations were used to determine the magnitude of that energy, it appears that exact numbers might not be needed to establish an approximate result.

It was guessed that the average received signal strength might be on the order of 10^{-14} watts (one microvolt at 100 ohms), antenna coverage about one arc-minute, receiver bandwidth about one MHz, and a MBR spectrum width of about 1,000 GHz.

With negligable atmospheric attenuation in the microwave band, space attenuation of 10^9 (due to the dispersal of black body photons in a universe that expanded by a factor of 1,000, equal to the ratio of distance proportional to elapsed time of 3×10^{17} seconds divided by 10^{13} seconds squared) and an attenuation of 1,000 due to Doppler red shift (frequency decreased by 1,000, so energy decreased by that factor), the total attenuation would be about 10^{12}.

A sphere is about 2×10^8 greater than one circular arc-minute, and the power over a spectrum that is about 10^6 times greater than that of the received bandwidth, would result in an equivalent total power from all directions, and over the whole spectrum, at the receiving site of two watts, which is equivalent to 2×10^{12} watts at its source. Based on an estimated 10^{22} average size stars in the observable universe, there may be (as a crude estimate) an average of about 100 bodies for each star in the universe (a total of 10^{24}) receiving that much power for a total source power of 2×10^{36} watts.

That rate of energy is equal to the same number of Joules each second. (One watt equals one Joule per second.) According to BBT this situation has gone on for over 10^{17} seconds, and might be expected to continue for about 100 times that period or 10^{19} seconds. (The MBR energy should eventually be dissipated as it impacts the matter of the universe.) So it was guessed that the total energy from the decoupling might be on the order of 2×10^{55} Joules, equivalent to about 100 million equivalent suns, or 1/1,000 that of an average galaxy.

(The sun's mass is about 2×10^{33} grams which, according to $E=mc^2$, is equal to 1.8×10^{54} ergs or 1.8×10^{47} Joules. A universe having an estimated 10^{22} average suns would have a total energy of 1.8×10^{69} Joules.)

Because there is the equivalent of about 100 billion average galaxies in the observable universe, the energy of the decoupling may be on the order of 10^{-14}, or one part in one hundred million million, of the estimated equivalent energy of the observable universe; a minute amount compared to what might be expected of Gamow's great event. (Calculations based on the Stefan-Boltzmann law put the expected black body energy of the decoupling at about 2.7 x 10^{67} Joules, equivalent to about 10^9 galaxies or about 1/100 of the estimated total energy of the universe.)

If, as believed by many BBers, the universe were flat or closed, the presence of dark matter might provide as much as 99% of the mass of the universe. If so, the energy of the decoupling would be a correspondingly smaller fraction of the total energy of the universe; as little as one part in 10 million billion.

Based on recent data from Cosmic Background Explorer (COBE) satellite experiments, the average "brightness" of the MBR is about 0.45 x 10^{-4} ergs per second per centimeter squared per steradian per centimeter. Based on the assumption of that level of signal over the Earth's surface from all directions of space and over a bandwidth of one to 20 cycles per centimeter, and based on the Stefan-Boltzmann law that energy is proportional to the fourth power of temperature, the calculated total energy of the decoupling would be about ten orders of magnitude above that of the earlier estimate, about 2 x 10^{45} Joules or about 1/10,000 of the estimated total energy of the universe. If this estimate is correct it might be large enough to avoid a significant problem related to low BB decoupling energy as based on received MBR signal strength.

Even if the above figures prove to be erroneous, it should be remembered that MBR photons should not be raining on us from all directions. In any conceivable BB universe other than the closed case, which has been shown to be impossible, they would have long ago been dispersed to far beyond other matter, out to the edge of space, and could not be detected by our receivers. For the same reason they could not interact with the matter of the universe to cause its thermalization. Black-body photons could not be arriving directly from the decoupling, nor could they be arriving as a result of their having thermalized the universe.

According to BBT, because the closed curved space of the universe is expanding, all the matter of the universe is departing from the BB site (which is everywhere), and thus from each other, in all directions (except for matter such as that within galaxies and clusters of galaxies that are held together by mutual gravitation). Therefore, photons from the BB are thought to be arriving at the Earth (and at all other bodies of the universe) from all directions. But that reasoning can only apply to a universe of the closed space of positive curvature. In an open or flat universe, having either negative curvature or no curvature, if it were possible to be receiving photons from the BB decoupling they could only arrive from the direction of the BB. The reception of BB photons from all directions can only be attributed to a closed BB universe. But, due to time constraints and other considerations, that case has been shown to be impossible.

Regardless of the above, MBR from the decoupling is still accepted by BBers as proof of the BB, and its uniformity as proof of the smoothness of the universe. However, reports over the past decade of uniformity within one part in 10,000 have become an embarrassment to many BBers, and recent data from COBE satellite Differential Microwave Radiometer (DMR) experiments have increased the severity of the BB smoothness problem. They indicate the MBR to be about 5 times smoother than earlier estimates; about 20 parts per million. Because that degree of uniformity is inconsistent with the discoveries of ever increasing nonuniform distribution of galaxies in space, cosmologists may be forced to find new rationale for MBR from space.

(Some of the newer inventions of BB theorists, such as domain walls, cosmic strings and sheets, and another flight of fantasy called "textures," represent irregularities that, if taken seriously, might also be inconsistent with the observed smoothness of MBR.)

The reader should be aware that reports of smoothness of the MBR have been corrected for the drift of our galaxy toward the "Great Attractor" at about 600 km per second, for our solar system's motion within our galaxy of about 220 km per second, and for the Earth's orbital speed of about 30 km per second. The directions of these motions, each quite different, are such that our net velocity with respect to the received MBR is about

390 km per second. That motion shows up as a measured signal difference in opposing directions of space equivalent to about .0035 degree K. This temperature differential is significant to the consideration of the thermalization of surrounding space: Regardless of the source of its energy, if surrounding space is thermalized, a major portion of the thermalized matter must be beyond the immediate vicinity of our galaxy (with a distribution that provides an average energy level equivalent to 2.7 K) in order for this differential temperature to be present.

The question might be asked, "If these signal are not from the decoupling what is their source?" The answer to that is not known. Electromagnetic radiation in some portions of the spectrum from a number of sources throughout the universe have been suggested.

Richard Gott, though a firm believer in BBT, has suggested that MBR might originate as thermal radiation from the event horizons of many black holes that exist throughout the universe. Hawking radiation resembling black-body radiation may be scattered evenly throughout the universe. Stephen Hawking himself has also suggested that.

But if radiation from such sources came directly to us it could not have a characteristic black-body spectral distribution. Even if its sources were black-bodies all of the same temperature, due to their dispersal in space, the spectrum would be "smeared." The only manner in which a black-body spectrum could be received as a result of those sources is by thermalization of surrounding space.

It seems reasonable to suggest that, regardless of the source of the necessary energy, the temperature of surrounding space has become equalized. If that has happened, it has equalized at a temperature somewhat above zero degrees absolute (all matter would collapse at zero degrees), and 2.7 K might be a reasonable value for that temperature. It just happens to be within an order of magnitude of various temperatures that have been predicted by early BB theorists, thus generating a lot of enthusiasm for BBT.

Another band of electromagnetic radiation, other than microwaves, that is known to be received uniformly from every part of the sky is X-ray. It is received within about one percent of equal intensity from all directions in the range of 1 to 10 Angstroms.

According to University of Washington professor of astronomy Bruce Margon, most of that background radiation has been found to emanate from a large number of quasars at great distance, each contributing a small fraction of the total. Other sources of X-ray include pulsars, that produce extremely regular pulses of X-ray, and may also include black holes, neutron stars, supernova remnants and hot interstellar gas.

If X-ray background radiation were from a quasar at a distance of about 9.5 billion light years (for example) a red-shift of about five would be expected, putting the source of the transmitted radiation in the range of about 0.2 to 2 Angstroms, still within the X-ray range. But, if some of this background radiation were from the great decoupling, as might be expected from a BBT that predicts infrared radiation and other radiation (and neutinos) from that era, its red-shift would be about 1,000, putting the transmitted range at 0.01 to 0.001 Angstrom. Those wavelengths extend to the area of short wavelength gamma rays that might be difficult to explain. If it came from an earlier BB era its wavelengths would be even shorter and even more difficult to explain.

In addition to X-rays, bursts of gamma radiation from unknown sources are detected as often as daily. They last from a fraction of a second to a couple of minutes. Their sources are unknown but, because they arrive from all directions, they may be from high energy extragalactic sources, or they may be from particle-antiparticle annihilations at much closer ranges.

Active galactic nuclei (AGN), such as quasars and Seyfert galaxies, produce radiation over a wide range of wavelengths, including the gamma range. However, quasars at great distances would have large red shifts, putting the sources of AGN gamma rays at very short wavelengths. Perhaps such short wavelength gamma rays provide further reason to question the correctness of conventional red shift calculations.

Other sources of gamma radiation include pulsars that produce regular pulses, the radioactive decay of atoms produced in supernovae and distributed throughout our galaxy, and electron-positron annihilation occurring within our galaxy. There may also be low level gamma ray background radiation from beyond our galaxy.

Currently the Compton Gamma Ray Observatory (CGRO) satellite, with four gamma ray experiments aboard, is in orbit. One of experiments, EGRET (for Energetic Gamma Ray Experiment Telescope), detects gamma rays by converting them to electron-positron pairs and sensing their direction of arrival by means of a spark chamber. The data obtained from these CGRO experiments may soon shed new light on the various sources of gamma radiation.

If the early BB universe is proposed as the source of infrared radiation (and neutrinos), perhaps it would also be reasonable to propose it as the source of radiation at other wavelengths, including X-rays and gamma rays. But it seems more reasonable to believe that microwave, X-ray and other bands of radiation that are received uniformly from all directions of space, are products of other processes throughout the universe.

Light Elements

According to many BB cosmologists there are three primary pieces of evidence that provide all but certain proof of BBT. The first of these is the Hubble expansion of the universe. But because that expansion is equally supportive of other theories, such as SST, that evidence is inconclusive. The universe might have been expanding at or near the Hubble rate for very many billions of years. The second major piece of evidence is the presence of MBR. But it has been shown in the previous chapter that there are serious flaws in that evidence. Perhaps the most significant of those flaws are that the extreme smoothness of that radiation is inconsistent with observed very large scale galactic formations, and that MBR from the decoupling could only occur in the closed BB universe case, which time constraints and other factors have shown to be impossible. The third major piece of evidence is said to be the abundance of light elements in the universe. A brief discussion of the integrity of that evidence is presented in this chapter.

(In addition to those three pieces of evidence, some cosmologists have included the recently confirmed limit of the number of families of fundamental particles to just three as further evidence in support of BBT. However that evidence, like that of Hubble expansion, may be equally supportive of other cosmologies.)

Although most BB cosmologists agree that the presence of MBR is the most supportive evidence of BBT, American physics professors David Schramm and Gary Steigman have recently said, "The strongest support for the big-bang model comes from studies of primordial nucleosynthesis; the formation of elements." They tell us that these studies have predicted the abundance in the universe of several light elements; helium 3, helium 4, deuterium (the heavy isotope of hydrogen), and lithium. "The behavior of atom nuclei under the conditions of big-bang nucleosynthesis is not a matter of guesswork; it is precisely known;" all the forces and particles of quantum theory, and the generation of these elements, occurred as a known function of time, temperature, density and pressure since the BB.

(The reader is reminded that the sequence of events referred to here might merely be a contrived chronology generated by the combined efforts of a number of dedicated BB theorists.)

The reported ratios of the light elements, calculated from a postulated ratio of neutrons to photons (seven to one) at about one second after the BB, are exactly as presently observed (helium about 20%, deuterium about one part in 10,000 and lithium about one part in ten trillion.)

BB enthusiasts have repeatedly attempted to use a postulated ratio of helium to hydrogen in the universe as further evidence of the validity of BBT. According to calculations by Rees in 1976, Davies in 1981, and Carr in 1982, after the first second or so after the BB "one expects" roughly 25% of the mass of the universe to be helium and all the rest, but "a tiny residue of deuterium," to be of hydrogen.

Except that his ratio was about 50% each of helium and hydrogen, Gamow made similar statements in the 1950s. An estimate in the 1960s by Fred Hoyle and others came in at 36% helium, later adjusted to 25%. In 1988 we find Schramm and Steigman presenting their ratios of elements with similar claims of evidence for the validity of BBT. In each case the "predicted" ratios happened to agree with the currently understood composition of the universe, and the assumed baryon to photon ratio (the baryon number) has been selected to produce calculated results that agree with that composition.

But of course these reports haven't been predictions at all. All of these estimates have been made with full knowledge of the composition of the universe as understood at the time. The ratios of the elements were worked out after the observations were made, and are based on a hypothetical baryon number. It would be more correct to call them retroactive verifications (more "retrodictions") of BB theory, after appropriate adjustments to match observations.

In fact, early predictions included heavy elements as a result of BB nucleosynthesis (fusion). When it was later determined that heavy elements were the product of fusion within the stars, BBT was adjusted accordingly. Furthermore, because it is known that hydrogen is converted to helium in stellar nuclear reactions, there is no reason to insist that a BB is required for its origin in a universe that might be very much older than the hypothesized age of a BB universe.

Recent findings have resulted in fears that BBT might require further adjustments to accommodate the generation of additional light elements, and possibly even some heavy elements. Observations of a very old "fossil" star located outside of the plane of our galaxy have resulted in the discovery of both boron and beryllium in it. That star has only about 0.2% of the iron and less than one percent of the oxygen found in the sun, indicating that it is about 15 billion years old. By means of Hubble Space Telescope observations, these findings have been confirmed in three of the oldest stars within our galaxy, that are said to be about 13 to 15 billion years old.

(The age of those stars has been estimated by astronomers who probably are BBers, and their estimates, if made in the usual manner, would have been influenced by their belief in a BB that occurred at most about 15 billion years ago. The actual ages of those stars might be much greater.)

In those stars the ratio of beryllium to iron was found to be 1,000 times greater than it would have been if it had originated in stars. That ratio indicates that the beryllium might have been produced either by BB nucleosynthesis or by the action of cosmic rays on "star forged" elements. Cosmic rays can split atoms to produce elements such as boron and beryllium. (In this process elements are produced by fission rather than by fusion.)

If beryllium can be produced by cosmic rays, theory indicates that its ratio to boron would be one to 12. But observations of boron in those stars indicates that ratio to be about one to six, meaning that (according to BBT) some of it might have come from BB nucleosynthesis. However, previous BB theory limited the generation of beryllium by BB nucleosynthesis to only one part in 10^{16}.

The results of these discoveries concerning boron and beryllium therefore mean that some new adjustments might have to be made to BBT. Accordingly, near instantaneous suggestions have been forthcoming. To wit, it has been suggested that at about the first minute after the BB, the universe might have been "lumpier" than previously thought, and beryllium was produced in the higher density regions of the universe. (However, it is felt that lumpiness at that time, would have cleared up long before the decoupling. MBR would still be smooth, thus avoiding another dilemma for BBers.)

But of course that arouses suspicions that even heavier elements might also have been produced in the lumps. Some astronomers are now suggesting that many elements of the periodic table might have been produced in these lumps. BB nucleosynthesis might now have completed a full circle regarding the generation of the elements.

If cosmic rays can split atoms to produce boron and beryllium, certainly they must also be able to produce other elements, perhaps including lithium. This is an important point. The reason the presence of lithium in the universe is so important to BBers is that it can't survive the high temperatures inside of stars and, thus, they have concluded it can only have been generated by BB nucleosynthesis. That in turn means there had to be a BB. But if boron, beryllium and other light elements, including lithium, can be generated by the action of cosmic rays that premise is refuted.

BBers have also insisted that deuterium could only have been produced in BB nucleosynthesis. But, like lithium, it may be possible for deuterium to be produced by other processes throughout the universe. Peeples, Schramm, Turner and Kron have said that, "significant amounts" of deuterium "cannot be produced in known noncosmological processes" (meaning non-BB fusion processes). But BB cosmologist Joseph Silk has stated that, "It is possible to conceive of other nonstellar sources of deuterium at early stages of evolution of galaxies" and, "The net result of attempts to synthesize deuterium in the BB remains distressingly inconclusive ... just because deuterium is not produced in ordinary stars does not rule out a possible pregalactic phase involving massive stars that might have produced deuterium."

It also seems quite possible that both light and heavy elements can be produced in other events, such as supernova explosions. (A supernova is the remains of a massive star that has exploded at the end of its life. A nova differs in that it is the result of the impact of the two bodies of a binary pair.) Stephen Weinberg has agreed, saying, "We can imagine that this much deuterium was produced in "recent" astrophysical phenomena—supernovas, cosmic rays, perhaps even quasi-stellar objects." Geoffrey and Margaret Burbridge, William Fowler and Fred Hoyle have written that heavy elements could be built up in stars, particularly in stellar explosions such as supernovas.

(University of California, Berkeley professor of astronomy Stuart Bowyer has very recently reported data indicating ionized plasma in the Capella system—two coronally active yellow giant stars in our galaxy—at a temperature of close to six million degrees C, which "confined by magnetic fields may undergo fusion near one or both of the stars.")

Adding further doubts about BB nucleosynthesis, University of Texas at Austin astronomer Jeff Kanipe has reported that recent measurements (since 1988) have confirmed that the abundance of helium in galaxies is less than that allowed by the standard BBT model. Other investigators have recently agreed that the generation of helium, deuterium and lithium by BB nucleosynthesis would require more baryonic matter in the observable universe than is seen by astronomers.

This long story about BB nucleosynthesis, cosmic rays and light elements has been presented, not only to demonstrate the tenacity of BB theorists' adherence to their convictions, but, more importantly, to point out that the generation of lithium and deuterium, which is said to not be possible in stars, might be the result of other processes—some that may yet be discovered. The abundances of lithium, deuterium and even helium in the universe is not necessarily dependent on BBT.

The third major piece of evidence in support of BBT is thus subject to serious question. As with the other two pieces, it is far from conclusive.

Many years of theorist's efforts have been expended on the

development of schemes in support of BBT, including the nucleosynthesis of light elements. As in the case of other aspects of BBT, if a portion of that effort had been spent on the development of other cosmologies, it is quite possible that there would by now be any number of plausible alternate theories for the generation of light elements in the time and space of the universe.

ELEVEN

Red Shift

In the late 1920s and early 1930s American astronomers Edwin Hubble and Milton Humason, working at the Mount Wilson Observatory, provided convincing evidence that other relatively close galaxies are departing from ours at velocities approximately proportional to their distances.

The accumulation of that evidence was not an easy task. The distance of each galaxy studied had to be painstakingly estimated by other means. Years of effort were expended in accumulating that data. Even after many intervening years the exact rate of expansion of the universe, as expressed by the Hubble constant, has not been firmly established. Past estimates of that constant have varied over a wide range. Until recently values ranged between about 15 to 30 km/sec/MLYs (kilometers per second per million light years), but recently improved methods have provided an estimate that can be used with considerably more confidence.

This new best estimate is about 80 kilometers per second per megaparsec, which equals about 25 kilometers per second per million light years. The current consensus of opinion of a number of prominent astronomers, including John Huchra, Wendy Freedman of the Carnegie Observatories, and Gerard de Vaucouleurs of the University of Texas, supports this value.

If the universe had expanded at a fixed rate (the Hubble rate) since the BB occurred, its present age would be equal to the speed of light (300,000 km per second) divided by the Hubble constant. That age is called the Hubble age or Hubble time, T_H. For a Hubble constant, H, of 25, it would be 12 billion years. But that is not the age of the BB universe. As was mentioned in Chapter 6, its age could be considerably less depending on which BB case is preferred. For the flat universe case the age would be two thirds of T_H or 8 billion years, for a closed universe it would be somewhat less than that value, and for an open universe it would be between that value and T_H.

However, in order to keep the following discussion simple, an example of a flat BB universe having an age of 10 billion years (BYRs) will be assumed. That age would require a Hubble constant of 20 km per second per million light years and a Hubble time of 15 billion years. This assumed age of 10 BYRs, which is more in keeping with the chronology of BBers in the past, is 25% greater than that which might be supported by the new data.

Due to the expansion of the universe, the rates of departure of other galaxies from ours result in Doppler effects on radiation received from them; a lengthening in the wavelength of the received radiation (with frequency decreasing in a reciprocal relationship). This effects all bands of electromagnetic radiation that might be emitted, from gamma rays through radio frequencies. Because the spectrum of visible light from distant bodies would be shifted toward the red, that is, toward longer wavelengths, that shift is called red shift.

Red shift has a simple mathematical definition. According to Hubble's law it is equal to the shift in wavelength divided by the radiated wavelength. It is measured by knowledge of the frequencies of spectral lines of elements that are present in the radiation source. It is calculated by dividing the wavelength of a received spectral line less the wavelength of that emitted spectral line (giving the shift in wavelength) by the wavelength of the emitted spectral line. Although this can be simply stated, measurement of wavelength shift is not an easy task. The determination of the red shift of a distant galaxy requires great skill and effort.

Galaxies that are relatively close to ours have a relative velocity that is only a small fraction of the speed of light. When their red shift has been measured, their velocity can be determined by the simple expression v/c equals Z; their velocity as a fraction of the speed of light equals their red shift. Their distance is equal to v/c times T_H, or v divided by H.

(Hubble in 1936, using the best equipment available at that time, was only able to determine galactic velocity out to Ursa Major II, then thought to be about 260 million light years distant, but now thought to be several times that far. He determined its relative velocity to be about 42,000 kilometers per second; v/c=0.14.)

In our example of a 10 billion year old BB universe, if a galaxy were found to have a red shift of 0.1, its velocity relative to us would have been 0.1c (or 30,000 kilometers per second) at the time the light received from it had left it. For an age of 10 billion years, that galaxy would have been about one billion light years from us at the time the light received from it had left it. Because its light would have taken one billion years to reach us, and assuming, as BBers would, that it was "born" shortly after the decoupling, we see it as it was one billion years ago; that is, when it was 9 billion years old. "Look back" is one BYRs or 10%. If that galaxy continued to travel at approximately 0.1c during the one BYRs it took for its light to reach us, it would have traveled an additional 0.1 billion light years (BLYs) and now be 1.1 BYRs from us.

When the relative velocity of a galaxy is more than a small percentage of the speed of light, Special Relativity must be taken into account. The impact of that theory is illustrated in the graph of velocity (as a fraction of the speed of light) as a function of red shift in accordance with Equation 4 of Figure 4, derived from the Lorentz transforms discussed in Chapter 2.

According to Figure 4, if Z (red shift) is small, v/c is approximately equal to Z, and the smaller Z is, the more nearly v/c approaches its value. That agrees with the expression given above for small velocities. The plot of Equation 4 in Figure 4 also illustrates that Einstein's prohibition of speeds greater than that of light is not violated; no matter how large Z might be, v/c never exceeds unity, i.e., the velocity of light is never exceeded.

Under BBT a further complication is encountered for distant bodies. Except for a fixed-rate universe case (which is not acceptable to BBers), the proper age of the universe is not used to calculate distance. For example, if the Hubble constant, H, was believed to be 30 km/sec/MLYs, and the universe believed to be flat, Hubble time, T_H, would be 10 BYR and the age of the universe 2/3 T_H, or 6-2/3 BYRs. In that situation the distance should be v/c times 6-2/3 BLYs. For a quasar having a red shift of 3.5 and thus a v/c of 0.9 its distance would only be 6 BLYs; a result that is unacceptable to BBers.

In order to avoid that problem, an assumed elapsed time since the BB is used, which forces the age of distant quasars to be compatible with whatever age has been assumed for the BB universe. The assumed age normally used is the Hubble time, which of course is erroneous for all but a fixed-rate universe. That error results in a new BB problem that is illustrated by the following example.

A quasar having a red shift of 3.5 is thought to have a velocity relative to us of about 0.9c, or 270,000 km per sec (from Equation 4 of Figure 4). If it is assumed that the BB happened 10 BYRs ago, that quasar is assumed to have been about 9 BLYs distant when the received light left it. "Look back" is 90%; its light would have taken about 9 BYRs to reach us. Assuming a BB universe of a fixed rate of expansion (in accordance with the illustration of Figure 2 and as normally utilized by BBers in their calculations) during that 9 BYRs, if that quasar still existed, it might have traveled another 8.1 BYRs, and would now be 17.1 BYRs from us.

Although red shift indicated the relative velocity of the quasar to be 0.9c, its present distance from us (or that of its remains) might be 17.1 billion light years. If that travel had occurred in the 10 billion year life time of the BB universe, its speed relative to us would be 1.71c, which is in conflict with General Relativity and with the speed indicated by its red shift. As will be discussed in the next chapter, an attempt can be made to solve this problem by explaining that it would not occur if events were based on a universe of decelerating expansion, but that explanation is not adequate.

If this particular problem is ignored, calculations based on red shift might otherwise seem quite reasonable. However, careful consideration of the results of the usual interpretation of red shift turns up several additional problems.

One of those problems, which has been previously discussed, is called the age paradox. The current best estimate of the Hubble constant results in a flat BB universe age of 8 BYRS, a closed BB universe of slightly more, and a somewhat open BB universe age of slightly more than 8 BYRs. Because the age of some stars and galaxies is estimated (by independent means) to be as much as 15 to 20 billion years, those figures would tend to convince one that the standard BB cases are not credible.

Conventional interpretation of red shift observations indicates that large numbers of quasars are at great distances from us, resulting in the appearance of quasar "clumping" relatively soon after the BB. But the clumping of quasars in all directions would indicate that we are at the center-of-the-universe. That situation, which has been referred to as the Copernican problem, conflicts with the basic tenet of the smoothness of the Big Bang universe. The universe may be isotropic, but it can't be homogeneous; it may look the same in all directions, but it doesn't look the same everywhere.

The postulated smoothness of the distribution of matter of the universe and the curvature of its space in accordance with BBT provides the basis for the concepts of space expansion and for a universe without a center—the BB happened everywhere. But the clumping of quasars at great distances as determined by current interpretation of red shift denies homogeneity and a centerless universe. It puts us at the center of a nonuniform universe in direct conflict with BBT.

The clumping of distant quasars also requires the formation of large numbers of them too soon after the BB. Cosmologists believe that it might have taken billions of years for quasars to form, and yet their red shifts indicate that they are seen as they were within as little as one billion years after the BB.

In the past, the smoothness of the received level of microwave background radiation has been thought to support the smoothness of the universe. However, that radiation has been found to be too smooth to account for the presence of clusters of galaxies and for the formation of quasars so soon after the BB. Cold dark matter (hypothetical non-baryonic matter having no postulated characteristics other than gravitational attraction) had been proposed as a solution to that problem. But the extreme smoothness of MBR that has recently been established, that is incompatible with the discovery of quasars of great age and of gigantic galactic formations, has discredited cold dark matter theory in the eyes of many cosmologists.

The BB that happened everywhere is explained as an inherent characteristic of positively curved closed space. That provides the rationale for photons from the early universe arriving from all directions as MBR. But if the BB happened all over, that rationale might be expected to apply to all the matter of the universe. All of it, including quasars, might be distributed more evenly throughout space.

Like the stars and galaxies around us, rather than being clumped at great distances and of great age, quasars of various ages would be scattered throughout the universe. The observed distribution of young blue stars, as well as that of older cooler stars, throughout the universe support that even distribution of stellar matter. (A smoother distribution of quasars might help to support the smoothness of a BB universe, but it might support other theories as well.)

A lack of correlation between quasar luminosities and distances as determined by red shift data has been reported. A lack of spectrographic differences between quasars of different red shifts has also been reported. Both of these factors tend to indicate that quasars are less distant and closer in age than indicated by their red shifts. Spectrographic similarity also tends to deny the quasar evolution that is often presented as evidence in support of BBT.

The present interpretation of red shift also results in high relativistic velocities and distances that require unbelievably great masses and brilliances of distant quasars. The highest red shift observed to date, about 4.7, indicates a velocity of 94% of c. In addition, rapid variations in the level of radiation of distant quasars (in periods of less than one day) require their sizes to be unbelievably small, and thus their brilliances and densities to be unbelievably great.

An additional red shift problem has to do with quasar flares that appear (as observed by radio telescopes) to exceed the velocity of light. It is impossible to account for those that might actually exceed c. But it can be shown (by simple and straightforward mathematics) that flares having relativistic velocities that are ejected at angles of less than 90 degrees toward (or away from) the observer can create the appearance of superluminal velocities. However, it is difficult to account for the relatively large number of quasar flares that exhibit this phenomenon.

Because of the great energies required to propel flares to near superluminal speed, one might expect them to be observed only infrequently. It may be more reasonable to conclude that the appearance of superluminal speeds is due to the present interpretation of red shift measurements. The mathematics that is used to provide the appearance of superluminal speed is directly dependent on the assumed distance of the quasar under consideration. That distance is in turn dependent on the interpretation of red shift.

The problem concerning quasar flares can be demonstrated by the following example (which may not be totally realistic, but illustrates the point) of a quasar flare at a velocity near to the speed of light traveling toward us, but at an angle of 36.87 degrees from radially (using a 3-4-5 right triangle for this example). Simple trionometry can show that, when observed at one year intervals, that flare would appear to travel an arc equivalent to almost three light-years in each year, or at a speed of almost 3c. That apparent tangential speed would also be observed for a quasar flare traveling away from us (and appearing to be in the opposite direction) at an angle of 36.87 degrees from radially. The radial speed of the receding flare would be almost 0.8c from us, which (if it could be observed) should result in a red shift of almost 2. That of the approaching flare would be almost 0.8c toward us, and should result in an equivalent blue shift.

Because flares might be expected to depart in opposite directions from a quasar with approximately equal speeds, the above situation might seem plausible, but it is erroneous.

Let us assume the same speed for a pair of flares of opposite directions, each with velocities of almost c (at the angles and speeds discussed above), that are associated with a quasar having a red shift of $Z = 3.5$, and thus a relative velocity of 0.9c away from us. In this case, the flare traveling away from us would have a radial velocity of only about $0.8c – 0.9c = - 0.1c$ relative to the quasar, and the flare traveling toward us would have a radial velocity of about $0.8c + 0.9c = +1.7c$ relative to the quasar. These are obviously conflicting and erroneous conclusions.

The only reasonable explanation that can be suggested for these results is that the present interpretation of red shift in determining the speed and distance of massive bodies is incorrect. (It is suggested that this problem might be resolved by determining and analyzing the shifts of the wavelengths of radiation from flares of quasars having detectable flares in opposing directions in addition to that of their source quasar. Reports of an investigation of that type have not been discovered in the literature.)

BB advocates might explain some of the anomalies regarding red shift interpretation as due to the positive curvature of space. But that explanation cannot be applied to the open or flat universe cases. Although some BBers believe in the closed universe (that is ruled out by age, density of the universe and other considerations), some believe in an open universe (having negatively curved space) and many believe in the flat universe case (in which space is uncurved), including those who have accepted inflation theory. But the characteristics of neither an open universe nor a flat universe can properly be explained by characteristics that apply only to a closed universe of positively curved space. Their use of those characteristics as an explanation for red shift problems is therefore invalid.

It is suggested here that a solution to many of the problems related to red shift may lie in proper consideration of the effect of gravitational red shift on radiation as it leaves very massive sources, as quasars and Seyfert galaxies are believed to be. (Seyferts are thought to be similar to quasars but of lower luminosity.) Because the usual red shift calculations (based on Formula 4 of Figure 4) neglect the addition of gravitational red shift to Doppler red shift, it may not tell the whole story.

According to General Relativity, gravitation causes a tiny red shift in the radiation we receive from the sun. (It equals 2G times M divided by r times c squared, where M and r are the mass and radius of the sun, and G is the gravitational constant.) The same phenomenon slows the frequency of radiation enough to prevent its escape from black holes, that is, red shift becomes infinite. It also might be responsible for very large red shifts of radiation from other massive bodies. This gravitational red shift is known as Einstein Shift.

Astronomers generally recognize at least four relatively stable states of large stellar bodies of the universe. The first of those states is that of main sequence stars (like our sun) in which nuclear reactions are taking place. The second of those states is that of white dwarfs that are formed when relatively small stars (like our sun) cease their normal processes and collapse to that state. A third state is that of neutron stars that result from the collapse of stars somewhat larger than the sun, and a fourth is that of black holes. Stars that have a mass more than several times greater than the sun are believed to collapse to this state. Although their existence is not entirely proven, theory and observational evidence tend to support the reality of this state of massive matter in space.

In States 1 and 2, and perhaps in State 3, General Relativity gravitational effects on radiation might not add appreciable red shift to that resulting from their relative velocity. But in State 4 it is believed that the effect of gravity is great enough to prevent direct radiation, that is, to cause infinite red shift. That suggests the possibility of an additional fifth state of objects that has an intermediate effect on red shift; not great enough to prevent radiation, but great enough to significantly slow it.

It is reasonable to think of large stars that ultimately collapse to become black holes as initially having a Schwarzchild radius, or event horizon, that is far inside its surface, where its effect would be of little significance. As the star collapses, and its mass and density increases, its event horizon becomes progressively closer to its surface, and, when collapse is complete, the event horizon has moved out beyond the surface of the black hole. At that time, regardless of how hot and how radiant the mass might be, the event horizon, a phenomenon of gravitational force, prevents the escape of radiation.

It follows that a main sequence star may be thought of as having its event horizon only a small percentage of the radial distance from its center, a white dwarf perhaps as having its event horizon a greater percentage of its radius from its center, and that of a neutron star having an even greater percentage of its radius from its center. It is suggested that quasars may be objects that have their event horizon at a large percentage of its radial distance from their center, but not beyond their surface.

(Schwarzchild radius is equal to $2GM/c^2$. For our sun its value would be just a few kilometers.)

Perhaps massive stellar bodies of the proposed fifth stable state collapse similarly to black holes, but because they aren't sufficiently massive to becomes full-fledged black holes, their development ceases and their Schwarzchild radius remains below their surface; far enough below the surface to allow a large amount of radiation to escape, but close enough to the surface to slow the escape of that radiation. The addition of that gravitational red shift to Doppler red shift of radiation from these bodies would result in the appearance of excessive velocity and distance.

It is suggested that there is a family of such objects that have the equivalent of event horizons at various depths below their surfaces, resulting in quasars having a variety of ratios of gravitational red shift to Doppler red shift, including some for which the former may be considerably greater than the later.

Perhaps some of these objects gradually accumulate nearby matter as black holes do, and eventually become black holes; perhaps a relative scarcity of matter in the vicinity some of them retards their growth, keeping their event horizon below their surface for an extended period; and perhaps matter in the vicinity of some is so sparse that they never become black holes, and their event horizons remain below their surfaces.

That concept is in agreement with stellar theory, as can be confirmed by many sources, including the following quotation from the McGraw Hill *Encyclopedia of Science and Technology* under the subject of Gravitational Red Shift, "neutron stars (and white dwarfs as well) which had been formed earlier could accrete enough matter to become more massive than the maximum mass of a neutron star. In these cases the only known alternative is for such stars to collapse to a black hole." But if the matter that is available for accretion is not sufficient to form a black hole, what might be the result?

As shown by the formula presented above, gravitational red shift is proportional to the mass of a body and inversely proportional to its radius. Calculations would show that radiation from the sun has a red shift of 0.001 nanometer (nm) at a wavelength of 500 nm (equivalent to a Z of 0.001/500 or 0.000002) and a white dwarf with twice the mass and 1/15 the radius of the sun would have a red shift of 0.03 nm at 500 nm (equivalent to a Z of 0.00006), or 30 time as great. These are relatively insignificant red shifts. But, for example, if there were an object having

500 times the mass of the sun and 1/500 its size, its gravitational red shift would be 0.5. That is equivalent to a velocity of almost 40% of the speed of light as determined by the conventional method. Obviously the Einstein Shift of massive stellar objects should not be ignored!

The masses and the luminosities of quasars necessary to produce the levels of radiation that are received from their estimated distances is incredible—truly beyond belief. Some quasars, according to estimates of distance based on current interpretation of their red shifts, have been reported to be as bright as a quadrillion ($10^{15)}$) suns—a ridiculously high number—equivalent to the luminosity of 10,000 average galaxies. If quasars are closer than calculated by the current interpretation of red shift measurements, as would be indicated by the proper consideration of their gravitational red shifts, these anomalies might be eliminated. Their speeds, distances, masses, luminosities, and clumping might be within reason.

Observed fluctuations of radiation from some quasars are too short to be consistent with enormous massive bodies at enormous distances. Variations of visible, infrared and radio frequency radiation might indicate dimensions as small as one light-day or rotational rates as short one day. It is suggested that nonuniformity of surface luminosity, perhaps giant flares, and faster rotational rates of bodies that are closer and less massive than those that have been perceived in the past, are responsible for the observed large variations of radiation intensity.

The turbulence of the surface of the sun is relatively mild, and flares tend to loop back to its surface. Flares of neutron stars have greater strength and escape from fields that tend to confine them, some producing pulsar flashes as these stars rotate at high rates. Therefore, enormous flares of great velocities might also be expected to emanate from the massive bodies proposed here.

As has been stated, it can be shown that relativistic flares from very distant bodies can appear to be superluminal. But, because observations of quasar distances have been based on red shift calculations that do not include consideration of the gravitational red shift, the numbers of reported observations of superluminal flares may by excessive. Although the objects as proposed herein might produce high velocity flares, they might only rarely produce flares of sufficient velocity to cause the appearance of superluminal speeds. If those objects are more evenly distributed in space, as discussed below, the lower relative velocity of those that are determined to be closer would reduce the occurrence of flares that are perceived to be of superluminal speeds.

BB cosmologists, using the current interpretation of red shift measurements to gauge the distance of quasars, are convinced of the clumping of quasars at great distances, and that that clumping provides evidence in support of an evolving universe. However, as was discussed in Chapter 8, even in a BB universe wherein the BB had happened everywhere, quasars should not be clumped. They should be distributed throughout space as is all the other matter of space, including photons that are said to come from the decoupling of radiation from the matter of the universe about 300,000 years after the BB.

Some BB cosmologists have suggested that quasar clumping is the result of slowing or "running down" of the processes of the universe, that is, increasing entropy. A BB universe might be running down but it shouldn't result in the clumping of quasars. If gravitational effects cause a significant portion of the red shift of quasars as proposed herein, the Doppler portion of their red shift would fall on a lower, more linear portion of the V/c vs Z curve of Figure 4, resulting in their more uniform distribution in space. That could reduce, or possibly eliminate, the perception of the clumping of quasars in distant space and time.

As mentioned above, astronomical data shows little correlation between the apparent luminosity of quasars and their distance as determined by the usual interpretation of their red shifts, and spectrographs of quasars of different red shifts are the same. It is suggested that these observations are consistent with a more even distribution of quasars throughout the universe, that would result from proper consideration of the gravitational red shift of massive objects.

Observations of quasars having considerably greater red shifts than those of neighboring galaxies provide additional evidence that something is amiss with the present interpretation of the red shifts of massive bodies. Those observations indicate that a number of quasars are quite close to galaxies whose distances are fairly well known. There are several quasars in The Third Cambridge Catalogue that are extremely close to galaxies listed in the New

General Catalogue. (Examples are NGC 4651 and 3C275.1, NGC3067 and 3C232, NGC4138 and 3C268.4, NGC5832 and 3C309.1, and NGC7413 and 3C455.) Recent data has confirmed that the quantity of quasars found within small angles of galaxies greatly exceeds statistical expectations.

Astronomer Halton C. Arp, formerly at the Hale Observatory and now at the Max Planck Institute of Astrophysics in Germany, has said that the probability of so many chance associations is small. He has reported associated quasars and galaxies of quite different red shifts. Among them are quasar Markarian 205 (whose red shift indicates a velocity of 13,000 miles per second) and galaxy NGC 4319 (who's velocity is only about 1,000 miles per second) that are connected by a bridge of gas. Arp has said that the relationship between red shift and distance is a "frail assumption in which so much of modern astronomy and cosmology is built."

The acknowledgment by astronomers of the effects of Einstein Shifts (combined with Doppler red shifts as usually perceived) as might be expected of radiation from massive bodies in space would provide an explanation of how quasars can be associated with galaxies of much lower red shift.

An alternate solution to red shift problems has been suggested by those who support multiple smaller explosions throughout the space and time of the universe, rather than a single giant BB. They suggest that there may be associated areas of high gravitational force causing gravitational red shifts that result in the appearance of quasars at increased distance. The large structures of galaxies, including voids and sheets of galaxies, might appear to support this theory. However, detailed studies of patterns of wavelength shifts that might provide evidence supporting it have not been conducted. In the meantime one might guess that small bangs around us would result in blue shifts as well as great red shifts. That has not been observed.

Another solution to red shift problems (that was mentioned in Chapter 6) has been suggested that has to do with the possible effects of Einstein's discredited cosmic repulsion, now usually referred to as the cosmological constant. Brandeis University physics professor Larry Abbott and other investigators have suggested that even a very small positive cosmological constant would add to Doppler red shift, thus causing an over-estimation of speeds and distances of remote bodies. However, although that would scale down the velocity and distance of quasars, the velocity and distance of other objects would be scaled down proportionately. Thus it could not provide an explanation for the proximity of quasars to galaxies of lower red shift, and it could not provide an explanation for clumping. Quasars would still be clumped, but at lesser distances.

In summary, it is suggested that there is a family of objects, including quasars, that have the equivalent of an event horizon at various depths below their surfaces, resulting in a variety of ratios of gravitational red shift to Doppler red shift, including the possibility of objects having gravitational red shifts that exceed their Doppler red shifts. This postulated phenomenon would provide the solution to many problems that result from the present interpretation of red shift observations.

It would solve the problem of the extreme speeds of quasars, and thus their extreme distances, ages, masses and luminosities. Although some visible objects in space may truly be at great ("cosmological") distances, the observed rapid variations in luminosity of some quasars, that cause the appearance of extremely small size and great density of quasars, would be more compatible with closer, smaller bodies of lower densities and higher rates of rotation.

Quasar velocities would be on a lower more linear portion of a plot of velocity versus the Doppler portion of their red shift (in accordance with the results of the Einstein-Lorentz transformations), resulting in a more uniform distribution of quasars in space. The appearance of quasar clumping would be reduced or eliminated. That would, of course, help to support the BBer's insistence on a smooth universe, but citing quasar clumping as evidence of an evolving universe would no longer be possible.

Giant flares similar to solar flaring, combined with faster rotational rates of bodies that are much smaller than those that have been envisioned in the past, may be responsible for rapid variations of radiation intensity. Flares of great velocities might be expected from massive bodies, but if many quasars are closer to us and more evenly distributed, the apparent speed of emitted matter would be correspondingly slower; the relatively large number of cases of perceived superluminal flares would be reduced or eliminated.

Quasars having a variety of gravitational red shifts, and lesser velocities, distances and ages, would explain the lack of correlation of apparent luminosities and distances, the similarity of their spectrums, and the proximity of quasars to galaxies of lower red shifts. It is also suggested here that the differences in masses and radii of stars of some binary pairs is the cause of observed differences in their average red shifts.

One might conclude that because proper consideration of Einstein Shift of massive bodies might provide a solution to many of the red shift problems attributed to BBT, that solution might tend to discredit BBT. But, in fairness, it should be noted that a number of the points discussed might be utilized to support it.

A more even distribution of quasars might be interpreted to support the tenets of a BB everywhere and large-scale smoothness (homogeneity as well as isotropy). Reduced clumping of quasars would ease the Copernican problem; clumping places us at the center of the universe. A younger observable universe might provide sufficient time following the BB for quasar formation, and cold dark matter might again become a viable theory. Lower speed, and thus closer quasars, might also solve the speed-of-light and related problems that have been mentioned. An explanation for the proximity of quasars to galaxies might help support BBT. However, regardless of these points, on balance, the result of a closer more even distribution of quasars would seem to discredit BBT as normally portrayed.

Although the above discussion provides some ideas in support of the existence of a new class of massive stellar bodies, relatively little directly supporting evidence is available. Of course, it is possible that more evidence will be discovered. If, for example, it should be determined that objects previously identified as quasars cannot again be found, or the character of their radiation has changed rather suddenly, it may indicate that they have grown into black holes. (Perhaps such observations have already occurred but gone unreported or insufficiently publicized.)

Meanwhile, other than a lack of correlation of luminosities and distances, a similarity of spectrums, and the apparent proximity of quasars to bodies of lesser red shift, no additional directly supportive observational evidence is known. Although the postulated fifth state of stellar bodies would seem to answer many questions about red shift and the configuration of the universe, it may prove to be just another theory.

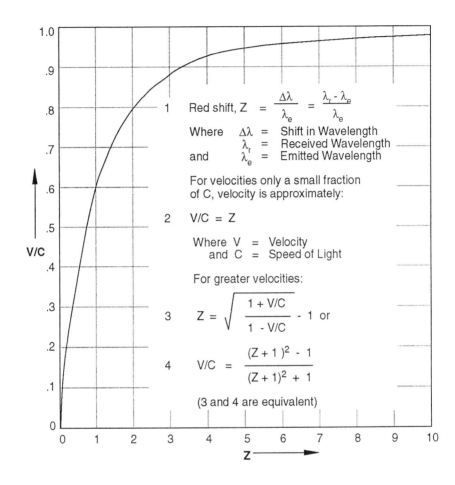

FIGURE 4: VELOCITY AS A FUNCTION OF RED SHIFT
(As a fraction of the speed of light as
derived from the Lorentz Transformations)

TWELVE

The Age, Size and Shape of the Universe

As previously mentioned, the most probable value for the Hubble constant (H) is about 80 kilometers per second per megaparsec (km/sec/Mpc) which is equal to about 25 kilometers per second per million light years (km/sec/MLYs). That results in a Hubble time T_H of 12 billion years (BRYs), which would be the age of the BB universe if its rate of expansion was constant since the BB.

This best estimate of the value of the Hubble constant is based on new improved methods of determination of the distance of remote galaxies. Early measurement of galactic distances were based on the regularly varying luminosity of stars called Cepheid variables. But, because of their relative low peak luminosity their usefulness as "standard candles" was limited to relatively close galaxies. The later use of type 1a supernovae that were found to reach the same peak luminosity, but have a peak luminosity several times greater than Cepheids, extended the ability of astronomers to estimate the distance of galaxies.

In the past few years a further improved method of measurement has been developed that utilizes the fact that the most luminous planetary nebulae in galaxies all have nearly the same peak luminosity. Because they are brighter than type 1a supernovae the range of measurement has again been extended. This new standard candle has provided measurements which have resulted in fairly good confidence of a Hubble constant (H) of approximately 25 km/sec/MLYs.

(A planetary nebula is the cloud of debris that is blown away from a violent transformation of a red giant—the remains of a burnt-out small to medium sized star—into a white dwarf.)

Although few if any BBers believe in a universe having a fixed rate of expansion, we read of an age of about 15 billion years in many articles written by or about them, corresponding to an H of 20 km/sec/MLYs. However, they are undoubtedly referring to a T_H of 15 billion years (BYRs), which implies a fixed-rate universe. Although it is rarely made clear, many of them believe in the flat universe case, for which the age of the universe would be two thirds of T_H, or 10 BYRs for that H. If they believe in a closed universe its age should be stated as somewhat less than 10 BYRs, and if they believe in an open universe its age should be stated as somewhat more than 10 BYRs.

However, according to this latest estimated Hubble constant, the age of the fixed-rate universe would be 12 BYRs, the age in the flat case would be 8 BYRs, in the closed case somewhat less that 8 BYRs, and in the open case somewhat more that 8 BYRs.

If the Hubble constant were at the extreme low end of its previously estimated range (of 15 km/sec/MLYs), the Hubble time (also called the Hubble age) would be 20 BYRs, putting the time of the BB at 13.33 BYRs ago for a flat BB universe; and if the Hubble constant were at its other extreme (of 30 km/sec/MLYs), Hubble time would be 10 BYRs, putting the BB at 6.67 BYRs ago for a flat universe.

As has been mentioned, estimates of the age of some stars and galaxies, based on other data (such as the ratios of abundances of heavy elements and ratios of radioactive elements), are in the range of 15 to 20 billion years. Because the universe can't be younger than its stars, it should be clear that, for even the lowest previously estimated Hubble constant, a closed or flat BB universe would have been impossible. The newly established H also rules out an open BB universe, including the fixed-rate case. Regardless of these simple, straight-forward calculations, which are based on their own theories, each BBer clings to a belief in his or her favorite BB universe case whether closed, flat or somewhat open.

Undoubtedly because of the increasingly contradictory evidence of aged stars and galaxies, in recent years BBers have been increasing their estimates of the age of the universe. That has forced their acceptance of a lower value of the Hubble constant, regardless of its lower credibility. A 15 BYR old flat BB universe requires an H of 13.33 km/sec/MLYs, which is about one half of its most probable value. Even if BBers accepted an extreme open universe case, a near fixed-rate case of a 15 BYR old universe (and none are known to do so), an H of 20 would be required, only 80% of the most probable value.

The reader is reminded that, although BBers normally profess a belief in a closed, flat or somewhat open universe, the chronology they normally present is that of a fixed-rate universe. The time line of the BB universe that is most often presented (as described in Chapter 4 and shown in Figure 2) represents a fixed-rate (undecelerating) universe that is 10 BYRs old, corresponding to a H of 30 km/sec/MLYs or about 98 km/sec/Mpc.

Based on Hubble's work, the earliest estimate of the age of the BB universe was only about 1.8 billion years (an H of 170 km/sec/MLYs). In the 1950s errors were found in the method of judging the age of stars that resulted in an increase of that estimate to about 5 billion years, which was the value George Gamow reported in his early work. (Following Hubble's death in 1953 astronomer Walter Baade, based on improved Cepheid variable data, found that distances calculated by Hubble had to be increased by a factor of 2.8.)

In the 1980s, because of evidence that some stars were as much as 10 billion years old, BBers had to increase the age of their universe to at least that amount. Robert H. Dicke in 1961 said that its age is about the same as the nuclear burning time of a star, and in 1970 Rees and Silk said that, "Estimates of the ages of stars suggest that our galaxy, and others like it, are unlikely to be less than 10 billion years old. Hence we are presented with a remarkable coincidence: most galaxies appear to be about as old as the universe." This was supported by Carr in 1982.

Due to confirmation of the age of some stars and galaxies to at least 15 billion years, and despite the fact that the value of the Hubble constant indicates a lesser age, BBers have recently found it necessary to increase their estimated age of the BB universe to that amount.

Regarding globular clusters of stars within our own galaxy, as long ago as 1974 Gott, Gunn, Schramm and Tinsley reported that, "Models of stellar evolution indicate that they are between eight and 16 billion years old." A star has recently been reported (HD 140283) that has only 0.2 percent as much iron as the sun, indicating its age to be about 15 billion years. As recently as June 1992 the literature has confirmed the age of some stars to be 16 BYRs, 4 BYRs more than the newly estimated Hubble time and 8 BYRs more than the calculated age of the flat BB universe. The relative abundances of thorium, uranium and plutonium isotopes in meteorites has provided evidence that the age of our galaxy might be as much as 20 BYRs.

The Earth is estimated to be on the order four and one-half billion years old. (Rocks have been found in northern Canada that have been dated at 4 BYRs.) The sun might have been in place a couple of billion years before that. The accumulation of the matter that makes up the stars of our galaxy might have taken a couple of billion years before that. The dispersal of that matter from other stars may have taken a couple of billion years before that. The life of those stars, in which some of the heavy elements of our solar system are believed to have generated, was probably a few billion more years. The accumulation of primordial matter (mostly hydrogen) for our galaxy might have taken another couple of billion years. (According to CDM theorists, galaxies take at least several billion years to form.) The dispersal of that matter from the BB may have taken another couple of billion years.

The total of those increments of time may add to well over 15 billion years, nearly twice as long as the most likely time since a closed, flat or somewhat open universe BB might have occurred. (Looking at this in a different way, it is difficult to believe that the 4-1/2 billion years old Earth, is more than one half as old as a closed, flat or somewhat open BB universe, as calculated by the current best estimate of the Hubble constant.)

The above scenario allows for only one cycle of stellar nucleosynthesis. However, it is likely that it may have taken at least several such cycles before our solar system formed in order to account for the variety and quantity of heavy elements (called "metals" by astronomers) that we encounter within the solar system. This is supported by reports such as that of American physicists Gulkis, Lubin, Meyer and Silverberg in 1990, "Because significant amounts of elements heavier than helium have been observed in the oldest known stars, the material most likely was produced in an even earlier generation of stars." (It has been estimated that as much as 2 percent of the mass of our sun consists of elements that came from previous generations of stars.)

But assuming that only one previous cycle was required, and also assuming that, except for the period of the life of our planet and one previous generation of stars, the above incremental estimates were high by a factor of two, the total would still be as much as 15 billion years, which is considerably greater than the age of the BB universe as estimated by the new Hubble constant.

Hale Observatory astronomers Maarten Schmidt and James Gunn recently reported a quasar having a red shift of almost 5. The spectrum of that quasar, which is thought by BB cosmologists to be about 95% of age of the BB universe (9.5 to 14.25 billion years), indicated the presence of carbon, nitrogen, oxygen and silicon. Those elements could only come from previous generations of stars. Spectral analysis of other galaxies judged to be as old as 15 billion years has indicated the presence of carbon monoxide lines. That compound also could only have come from earlier generations of stars. If the estimated age of those galaxies is correct, there had to have been at least one generation of stars prior to 15 billion years ago.

Edward Anders of the University of Chicago and Ernst Zimmer of Washington University in St. Louis have recently reported the presence of minute grains of diamond, silicon carbide and graphite in meteorites that have traveled through interstellar space for eons. Their source is believed to be remains of novae of red giants that may have triggered the formation of the solar system. It is believed that some of the silicon carbide grains came from at least four different red giants. If that proves to be correct, it would seem to provide physical evidence for more than one stellar cycle before the formation of the solar system.

If it is assumed that just two previous generations of stars were required prior to the formation of our solar system, the estimated age of the universe might increase by a few more billions of years, bringing the total to about 20 to 25 billion years. For each additional star cycle, several additional billions of years might be required; possibly 25 to 35 billions of years for three cycles, etc. If the opinion of some astronomers and cosmologists is correct, and the life of stars can be as great as 10 to 15 billion years, these numbers could be considerably greater.

This line of reasoning regarding just one previous star cycle tends to discredit BBT in regard to the estimated time since the BB, indicating that age to be incorrect by about a factor of two. But it seems probable that more than one star cycle has been necessary, requiring the age of the universe to be considerably greater; as much as several tens of billions of years.

During the past century ever larger stellar formations have been discovered by astronomers; first galaxies, then clusters of galaxies, clusters of clusters, sheets of galaxies and large voids in space. Recent results of data collected by satellite infrared detectors indicate the presence of immense galactic formations, including the "Great Wall" that is said to spread 500 million light years through space. There have also been reports of large scale structures of galaxies that span almost one billion light years. It has been estimated that, if the missing mass was sufficient to provide the density variations required to "seed" these formations, their evolution might have required as much as 100 billion years.

University of Pennsylvania cosmologist Paul Steinhardt, well known for his work with both Guth and Linde on inflation theory, is quoted as saying, "There wasn't enough time in the history of the universe for gravity to pull together these structures." Princeton University astrophysicist Jeremiah Ostriker is quoted as saying that these results "sound the death knell" for CDM theory, the missing matter that is required, not only to support the closed or flat BB universe cases, but to account for the presence of galaxies, clusters and larger formations of galaxies. If only tens of billions of years were required for these formations, it would not only rule out a closed or flat BB universe, but the entire BB concept.

Regarding the quasar mentioned above having a red shift of about 5, and thus an age of about 9.5 to 14.25 billion years by BBT estimates, it is difficult to explain how quasars of such great age might have formed from the hypothesized cold dark matter in a period of about one-half to three-quarters of a billion years following the BB decoupling.

There have also been recent reports of evidence of the polarization of the light received from distant quasars. Polarization of their light indicates that they had relatively strong magnetic fields at the time it left them. Some of these quasars are reckoned to be observed as when they were only one tenth the age of the BB universe, far sooner after the BB than such fields could have developed.

Some sources have estimated that it takes 200 to 250 million years for our sun to complete an orbit around our galaxy. Others have estimated our sun to be about 30,000 light years from the center of our galaxy and its speed in orbiting that center is estimated at 200 to 300 km per second. If the age of the universe were on the order 10 billion years old, these estimates would indicate that our galaxy could have completed only 40 to 50 revolutions since the BB.

Intuitive judgement based on observation of the results of rotational motion suggests it is unreasonable to believe that the spiral form of our galaxy (or other spiral galaxies) could have developed in so few rotations. It would seem much more consistent with life's experience that many more rotations would have been required to generate the observed galactic configuration. Perhaps several hundred rotations would be more credible. If that judgement is correct, a galactic age on the order of 100 billion years would be required. Because the rate of rotation undoubtedly would have accelerated as the galaxy formed, rotations would have taken longer in the past, possibly indicating an even greater age for our galaxy.

These various bits of evidence and logic tend to support a universe of at least tens and perhaps hundreds of BYRs old, discrediting a BBT that postulates an age of 10 to 15 BYRs.

In the next nine paragraphs, three examples of the relationships of quasars to the Earth are presented. (The numbered items in parentheses in these paragraphs refer to corresponding items of Figure 5.) All distances and velocities given are approximate. The speed of light is represented by c, a billion years by BYRs, and a billion light years by BLYs. (The material of those nine paragraphs is rather tedious. It might be skimmed over lightly without too much loss to the reader.)

This discussion is based on the manner in which BBers are accustomed to calculations based on red shift data, that is, they assume a fixed-rate universe for their chronology but a flat universe for other physical characteristics. For simplicity, an age of ten BYRs assumed in this discussion. Similar problems could be illustrated as well if an age of 15 BYRS, as preferred by some BBers, were utilized.

(It is of course erroneous to consider a flat universe as having a fixed rate of expansion as in these examples. But because BBers customarily commit that error in their chronology, perhaps it is permissible to incorporate that lack of logic here in order to further illustrate the fallacies of the widely accepted BBT.)

As mentioned in the example of the previous chapter, astronomers have observed a quasar having a red shift of about 3.5. The velocity of that quasar relative to us is 90% of the speed of light (0.9c) so that its distance from us was 9 BLYs (1 of Fig. 5a) when the light received from it was emitted. If the BB occurred 10 BYRs ago, the photons received from that quasar left it only about one BYRs after the BB, and its distance from the BB at that time was about one BLYs (2 of 5a).

In this first example (which is the same as that presented in the previous chapter), it is assumed that our galaxy and the quasar were traveling in opposite directions from the BB. If the received radiation left the quasar when it was 9 BLYs from us, during the 9 BYRs its radiation traveled to us, in a fixed rate universe the quasar must have traveled another 8.1 BLYs (3 of 5a), so it would now be 9.1 BLYs from the BB (4 of 5a). Therefore it would now be 17.1 BLYs from us (5 of 5a). We could, of course, have no knowledge of what happened to it in that 9 BYRs. University of Leiden astronomer Maarten Schmidt said that such a quasar would have burnt out by now. But, even if it burnt out or blew up, some of its remains would nevertheless now be at 17.1 BLYs from us.

If that quasar, or some of its dust, is now 9.1 BLYs from the BB and 17.1 BLYs from us, the distance our galaxy traveled since the BB (6 of 5a) must be 8 BLYs. Its speed from the BB (7 of 5a) must be 80 percent of the speed of light (0.8c), the speed of the quasar from the BB (8 of 5a) is 0.91c, and its speed from us (9 of 5a) must be about 1.71c.

Similar calculations for a quasar of a different red shift, but also traveling in the opposite direction as we are from the BB, provide conflicting results. This second case is of a quasar having a red shift of 2, Figure 4 tells us that its velocity relative to us is 0.8c. If the BB occurred 10 BYRs ago the quasar's distance from us at the time the received light left it (1 of 5a) was 8 BLYs. That light left it about 2 BYRs after the BB when its distance from the BB (2 of 5a) was about 2 BLYs. During the 8 BYRs it took for its light to reach us the quasar traveled another 6.4 BLYs (3 of 5a), putting its remains about 8.4 BLYs from the BB (4 of 5a) and 14.4 BLYs from us (5 of 5a). Those figures put us at about 6 BLYs from the BB (6 of 5a). That distance was traveled in 10 BYRs, so our speed from the BB (7 of 5a) would be about 0.6c. The speed of the quasar from the BB (8 of 5a) is 0.84c and its speed from us (9 of 5a) is about 1.44c.

Not only do the results in these two examples show the quasar to Earth relative velocities to be greater than the speed of light, but they show a different speed of the Earth relative of the BB depending on the speed of the quasar as determined by its red shift.

If we consider a third case that is similar to the first example, except that the directions of travel from the BB of the quasar and the Earth are the same, as illustrated in figure 5b, the results are quite different. In this example (1) the distance the quasars traveled relative to us since their radiation was emitted, (2) their distance from the BB when it was emitted, (3) distance the quasars traveled during the transit of the radiation, and (4) its present distance from the BB are the same as in the first example above.

But for a quasar having a red shift of 3.5, its present distance from us (5 of 5b) would only be about 0.9 BLYs and our distance from the BB (6 of 5b) would be 10 BLYs. Our speed from the BB (7 of 5b) would be that of light. The quasar's speed from the BB (8 of 5b) would be 0.91c, and its speed from us (9 of 5b) would only be .09c. Although in an expanding universe that is flat or near flat, and having a quasar and our galaxy departing in the same direction from a point in space, may be a legitimate BB case (an Euclidean universe), the above results are totally unacceptable. They show the distance between our galaxy and the quasar to be decreasing, which would result in a blue shift rather than the red shift on which the example was based.

The results of these examples are confusing, to say the least. It seems inappropriate that relative speeds are calculated to be greater than that of light, that calculations based on the observations of different quasars result in different speeds of our galaxy relative to the BB, and that the Earth and a quasar traveling in the same relative direction from a point in space results in a decrease of their distance.

Furthermore, because quasars are observed in all directions from us, the examples given are far from representative of the whole universe. If we were to expand this discussion of a unidimensional situation to include realistic three-dimensional space (again, an Euclidean universe), wherein the quasars under consideration were traveling in many directions from us, even greater anomalies would become apparent, including speeds much greater than c.

The results of the above examples appear to discredit BBT. However, as BBers might quickly point out that, in a flat universe, in which expansion is decelerating, distant quasars would not presently be traveling at the speeds indicated above. Although they customarily utilize a fixed-rate universe to illustrate BB chronology, they base other aspects of their theory on a decelerating (closed, flat or somewhat open) universe in which those distant quasars would not have reached the speed of light. That would appear to be true of a sufficiently decelerating universe, and it must be true of a BB universe in which Einstein's prohibition applies.

(However, some theorists apparently believe that Einstein made yet another mistake and have rejected that prohibition. Both Guth and Linde have decided that inflation could incorporate speeds greater than light, and Oxford University mathematician and theoretical physicist Roger Penrose, a colleague of black hole theorist Stephen Hawking, told us (in 1970) that inside the event horizon of a rotating black hole, matter is falling inward at the speed of light while it is being dragged along in the vortex of the black hole, and thus can have a net velocity well in excess of c.)

But even if the superluminal speeds that have been calculated above were to be ignored, other problems can't be so easily dismissed. Calculations showing different speeds of our galaxy relative to the BB depending on which quasar is observed, and showing a decrease in distance between the Earth and a quasar traveling in same direction, are more difficult to explain.

BB cosmologists might respond to these difficulties by saying that they can be explained by the positive curvature of space, and that the calculations presented above are faulty because space is expanding and there wasn't a single BB site, but that it happened all over. But those arguments wouldn't hold up.

As has been proposed in the previous chapter, the current interpretation of red shift that ignores the gravitational effect on radiation from massive bodies is the true source of these anomalies. An attempt to rationalize them by invoking positively curved space is not logical. It has been shown that the age of the universe (as demonstrated by evidence such as the age of galaxies, the required star cycles, the time required for gigantic galactic formations, and the lack of sufficient missing matter) rules out the closed universe and flat universe cases; and even a "very open" BB universe is highly improbable.

According to standard BBT, a flat universe has no overall curvature and, if the density of the universe is less than that of the flat BB case, it has some degree of negative curvature. Therefore, for a flat or open universe, positive curvature can't be used as rationale to counter the anomalies presented above. If space isn't positively curved the BBer's belief in expanding space, and a BB that happened all over, can't be supported. In a BB universe without positive curvature, that has heavenly bodies departing from each other in all directions at speeds in proportion to their distance from each other, there must be a BB site.

If that BB occurred about 10 billion years ago, it might be expected that the diameter of the universe would now be about 20 billion light years. (Because it isn't consistent with their curved expanding space and "BB everywhere" concepts, BBers never refer to the radius or diameter of the universe, but only to its "size," which in this case would be 10 billion light years.) Because astronomers with modern telescopes believe they are able to detect quasars out to almost 10 BLYRs in a 10 BYR old universe (and to almost 15 LYRS in a 15 BRY old universe) if our galaxy were near the edge of the universe we might expect to detect a lesser density of quasars in that direction than in the opposite direction. But that hasn't been experienced.

In fact, in a flat or open BB universe, if quasars and radio galaxies are fairly uniformly distributed in our sky and if they appeared to have been more prevalent several billion years ago, as red shift measurements are thought to indicate, that would provide reason to believe our galaxy is close to the center of the universe, the site of the BB. Our velocity of departure from that site would be a relatively small fraction of the speed-of-light.

G. F. R. Ellis in 1975 said, "It would certainly be consistent with the present observations that we were at the center of the universe" and Joseph Silk said in 1980 and 1989, "If the universe possesses a center we must be very close to it ... otherwise we would detect more radiation from one direction than from the other direction." (But Silk, a firm believer in homogeneity, doesn't seriously consider that possibility.)

If we are relatively near the site of the BB, and that explosion wasn't quite uniform, which would seem likely, perhaps we can find some "debris" of the BB. A less than marvelously perfectly formed explosion might be expected to leave some irregular concentration of mass at or near zero velocity. Unless it happened to be hidden from view by our own galaxy, there is a chance that evidence of the BB could be detected. However, as of this date, it appears that no convincing evidence of BB debris has been reported.

(In recent years some strange configurations of matter in space have been discovered. Among these are "sheets" of galaxies and gigantic voids. Perhaps one of the strangest of them is the "Great Attractor" toward which our galaxy appears to be traveling at a rate of about 400 km per second. If there was a BB, perhaps our galaxy and its neighbors were among the slowest to leave it and, therefore, in the unlikely event that at least our portion of the universe happened to be closed, they might be among the closest of those returning to the Great Attractor, the site of the BB. Wouldn't that be an exciting development!)

It must be remembered that much of the above confusing discussion applies only for a BB universe. If BBT is incorrect and, for example, if SST applies, much of the above would be irrelevant. It should also be remembered that, in a BB universe in which the BB happened everywhere, quasars would be scattered throughout the universe. The appearance of clumping, that might be taken to indicate that we are near the center of the universe, may be the result of current red shift interpretation that ignores gravitational red shift, or the result of other unknown phenomena.

Until many questions are answered, especially those regarding the proper interpretation of MBR, red shift and large-scale irregularities of the universe, BBT will have serious problems regarding the age, size and shape of the universe. If there had been a BB, there is considerable doubt that its space is positively curved, or hardly curved at all. On the other hand, there is a minute chance that we are near its center, the site of a BB.

But the universe undoubtedly is very much older than 10 billion years, and very much larger than 20 billion light years in diameter. It's probably old enough for more than one previous generation of stars to have lived and died. It's certainly old enough to rule out any BB closed universe case, undoubtedly old enough to rule out the BB flat universe case, and probably old enough to rule out all of BBT.

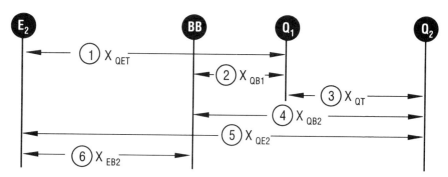

FIGURE 5a. E & Q in opposite directions (not to scale)

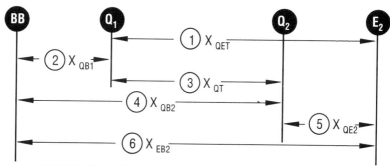

FIGURE 5b. E & Q in the same direction (not to scale)

BB Site of the Big Bang **Q₁** Quasar when radiation left it

Q₂ Quasar now **E₂** Earth now

① X_{QET} Distance radiation traveled during its transit

② X_{QB1} Distance of Quasar from BB when radiation left it

③ X_{QT} Distance Quasar traveled during radiation transit

④ X_{QB2} Present distance of Quasar from BB

⑤ X_{QE2} Present distance between Quasar and Earth

⑥ X_{EB2} Present distance of Earth from BB

⑦ V_{EB} Velocity of E relative to BB—$V_{EB} = X_{EB2/10}$

⑧ V_{QB} Velocity of Q relative to BB—$V_{QB} = X_{QB2/10}$

⑨ V_{QE} Velocity of Q relative to E—$V_{QE} = X_{QE2/10}$

FIGURE 5: QUASAR/EARTH/BIG BANG RELATIONSHIPS –
2 special cases for Euclidean (Flat) universe

THIRTEEN

Matter vs. Antimatter

Quantum mechanics fails to provide a satisfactory answer to a serious problem regarding the generation of matter in the universe. That problem, which is also unanswered by General Relativity, classical physics or by other accepted theory, is how the excess of matter over antimatter that is found in the universe might be accounted for.

According to quantum theory, when vacuum energy is transformed into matter, particles and antiparticles are produced in equal quantities. If that is so, why has our universe been left with so much more matter than antimatter? Some past attempts to solve this problem are summarized here.

Astrophysicist Adrian Webster in 1974, in attempting to explain the processes of the BB, suggested that in the early stages of the BB that "the equilibrium between the photons and the pairs of particles was disrupted; positrons and electrons that recombined to produce photons were no longer replaced by the reverse action. The positrons were steadily annihilated leaving a small excess of electrons" but he later asked, "why was there a residuum of real particles (the protons, electrons and neutrons) that constitute the matter in the universe at the present time?" And he admitted that he knew of nothing in physics that would lead us to believe there should be an excess of either matter or antimatter, and threw in the towel with, "the most likely possibility is that the excess was always there and that it has been a characteristic feature of the universe at all times."

University of California cosmologists Silk and Barrow in 1980 guessed that, in the first 10^{-35} of a second after the BB "when the processes that mediate the the decay of protons are abundant," they might have decayed leaving an excess of matter over antimatter of one part in 10^8 but no real explanation was given how that occurred.

Princeton Institute for Advanced Study particle physcist Frank Wilczek later (in 1980) suggested that the asymmetry between matter and antimatter came about because the law of conservation of baryon number was occasionally violated. According to Wilczek that involved hypothetical massive unstable X particles, vector bosons 10^{15} times more massive than protons, that existed before 10^{-35} second, just before the formation of quarks in accordance with GUTs.

Prior to 1980, a theory of symmetry called CP, for charge conjugation and parity (space inversion), that applied to the behavior of antiparticles versus particles, had been hypothesized. (CP symmetry means mirror image symmetry: if an experiment is conducted and watched in a mirror and then another experiment conducted that is the mirror image of the first experiment, replacing all particles by their antiparticles, the results would be the same as in the mirror image of the first experiment.) It was later found that the rules of CP symmetry are occasionally violated.

Wilczek suggests that in a small number of cases, upon their decay, X particles were among those that violated CP symmetry. When that happened the law of baryon conservation was violated, resulting in an inequality of particles and antiparticles. By the time the universe cooled to the GUT temperature, all of the X particles had decayed, leaving an excess of about one proton for every billion antiprotons. That happened in just the right ratio to leave the number of protons that remain in the universe today, neatly solving the excess matter problem. (The theory of CP symmetry is also responsible for postulating the existence of axions that might provide at least a portion of the dark matter of the universe.)

Others have suggested that evidence showing that K mesons

transmute to their antiparticles somewhat less often than their antiparticles transmute to K mesons would lead to the same result, but this and other similar schemes are still considered to be highly speculative.

B. J. Carr said in 1982 that GUTs predict "that the generation of a tiny asymmetry between the amount of matter and antimatter is inevitable, and it could well be sufficient to explain the excess of protons over antiprotons." But it turns out that GUTs require the decay of protons (in about 10^{30} seconds). But experiments performed to confirm their decay, and thus confirm GUTs, have failed to do so, tending to discredit the ability of GUTs to explain the excess of matter.

American physicists Dicus, Letaw, Teplitz and Teplitz in 1983 suggested that, in the first 10^{-35} second after the BB, the observed excess of matter was generated; and that is because, at temperatures above 10^{27} degrees, quarks can disintegrate into electrons and protons. They added that, "If the universe is cyclic each cycle can give rise to the excess of nuclear particles over antiparticles that is observed today."

According to some cycling BB universe advocates the collapse of the universe is like the formation of a black hole in which baryon number is not conserved. (We are told that all that is preserved in the collapse of black holes is mass, charge and angular momentum.) But it would seem that, based on the evidence presented herein, the possibility of a cycling BB universe has now vanished.

If Hawking's idea of billions of small black holes resulting from the BB is valid, as the matter of the early universe collapsed to form these black holes, he has suggested that, unequal amounts of matter and antimatter were caught in the gravitational clutches of each of them. Unequal amounts of matter and antimatter would then have disappeared into each hole. The subsequent collapse of these short-lived holes might have resulted in the excess of matter that is presently in the world. But it's not clear why matter and antimatter would be treated unequally on the average.

None of these attempts to explain an excess of matter over antimatter are convincing. Perhaps there's a flaw, an oversight or a misinterpretation of quantum theory that will be corrected, or a new theory, that will someday solve this problem. Because we observe more matter than antimatter, a credible theory for that might someday be discovered. In the meantime, all cosmological theories, including BBT, must await that explanation.

This mystery and other unsatisfying concepts of quantum theory, such as particle/wave duality and observer participation, leave plenty of room for uneasiness regarding its adequacy. Perhaps the philosophy of Niels Bohr, a key figure in the development of quantum theory, was sound. His opinion was that there isn't really a quantum world, virtually all knowledge is provisional, and quantum theory only provides an interim means of describing the behavior of the fundamental particles of nature. Richard Feynman agreed, saying that, "Scientific knowledge is a body of statements of varying degrees of certainty— some most unsure, some nearly sure, but none absolutely sure." Another wise man, French diarist Andre Gide, once said, "Believe those who are seeking truth, but doubt those who find it."

(In keeping with those thoughts, for each bit of scientific knowledge each individual, depending on their own judgement, might assign a "probability of certainty factor." For example, the statement, "The sun will rise tomorrow" might have a PCF of over 99.9999999%, but for "Black holes exist" the PCF might be about 99%. That practice could serve to remind us of the tentativeness of science.)

Einstein's reluctance to accept quantum theory was well founded. (Regarding probability amplitude, he once said, "God does not play dice.") Duality and other strange features of quantum theory might justifiably be considered as evidence of an imperfect or incomplete understanding of particle physics.

(Some later work provided support for Einstein's uneasiness with quantum theory. In 1952 American physicist David J. Bohm published his ideas based on Louis de Broglie's pilot-wave model, which provided an objective and deterministic account of quantum phenomena that was not dependent on observer participation nor subject to Heisenberg uncertainty. However, that alternative, that eliminated the paradoxes of the Copenhagen interpretation, has been ignored by most quantum theorists to this day.)

As Austrian born science philosopher Karl Popper had suggested in the 1930s, and as the history of science has shown, theories come and go. They are postulated and provisionally accepted. They might be modified over time, discarded if disproven, and replaced by better theory. Quantum theory will undoubtedly follow that pattern. Future developments will clear up the mysteries of uncertainty, probability, observer participation, duality, and even the excess of matter over antimatter may someday be satisfactorily explained.

FOURTEEN

The
Anthropic Principle

When some of the physical constants of nature, such as the speed-of-light and the mass of the electron or the proton, are adjusted to a dimensionless form, that is, by factoring them by other appropriate fundamental constants, or Planck's constant, the approximate values of some of them turn out to be related in unusual ways. For example, some of them seem to be related by various multiples of 10^{40}; the dimensionless gravitational coupling constant is equal to about 10^{-40}, the dimensionless Hubble age of the universe is equal to about 10^{40}, the ratio of the mass of the universe to that of a proton is about 10^{40} squared, and ratio of the mass of a proton to the mass of an electron, which is actually about 1,800, is considered to be approximately unity, the value of the zero-power of 10^{40} (but of course unity is the zero-power of any number).

Mankind has been fooled over and over again by such magic numbers in support of erroneous ideas. From chance numerical anomalies he has a tendency to select those that agree with satisfying results, and to distort data to support his views. Some of those dimensionless constants appear to support BB theories, but to what extent were they innocently and unintentionally selected or tailored to support the favored theory?

English mathematician and physicist Paul Dirac (one of the

founders of quantum theory who is responsible for the mathematics of electron behavior and for the invention of magnetic monopoles) suggested in 1938 that those relationships, the "Great Coincidences of the Dimensionless Constants," might have physical significance, i.e., they may be more than merely coincidental. Theoretical physicist R. H. Dicke became involved in this "large number hypothesis," and (in 1961) suggested that, if these numbers weren't as they were, human minds wouldn't have had a time and a place to evolve the ability to consider such things. For example, stars that produced the heavy elements that are essential to animal chemistry wouldn't have had time for that process if the Hubble constant were much larger, and life could not have evolved. Thus was born the concept of the Anthropic Principle.

Cosmologist Brandon Carter, who named the concept, in 1974 further developed the idea. He defined two categories of Anthropic Principle, the weak and the strong. The Weak Principle is defined by the statement that the universe happened to be such that it allowed us to be observers, and the Strong Principle is defined by the statement that the universe was somehow compelled to allow us to be here. The second of these might sound as though it were bordering on metaphysics or theology, but that was not Carter's intention. He presented more examples of constants of physics that he considered to be remarkable relationships.

Carter also introduced the idea of the World Ensemble, based on Everett's many worlds, in which there exist universes of all conceivable combinations of initial conditions and fundamental constants, but "observers" in the universe, such as ourselves, can only exist in those having certain special combinations of parameters. He suggested that cosmologists had previously shown an "exaggerated subservience to the Copernican Principle." (The comments of Chapter 12 regarding the possibility of our galaxy being located near the center of the universe might be favorably received by supporters of the Anthropic Principle.)

B. J. Carr in 1982 added that, if the relationships of the dimensionless constants pertaining to the BB weren't precisely as they were, the universe would be drastically different, and couldn't possibly support human life. Thus the universe was "fine-tuned" to provide for our existence. The Great Coincidences might be the result of physics as yet unknown to us, and possibly Copernicus wasn't exactly correct in thinking we occupied no special place in the universe. Perhaps the universe isn't isotropic and homogeneous after all. He later had second thoughts and suggested that, "the Many Worlds and Many Cycles explanations for the Anthropic Principle are rather bizarre" and he doesn't recommend them.

Paul Davies also subscribed to fine-tuning. In 1985 he commented on the "remarkable coincidence" that the strength of the BB explosion exactly matched the force of gravity such that the expansion rate of the universe is very close to the borderline between recollapse and rapid dispersal, i.e., very close to flat. If the physical constants of our universe weren't just as they are we wouldn't be here. As an example, if the gravitational constant were a little larger the stars would have burnt out too fast for life to evolve, and if it were a little smaller the sun would be too cool for life to start.

Physicist Heinz Pagels, also in 1985, mentioned that in theory (BBT) the density of the present universe could have been anywhere between one ten thousandth of and ten thousand times the amount necessary for flatness, and that in order for the universe to be as flat as it appears to be (somewhere between one tenth and twice the critical density, according to Pagles) the initial conditions of the universe had to be fine tuned to within one part in about 10^{18}. Pagels, who is not an advocate of the Anthropic Principle (and doesn't explain how he arrived at those numbers), said that, while such fine tuning might be possible, it doesn't provide a satisfactory explanation for the flatness of the universe.

Carr had said that because "the density is within a factor of 10 of the critical value now implies that its deviation from the critical value must have been even smaller at earlier times" and stated a smoothness within one part in 10^{16} at one second and one part in 10^{60} at 10^{-43} second after the BB. Unlike Pagels, he presented this as evidence of fine tuning, and thus of the Anthropic Principle.

To summarize, some BB cosmologists have reached the conclusion that, rather than conditions just happening to be such as to allow the appearance of life on earth, from which man eventually evolved, the BB and everything following it had been precisely tailored for the development of intelligent life. Philosopher Richard Swinburne, in 1989, finally took the bull by the horns and suggested that divine intervention may have played a part in fine-tuning the universe for our occupancy.

In contrast to the Anthropic Principle position on life in the universe, there might be at least 10^{22} planets; an average of one for each of an estimated 100 billion stars in each of an estimated average of 100 billion galaxies within telescopic range of our planet. If there were a possibility of life, as a wild guess, on one in a billion of those planets, there could be life of some form on as many as a 10,000 billion of them. It would certainly seem possible that, as another wild guess, at least one in a billion (10,000) of them are old enough and have environments sufficiently hospitable to have evolved some form of intelligent life.

There might therefore be a slight chance (one in 10 million) that intelligent life on a planet within our own galaxy could be smart enough, and close enough, to ponder cosmology while scanning our galaxy with their telescopes. It is also possible that their knowledge of science is far in advance of ours. Perhaps they have already found the answers to the cosmological questions that plague us. Unfortunately they may be so distant (tens of light-years) that we can't expect to receive any answers from them for decades, and must continue to search for our own answers.

If the above guesses were both one in 100 million instead of one in a billion the estimated chance of intelligent life on another planet in our galaxy might then become about one in 100,000.

(At least a few scientists, including popular science celebrity Carl Sagan, don't consider chances of contact to be too remote. Messages have been placed on spacecraft that have left the solar system, and the antenna array of Project Cyclops is listening for signals from space. One astronomer has recently guessed that there might be as many as one billion inhabitable planets within our galaxy. Perhaps those that are already inhabited and those that are inhabited by intelligent life are much greater than the above figures might indicate.)

As cosmologists Robert Shapiro and Gerald Feinberg in their book of 1980 *Life Beyond Earth* have suggested, those who embrace the Anthropic Principle are akin to microscopic rotifers living in a muddy little puddle who view the world as having been designed to meet their needs. Cosmologists, more so than bugs, should be aware that there is much evidence of life adapting to harsh environments, but little evidence of environments changing to meet the needs of organisms. Astrophysicist/cosmologist David Schramm (now at Fermilab) added that, "When you invoke the anthropic principle, you're saying you don't know how to solve the problem."

As with other portions this paper, the above brief comments on the Great Coincidences of the Dimensionless Constants, fine-tuning and the Anthropic Principle, tend to trivialize the works of some great minds. But in this case it seems that those involved, in their enthusiasm for BBT, headed off in a direction having little to do with science, and were destined to cross the border into theistic territory. They apparently feel that they have uncovered some of God's methodology for producing life and humanity on the Earth.

FIFTEEN

The
Cult

As stated in the introduction there, of course, isn't really a cult. But to the uninformed outsider there might just as well be a BB cult. External appearances might easily be interpreted as evidence of its existence.

Based on media coverage, if one didn't know differently, and didn't know that he is an amazing genius, one might suspect that Stephen Hawking was the current high priest of the Big Bang. If one weren't aware that many other BBer cosmologists were intelligent, highly educated, and otherwise normal human beings, one might think that they were members of a whole hierarchy of Big Bang priesthood, including bishops and cardinals under Supreme Priest Stephen.

There also seems to be some BB prophets and saints, and even a Messiah. The Messiah would of course be Einstein. He, apparently unintentionally, started the entire movement. Perhaps the greatest brain of history, and a beautiful person, Einstein the Divine can only be regarded with extreme reverence.

The priests work in their parishes, called universities, where they perform cosmological rituals for the parishioners and strive to write holy equations in support of the Big Bang Faith. A doctor of philosophy degree in mathematics or theoretical physics is required of The Priesthood, but both of those degrees are highly desirable.

Among the early saints was mathematician Alexander Friedmann, who undoubtedly was inspired by divine cosmological revelation to interpret Einstein's equations and thus provided a basis of the Big Bang expansion of the universe so that the masses (mere mortals) might understand. Another saint, Lemaitre, who is called the Father of the BB, also had a revelation. He was called to trace the expansion of the universe back to its explosive creation. He named the start of time, space, energy and matter the Creation of the Primeval Atom.

Like early Christianity, things didn't start out very rapidly for the Big Bang Cult. It wasn't until the great prophet Gamow, a disciple of Friedmann, and undoubtedly also destined for sainthood, came to us and set forth further details about the explosion that was to be called the Big Bang. The masses hungered for something they could cling to and, with its trendy new name, the Big Bang brotherhood flourished. (Out of proper respect, the new name is always capitalized.)

The Big Bang has it Scriptures, as revealed by its saints and prophets. Everything that has happened from the first instant of time has been painstakingly recorded for posterity. What occurred and the exact conditions under which it occurred, from the Creation to this very moment, has been precisely preserved by the chosen few so that the priests can spread the word to the masses.

Faith in the Big Bang has been reinforced by revelations of divine expansion to Elders Hubble and Humason, by revelations of divine radiation to Elders Wilson and Penzias, and confirmation of divine light elements by the prophet Gamow himself. The words "remarkable" and "amazingly" are among the most common adjectives used in the Scriptures to describe such events, and rightfully so, for who could not be in awe of the wonders of the Big Bang.

Some of the Big Bang saints and prophets were not immediately accepted. Among those were Saint Planck. His unorthodox vision of the Holy Quantum for many years went unrecognized for its True Holiness. It was not until after several additional prophets came, that the Priesthood agreed to integrate the Quantum into the Doctrine of the Cult. Among this group of Quantum Prophets were Bohr, Pauli, Heisenberg, Dirac, Feynman, Gell-Mann, and Weinberg. It took the persuasion of their detailed revelations to convince the Big Bang hierarchy that they were true prophets worthy of acceptance. The Quantum is now revered by the brethren.

After their embarrassingly reactionary reluctance to accept those later day saints and prophets, for which they have done penance, the Priesthood, for fear of denying a new revelation from the Almighty Big Bang, is now more receptive to new revelations. They now seem eager to accept those who have had a revelation or seen a vision, regardless of how radical those might be.

Among other more recently accepted are Guth, Steinhardt and Linde who's revelations have providing finer detail about the Instant of Creation. With the help of inspired followers like Pagles and Davies (now bishops) these revelations have been integrated into Holy Theory.

Questioning the tenets of the Faith, such as Isotropy and Homogeneity, the Expansion of Space, and Big Bang Everywhere, is frowned on. Such questions are analogous to a Christian priest questioning the virgin birth. Any consideration of such topics must be carefully presented as purely hypothetical intellectual pursuits. The council that rules on matters of Sacred Doctrine includes Cardinals Peebles and Schramm.

But the Big Bang is a benevolent and humane cult. Stretching on the rack and burning at the stake of pagans and heretics are frowned on. Those who reject the faith are merely ostracized. They and any who seriously question the dogma are excommunicated; banished from recognition in the halls of higher learning, and denied the opportunity for Cosmological Brotherhood.

It's not for common parishioners or parish priests to question the Doctrine of the Cult. Those who don't worship at the Shrine of the Bang are to be shunned. But converts are welcomed. Sciama once believed in the evil Steady State, which is the equivalent of Satan worship. Nevertheless, his past sins were forgiven and he has risen in rank to become Cardinal Dennis.

Icons of earlier pagan saints such, as Euclid, Copernicus and Newton, have been thrown out of the temples and the true orthodoxy may have been established for all time. As Supreme Priest Stephen asked in his Cambridge professorial inaugural lecture, "Is the End in Sight for Theoretical Physics?" Faith in the Big Bang may soon provide us with all the answers.

Of course the above is just for fun. But the truth is that the cult concept is somewhat analogous to the facts. The BB is almost universally accepted in the scientific community, and thus by the media and the general public.

One might expect the media and the public to accept a theory on the authority of respected worldwide leaders in cosmology, but the fact is that those scientists have accepted it on faith; primarily on faith in the skills and judgements of their predecessors and colleagues. That it is at least partly a matter of faith also becomes apparent when one considers the popularity of the Anthropic Principle among cosmologists. The tenacity of belief in the BB appears to be the manifestation of man's inherent desire for answers concerning his origin and that of the world, that might have more to do with metaphysics than science.

The many flaws that have been found in BBT are all but ignored. They are treated one at a time and dismissed one at a time; never gathered and examined for their overall impact, as this book attempts to do. Almost invariably researchers who discover and announce a flaw conclude their paper with a statement minimizing its importance to BBT. It may seem odd for a scientific researcher to discredit his own work in that manner, but there are some valid reasons for those disclaimers.

Few intelligent and considerate young scientists, who respect and honor their teachers and mentors, want to directly confront them with ideas that conflict with what they have taught. They don't want to appear disrespectful, ungrateful or heretical. In fact, they want to appear to be just the opposite—respectful, grateful and orthodox.

But there is more. These young scientists, who are naturally quite ambitious, are also concerned about their future. There are the matters of ratings and recommendations to consider. The young scientist's future is dependent on grading by his professors and/or on the recommendations of his professors for grants for the continuation of his work. To the professors basic cosmology is a closed issue; BBT is all but a proven fact. It becomes obvious to a student that endorsements of studies that might lead to contrary information are not very likely. Thus investigations into new areas go unrequested and unsupported.

(Thomas Gold clearly recognized this problem in a May 1993

issue of *OMNI* magazine entitled *Heresy! Modern Galileos*, referring to this as scientific herd instinct; when articles are reviewed by colleagues, decisions regarding grant applications are determined by this herd instinct.)

But it's not just young scientists who are reluctant to appear rebellious. Even senior scientists educated in the environment of BBT can be overwhelmed by the preponderance of biased cosmological opinion. Older researchers also are aware that their future is dependent on the approval of others in their field. Evidence of this among older and respected leaders in cosmology shows up in the form of disclaimers in articles that report evidence that is contrary to standard BBT. Some examples of these that have occurred within the past couple of years are presented in the following paragraph.

In an article in *Science News* of May, 1991 reporting that the CDM theory can't account for how "primordial matter" could have developed fast enough to produce the very early quasars that have been found, James Gunn was quoted as saying that reports of early quasars "cannot overturn - or even force major alterations in - accepted cosmological theories." In *Science* of September, 1991, on the same subject, Jeremiah Ostriker was quoted as saying, "Although of course none of that casts any doubt on the Big Bang itself." In *Science News* in September, 1991 in an article reporting far greater abundances of beryllium in old stars than BBT predicts, David Schramm is said to have emphasized that a lumpy universe would still allow for a BB type explosion. In *Science* of January 1992 on that subject he is quoted as saying, "The data so far do not force one away from the standard picture."

An additional factor is also at work. Close personal ties among physicists, astrophysicists, astronomers and cosmologists are the norm. What might be called cosmological incest is rampant in the world of cosmology. In the area of London, and especially at Cambridge University, we have had Barrow, Bonnor, Carr, Carter, Chadwick, Davies, Dirac, Eddington, Ellis, Gamow, Hawking, Lynden-Bell, Penrose, Rees, Rutherford, Salam, Sciama, Silk, Webster and others.

Glashow studied under Rutherford, Dirac was Sciama's teacher, Sciama was Hawking's tutor, Sciama and Rees worked together, as did Rees and astrophysicist Lynden-Bell. Penrose worked under

Sciama. Rees and Silk collaborated, and Silk and Barrow collaborated. Hawking has worked with Penrose, Sciama, and Ellis, and with Carter (on Anthropic Principle). Internationally, Gamow has collaborated with Hans Bethe; Hawking with Thorne, Guth, Linde and others. There have been some British heretics like Hoyle, Gold and Bondi (also of Cambridge), but have been duly dealt with.

The same pattern of interlocking careers has occurred in the United States. Some of American BBers have studied or worked at more than one U. S. university at various times. At Princeton there has been Compton, Dicke, Everett, Feynman, Geller, Gott, Gunn, Ostriker, Peebles, Pagels, Salam, Thorne and Wheeler; at MIT, Gell-Mann, Guth, Philip Morrison, Steinhardt, Sagan, Schramm, Schwarzchild, Webster, Weinberg, Wilczek and Yukawa. At Cal Tech there has been Feynman, Gell-Mann, Glashow, Gott, Gunn, Osmer, Schmidt, Smoot, Thorne, Kenneth Wilson and Zweig; at Harvard there was Glashow, Hucra, Sagan, Salam and Weinberg; and at the University of Chicago, Fermi, Gell-Mann, Sagan, Schramm, Turner, Wigner and Yang.

Wigner and Yang were assistants to Fermi. Dirac married Wigner's sister. Thorne, Rees, Everett and Feynman were students of Wheeler, and Tryon was a student of Weinberg (at Hunter College). Ostriker and Cowie have collaborated. Peebles was a student of Dicke, and they have worked together. Silk and Peebles have collaborated (at Berkeley), as have Ostriker and Peebles (at Princeton). Weinberg, Salam and Glashow shared a Nobel prize. Weinberg and Glashow were high school and college school mates. Schramm, Gunn and Steigman have collaborated. So have Schramm, Gunn and Gott; Schramm, Steigman and Wigner; Guth and Steinhardt; and Thorne and Misner (of the "mix master" universe). Lynden-Bell, Gunn, Sandage and Schmidt have worked, sometimes together, at the Hale Observatory.

These are some examples of the associations that have occurred during the history of BBT. The combination of camaraderie, peer pressure, admiration and respect for each other, desire for acceptance and prestige, and economic considerations has caused a close fraternity among these scientists. To many of them basic BBT is a closed issue. A dissenter has little chance for research money, publication or even notice in the cosmological community. This has resulted in a great cost in misdirected brain power, time and money, and has hindered investigations into alternate cosmologies.

Although serious scientists have ever attempted to maintain their objectivity, science has proven on occasion to be the result of opinion and prejudice rather than objectivity. That certainly appears to be true of cosmology. The cult concept is supported by the fact that BBT sometimes seems to have more in common with religion than with science. Unlike science, that attempts to build on a foundation of the solid observational data, it is an elaborate construction that has been developed from a limited number of facts.

In an article on the problems of modern physics cosmologist Robert Oldershaw (in 1990) has said, "theory is far outpacing experimental observations ... a hypothesis can become to be regarded as being so convincing and elegant that it simply has to be right ... A classic example is surely our relentless devotion to the traditional paradigm of the big bang in cosmology." Like religious zealots, BB cosmologists have stubbornly refused to accept information that conflicts with their beliefs.

SIXTEEN

Reaching

The primary undesirable result of the fraternization of BBT cosmologists is that it has resulted in special efforts to support BBT at the expense of possible alternate cosmologies. In this book that process is referred to as "reaching."

Since the invention of the BB cosmologists have spent untold effort to overcome its many problems. In that struggle a great variety of innovations have been attempted and, in many cases, biased efforts made to find confirming evidence and compatible explanations while contrary evidence is ignored. Each bit of data and logic that might discredit BBT is customarily overlooked or passed off as inconsequential.

Because the validity of basic BBT is considered by all but a few within the cosmological community to be a virtual proven fact, this breach of scientific method hasn't received any noticeable degree of comment. In fact, apparently proud of their efforts to support the accepted majority opinion, investigators have frequently called attention to these violations.

There are many examples of admissions of "reaching" for evidence and rationale in support of BBT throughout the history of BB. Some examples of these violations of scientific method are cited here.

The first of those noted here was provided by radio astronomer Adrian Webster who (in 1974) wrote, "The canonical big-bang-theory is the framework within which many astrophysicists are currently attempting to understand all the events in the evolution of the universe ... These questions and many others are all being attacked by trying to find explanatory processes in the universe described by the canonical hot-big-bang model."

Another example was provided by Rees and Silk who wrote (in 1970), concerning the smoothness of black body radiation pressure waves, "Some wavelengths will be attenuated more smoothly than others, so that the inhomogeneities of favored size will be preserved whereas those less favored will tend to be destroyed. The aim of recent work has been to determine what scales of perturbation are most likely to survive the various damping until the scattering of photons comes to an end."

Because of their commitment to isotropy and homogeneity the discovery of large-scale nonuniformity in the distribution of galaxies became a major problem to BBers. Therefore there are many examples of reaching regarding this topic. Rees and Silk said (in 1970), "It would be conceptually attractive if there were processes that could transform an initially chaotic universe into one that displayed the large-scale uniformity of a Friedmann model." Rees added (in 1976) that "large-scale uniformity is a most remarkable circumstance—one might have thought that a chaotic early universe would ... be more likely." Davies explained (in 1984) that quantum fluctuations grew in just the right way to produce large-scale uniformity without small-scale uniformity," and Linde rationalized (in 1985) that "the computed irregularities are too pronounced. But the models used are crude, and a more refined approach could prove successful" to explain large-scale uniformity while allowing small-scale nonuniformity.

Also on the topic of smoothness, Barrow and Silk told us (in 1980), "The search for the smoothing processes that would require fewer special conditions is part of the continuing work in chaotic cosmology," apparently then referring to inflation.

Regarding inflation, as explained by quantum concepts, Pagles wrote (in 1985) that, "fluctuations were now too big by factors of 1,000." But "clever physicists found field theory models that gave even the right size for fluctuations. For the first time, a rather simple theoretical model based on field theory could explain the origin and evolution of the fluctuations from which galaxies could eventually form." Regarding any doubts about the validity of inflation, CDM or other theories in support of BBT, David Schramm, one of its most ardent defenders, is reported to have made the following scientific comment: "Just because you can't predict tornadoes doesn't mean the earth isn't round."

As noted in *Science* of November 1991 the vast formations of galaxies that have been found in recent years, "The bigger those structures get, the harder it becomes for cosmologists to figure out how they could have coalesced in the limited time since the big bang." It is assumed, as it is in virtually all cosmology articles, that the occurrence of the BB is not to be questioned; only how the universe can be explained within BBT. The same article quoted Steinhardt as saying that, "There wasn't enough time in the history of the universe for gravity to pull together these structures," and continued, "Steinhardt and many of his colleagues nevertheless hold out hope for the cold dark matter model." That article also reported that Schramm is working to find "seeds" that can organize matter "efficiently enough to explain the structures now being mapped."

On a more grand scale, in his book *The Big Bang* (1980), Silk told us, "Today the central questions of cosmology and cosmogony are being explored within the framework of Big Bang theory." In the forward of that book, written by Sciama, we are told, "no doubt future research will enable us to rationalize even the Big Bang itself." Also illustrative of reaching on a grand scale, Linde has been quoted as saying (regarding his efforts to reconcile particle physics with inflation theory), "I could not believe that God would miss such a good possibility to improve the creation of the universe."

As evident from these examples, and many more that could be quoted, the process of "reaching" has continued throughout the history of BBT. But for every one of the many admissions of breach of scientific method in support of BBT that have been reported in the literature, there is obvious evidence of dozens of cases that haven't been confessed.

A major example of reaching is the search for missing matter. Those who believe that the universe is flat or closed have spent years in search of this stuff, and have proposed a vast array of matter including cold dark matter (CDM), massive "cold" neutrinos, hot dark matter (HDM, maybe fast moving "hot" neutrinos), burnt-out galaxies, low mass stars, large planets, black holes, magnetic monopoles, cosmic strings and sheets, gravitational waves, and much more exotic stuff such as WIMPS, MACHOS (formerly brown dwarfs), CHAMPS, axions, gravitinos, neutralinos, photinos, winos and zinos.

Probably many thousands of scientist man-hours have been spent in this quest to prove that the density of the universe is sufficiently high to provide for a flat or closed BB universe, and to prove the presence of CDM that is thought necessary to explain giant galactic formations. If sufficient matter is not found, space cannot have positive curvature. Without that curvature the BBer's case for photons from the decoupling arriving from all directions is without merit, and their most important evidence in support of the BB is invalid. The discovery of the missing mass is especially important to inflation theorist who postulate a flat universe.

As one example of extraordinary theoretical and experimental efforts that have been made to find the missing mass, Sciama has gone so far as to make precise predictions regarding tau neutrinos. His calculations showed them to have a mass sufficient to close the universe (30 eV), and a lifetime of 10^{23} seconds. However, satellite (Hopkins Ultraviolet Telescope) experimental searches for the radiation that would result from the decay of those neutrinos has produced only negative results.

Because of a recent realization that it would be impossible for all that CDM (even if it existed) to account for the development of the giant formations within the BB time frame, belief in CDM has been abandoned by some. Regarding the failure of CDM theory, Alan Guth, the originator of inflation, has suggested that CDM theory must merely be "modified for a better fit," and David Schramm is reported to have said that, even if there were found to be no fluctuations in the microwave background, BBT will survive; that eventuality could favor "more exotic and bizarre" BBT models.

Regarding BBT in general, Schramm is reported to have recently said, "We have the basic framework. We just need to fill in the gaps," and Peebles recently was quoted as saying, "By being a little more clever in the invention of theories a person can find a way around the problems and continue to look for a way to build within the Big Bang framework." Apparently BBers have no intention of mending their ways; in the future they will merely employ more cleverness in finding support for BBT. Peebles' comment might deserve a prize for providing the world's greatest endorsement of reaching.

A number of examples of reaching have been discussed elsewhere in this book. Notable among them is the development of the detailed time line described in Chapter 4. As cosmologist Ernan McMullin in 1981 reported that, "In the last decade much effort has been expended on applying quantum and elementary particle theories to the problem of how the universe developed in the first moments after the big bang. An immensely detailed scenario has been developed...." The energy levels, either experimental or theoretical, required for the creation of quantum particles, real or hypothetical, have been used to fit the time of their appearance into the BB universe scheme. McMullin has more politely used the word "developed" rather than "contrived" that is used in this book.

All of the various attempts to rationalize the problem of the excess of matter over antimatter could easily be seen as cases of reaching, and couldn't the whole idea of inflation be considered as one huge case of reaching? The extension of the idea from quantum theory that vacuum fluctuations can cause the spontaneous appearance of particle pairs on the scale necessary to provide rationale for the generation of the entire universe is quite a stretch. Inflation appears to be nothing more than a colossal desperate attempt to rescue BBT from several serious problems, including that of the singularity; an enormous violation of the law of conservation of mass/energy. It was invented and has been tailored to solve BB problems; and, like many other theorist's flights of fantasy, it cannot be proved or disproved.

In 1987 physicist Thomas S. Kuhn expressed the opinion that science is a political rather than a rational process. In a recent *Science News* article Ivars Peterson reported that some historians, philosophers and sociologists "argue that science has an undeserved reputation for objectivity. They maintain that social interests determine not only how science is done but also its content. Science itself is a matter of opinion—decided on the basis of personal or political beliefs, they insist. It is nothing but a social construction, perhaps even a group self delusion." Those opinions might be overly harsh regarding science in general, but they might apply to the field of cosmology where scientific method often seems to be considered an unnecessary annoyance.

However, because the majority of astronomers, astrophysicists and theoretical physicists who have been involved in cosmology for the past quarter century have diligently worked to provide theory and evidence in support of the favored theory, it's not surprising that most of the world is convinced of its truth. If a fraction of that effort had been used to investigate alternate ideas, there might instead now be a healthy competition between a number of viable cosmological choices; and it's possible that BBT would no longer be among them.

SEVENTEEN

Ripples in the Cosmos

On April 24, 1992, newspapers and, within the following couple of weeks, broadcast newsmen and science magazines across the U.S. announced a great discovery. It was "ripples ... at the edge of the universe" that "have provided the first evidence of how the stars and galaxies were formed."

This "strongest support yet for the birth of the universe" was hailed in the news as "one of the major discoveries of the century." The significance of this "unbelievably important" discovery "cannot be overstated." It's the "Holy Grail of cosmology" that, if true "would have to be considered for a Nobel Prize."

(Paul Steinhardt's reaction was quoted as, "These observations tell us about the universe back to the very beginning." Joseph Silk's reaction was, "It's the missing link." And it was later reported that Stephen Hawking said, "it is the discovery of the century, if not of all time.")

In that news release, reporting on the results of experiments aboard the Cosmic Background Explorer (COBE) satellite, not only was the importance of those "ripples" overstated, it was overstated by orders of magnitude; another example of reaching on a grand scale.

The writers of this news release appear to have gotten carried away with the enthusiasm of the experimenters for their work. University of California astrophysicist and COBE team leader George Smoot was reported as repeatedly declaring this to be "the golden age of cosmology" (a phrase that was used by David Schramm when reporting his reaction to earlier bad news for CDM).

Since its invention years ago a basic tenet of BBT has been that the cosmos began as a perfectly smooth mixture of primordial matter. In 1965, when microwave background radiation was discovered coming from all directions of space, it has been considered to be the most important evidence, not only in support of the BB, but in support of the smoothness of the BB.

Over the years following that discovery more and more sophisticated detection methods have found that radiation to be increasingly smooth. Until recently, when measurements indicated its smoothness to be better than about one part in 10,000, BBers were increasingly pleased with what they considered to be all but positive proof of a smooth BB. Their established beliefs in isotropy, homogeneity, Copernican Principle and Cosmological Principle had been confirmed beyond any possible doubt.

But as time progressed some of them have become increasingly concerned about too much smoothness. During the past decade greater and greater irregularities have been found in the matter of space; formations of giant voids and sheets of galaxies hundreds of millions of light-years across, clusters of quasars as distant as 10 billion years, and more recently, the Great Wall that is said to be half a billion light-years across. (The estimated size of the Great Wall was erroneously reported as 200 million light-years in the news reports.) As early as 1987 Princeton University astronomer Jeremiah Ostriker is said to have conceded that the conflict of these large galactic formations with the smoothness of the microwave background was putting a strain on standard BBT.

One news writer reminded his readers that, as embarrassment grew over the increasingly excessive smoothness of microwave background radiation, more reaching occurred by theorists who "obligingly adjusted their models to accommodate the ever smaller initial density fluctuations."

The presence of those extremely large scale structures and distant clusters not only deny the smoothness of the present universe, they deny it for the earliest stages of development of the BB universe. Even some BB cosmologists have expressed disbelief that galaxies and clusters of galaxies could have formed unless there had been relatively large irregularities in the density of the early universe.

Although some of the leading advocates of BBT have insisted that, on a larger scale, beyond the present giant irregularities the universe will turn out to be smooth, others have become increasingly concerned that there could not have been time for these structures to have evolved. As was mentioned in the previous chapter, even if the CDM postulated as necessary for a closed BB universe and for providing the "seeds" for the formation of galaxies and clusters was found to exist, there wouldn't have been time for these formations to develop. As Robert Oldershaw wrote in an article that is critical of cosmologist's certainty of BBT, "Even the strongest piece of evidence (the smoothness of MBR) has turned on it."

Because of increasing estimates of the age of stars and galaxies in recent years, BB cosmologists have been increasing their estimates of the age of the BB universe in order to overcome the awkward situation of stars and galaxies that are older than the BB universe. In recent years they have increased that age from about 10 to 15 billion years. However, due to very recent improved estimates of the Hubble constant that limit the age of a BB universe to maximum of about 12 billion years (and about 8 billion years for a flat universe), there still could not have been enough time for the formation of distant quasars and galactic structures.

But some BBers haven't given up hope on CDM theory. George Smoot, who announced the results of the COBE Differential Microwave Radiometer data on April 23, 1992, is included in that group. He is quoted as saying, "the temperature and size of the ripples also provide strong confirmation of the theory that as much as 90% of the matter of the universe is so-called cold dark matter."

(Smoot has recently stated that the early universe inflated, at greater than the speed of light, from an initial minute size to only about 100 meters, a very much smaller size than suggested by Guth or Linde. He also declared that "inflation is a transcendental concept linking the very small with the very large," thus, in one neat phrase, cleared up any doubts there may be regarding the superluminal expansion of the universe.)

However, in view of newly discovered age limitations and estimates of at least several billions of years required for the evolution of enormous galactic structures, many theorists have lost their enthusiasm for CDM theory, and agree with astrophysicist Jeremiah Ostriker's comment that these structures "sound the death knell" for CDM. Some estimates of the length of time required for the evolution of the Great Wall have been as high as one hundred billion years. If true, that would not only rule out CDM and a smooth BB, but would totally discredit BBT.

The new development, described in the subject news release regarding the discovery of small variations in the smoothness of background radiation with such great enthusiasm, reflects a complete reversal of attitude of BBers. Decades ago each report of increased smoothness was hailed as increased confirmation of BBT. But when smoothness was reported as one part in 1,000 some cosmologist began to express concern about that degree of uniformity. Through the years measurements have gradually increased, causing increasing concern, and recent measurements, approaching one part in 100,000, have become a serious embarrassment to BBers. The smoothness of MBR became too perfect.

However, it was inevitable that sooner or later, as more precise measurements were made, a limit to the smoothness of microwave background radiation would be reached. If a product of nature appears smooth on some scale (like viewing the surface of the earth's oceans from a spacecraft), when examined more and more closely it will eventually be found to have some degree of irregularity (like ocean waves).

Smoot was quoted as saying that, "after considerable computer processing," and the results withheld until his team could "check and recheck for possible errors in 70 million measurements at each of the three radiometers." Although computer processing can retrieve data from poor quality signals (which in this case were reported to be below the noise level of the instrumentation) unfortunately, neither computer processing or checking and rechecking poor data can make corrections for unknown system errors.

Certainly Smoot and his team are aware of those facts, and

tried to give them proper consideration. But, even if they had done so, isn't it obvious that these newly reported variations equivalent to plus or minus 15 millionths of a degree K in radiation from the BB decoupling are insignificantly small as compared to what might be expected as a result of the presence of the gigantic galactic formations that have been found in space?

Looking at these "ripples" isn't at all like "looking at God" as reported by the media. The variations reported are so minute that they might be expected regardless of the source of the radiation. They might originate from any number of sources, including unknown irregularities of the matter that surrounds the solar system, our galaxy, the local group of galaxies, and beyond.

(It would be of interest to know whether the variations correlate with any known galactic formations, including galactic concentrations and voids in space. Although it wasn't made clear how scaling of distance or size might have been established from angular data, ripples were reported to stretch across 500 million light-years of space. Perhaps there is a correlation with structures like the Great Wall or the newly reported Southern Wall that are estimated to be of about that size.)

But if black-body radiation emanated unimpeded from the BB decoupling at the speed of light (the speed at which photons travel) it would not be received by us, but would be far away, beyond the distant quasars. Therefore, if we are receiving it from the decoupling, it must have been bouncing around the universe for billions of years. If that were so, its reception would be expected to have variations indicative of the large irregularities of matter in space, not the minute variations that have been reported.

It should be noted that the news reports not only assumed an erroneous BB universe age of 15 billion years, they erroneously assumed a closed BB universe, and thus also assumed positively curved space and all that goes with it. That of course includes the expansion of space, as opposed to the expansion of matter, and that the BB happened all over. The uniform arrival of black-body radiation from the BB decoupling era can only be accounted for by acceptance of those tenets of BBT.

Those beliefs are implicit in the content of the press release. They are adhered to by BBers regardless of the obvious impossibility of a closed universe, and thus of the impossibilities of positively curved space, space expansion, and a BB that happened all over. If the BB universe is open, as it would have to be, space, if curved at all, is negatively curved. Therefore black-body radiation from the decoupling could not be raining on us. The entire premise of the press release is invalid, and this "evidence for the birth of the universe and its evolution" is misconceived. The reported ripples change nothing.

Smoot was quoted in the October 1992 issue of *Discover* magazine as saying, "If you are religious it's like looking at God … its the Holy Grail of Cosmology, its the birth of the universe, the handwriting of God." Perhaps more prophetically, Phillip Schewe of the American Physical Society, when asked if he had ever seen anything like this answered, "Not since cold fusion." In the original story in April 1992 Smoot had been quoted as saying, "I know I'm going out on a limb" but, blinded by enthusiasm for his work, he apparently had no idea how frail that limb might be.

EIGHTEEN

The Quest for Understanding

F or many years after its invention standard BBT seemed to
provide an answer to man's curiosity about the origin of the
universe. Due to his limited experience in the environment of
the Earth's surface, where he normally experiences rapid expansion only as the result of explosion, apparently he is disposed to
accept the cause of the expansion of the universe to be a gigantic
explosion. That idea was accepted with relatively little question.
So eager is man for answers to the origin, that the postulated
uniformity and symmetry of the results of this event, contradictory to all of his experience, was readily accepted. The
expectation of very large-scale irregularities that would normally
result from an enormous explosion was ignored.

But even more amazingly, scientists ignored the question of
the source of power that might have produced the BB. Joseph
Silk was witness to that. In 1980 he wrote, "The pioneers of
big bang theory were not greatly concerned about the singularity in space-time that was apparently required by the Friedmann
equation." An enormous violation of the law of conservation of
mass/energy, was accepted by BB cosmologists.

BBT depends on Einstein's General Theory of Relativity for
its theoretical basis, but how can a theory that is only partially
tested in our normal benign environment be depended upon in

a situation so remote from our experience as the near infinite temperature, density and pressure of the BB? Cambridge cosmologist Jayant Narlikar, one of the few remaining SST proponents in the world, asked, "How far has this theory been tested? To what extent can it be trusted in our extrapolation all the way to the bigbang epoch?" Cosmological philosopher Ernan McMullan warned against such an enormous extrapolation of laboratory physics in his statement, there are "good historical reasons to distrust the applicability of standard theories to extreme conditions."

With the advent of quantum theory it was hoped that it might rescue BBT from some of its problems. Since that time great effort has been expended in tailoring BB scenarios to fit quantum particle physics and quantum mechanics. Various features of quantum theory provided the basis for inflation scenarios. But how can this theory, which, like curved space, defies human intuitive understanding and has only been partially tested on a small scale in environments very different than that of the hypothetical BB, be depended upon to function on a grand scale in that alien situation? McMullin's quotation continued, "Furthermore, no adequate theory of quantum gravity has yet been devised. So there is every reason to suppose that present reconstruction of the early universe ought not to be taken too seriously as history."

Inflation theorists resurrected Einstein's cosmic repulsion to provide the energy for inflation's enormously expanding universe. But how can this formerly rejected term of Einstein's equations, that was originally thought to provide only the force necessary to oppose the minute gravitation in space be called upon to blow up the entire universe?

All of the theories of natural physical behavior that have been accepted over the previous few centuries have met the tests of human understanding and straightforward demonstration. It seems that in this century modern science has for the first time accepted theories that are contrary to everyday human experience. Richard Feynman, one of the great minds of modern physics said, "No one understands quantum mechanics," and such things as time dilation and curved space are not, in the usually sense of the word, understood by anyone.

Relativity and quantum theories may truly be acceptable for their predictive capabilities for Earthly phenomena but, until they can be subjected to controlled testing and reconciled with the intuitive mental processes that have served man so well in the past, full acceptance of them, even for Earthly processes, is suspect. Extending the application of General Relativity and quantum theory to cosmological phenomena as alien as the explosive birth of a universe isn't justified. The acceptance of BBT by cosmologists and the public alike can only be attributed to man's desire for answers to questions about his origin and that of the universe.

It seems that scientific method, that in essence consists of postulation based on the study of nature that is then verified by the results of controlled experimentation, has been discarded by cosmologists. It has been replaced by elaborate constructions that are said to have "elegance," apparently a preferred quality that has superseded scientific method. BB cosmology, believed by many to be a sound scientific structure, is built on a foundation of very few hard facts.

(A factor contributing to the wide acceptance of BBT in the Judeo-Christian world is that it is not terribly inconsistent with the creation of the world as told in the Bible. After hearing of the BB in 1951, Pope Pius IX is quoted as having said, "True science to an ever increasing degree discovers God as though God were waiting behind each door opened by science.")

It should be clear by now that we have an inadequate understanding of many subjects that bear on cosmology. An example of that is our lack of understanding of the presence of an excess of matter over antimatter in our part of the world. From all appearances that seems to be what exists, but quantum theory hasn't explained that. The inadequacy of the Grand Unification Theories and the lack of a Theory of Everything provide more examples of our lack of understanding. The unification of the electroweak and strong nuclear forces is far from an accomplished fact, and the difficulty of incorporating the force of gravity into a unified field theory seems overwhelming. If and when these theories are satisfactorily devised, any previous concept of cosmology might require a complete revision.

But man's greatest lack of understanding, that he so greatly yearns to satisfy, is of the ultimate origin of the universe and all therein. For a while it seemed that BBT had made a major step in that direction, but that was illusory. BB proponents criticized the old SST for side-stepping the issue of origin but, as time has passed, it became apparent that BBT, like SST, has only put off an explanation of the origin of the cosmos to an earlier time. In the end it must be realized that the question of the ultimate origin can't be answered. Unfortunately, neither BBT, SST, nor any other cosmology can satisfy that need. BBT seemed to do that for a time, but neither open, flat, nor one-shot or closed cycling scenarios have escaped the problems of BBT, and the same questions remain.

No cosmology can promise knowledge of the "first cause," and probably none ever will. The quest for ultimate answers to the origin of life and the universe is what drives men to science, philosophy and religion. Apparently a new theory can for a time quiet that longing, but sooner or later we realize that with each hard earned advance in science we have only moved one step closer to the ultimate cause. We must face the prospect of never reaching an understanding of the infinities of time and space. (Physicist-philosopher Paul K. Feyerabend has been quoted as saying, "this one-day fly, a human being, this little bit of nothing discovering the secret of existence is crazy.")

As we learn new facts of nature, they merely bring to light the next generation of questions, which is usually an even bigger and more complex set. We are left, and probably always will be left, to ponder the ultimate origin of energy, matter, space, time and life. John Wheeler said this more eloquently: "We live in an island of knowledge surrounded by a sea of ignorance. As our island of knowledge grows, so does the shore of our ignorance."

As astronomer Herbert Friedman wrote in *The Amazing Universe*, "no matter how far we push back the veil of ignorance to reveal the existing universe, we shall always be stumped by the basic issue: What lies behind creation?" And astronomer Bernard Lovell warned us, the problem of creation "can tear the individual's mind asunder." St. Augustine is said to have asked, "What was God doing before He created Heaven and Earth?" Which he answered with, "He was preparing Hell for those who inquire into such matters."

But it's not suggested here that we stop striving for answers to our questions. What is suggested is that we do so with open minds, ignoring the influence of the general acceptance of BBT and, based on what we know and what we don't know, see if we can't discover a simpler less troubled cosmology, and, in the meantime, live with our questions about origins.

NINETEEN

An Alternate Cosmology

Much of the evidence against BBT presented in the previous chapters is not new. Many of the items discussed have been brought up in the past but, taken one at a time, they have been glossed over and dismissed. However, now that they have been gathered and presented in a single document, their combined impact should be difficult to ignore. It would certainly seem that the credibility of BBT has been annihilated.

Upon consideration of that loss, one has to wonder what might replace BBT. If BBT has been proven invalid what is left? Without it there is a void for the majority of cosmologists and their faithful followers. A replacement is needed; a theory that will help to satisfy the desire for answers about the origin and evolution of the universe.

No one can be certain what that cosmology might be but, in order to avoid tearing down BBT without at least offering a replacement, an alternative cosmology is suggested here. It is based on the old SST originated by Bondi, Gold and Hoyle over 40 years ago, but it avoids the fatal flaws of that theory.

It has been said that the singularity problem of BBT provided the motivation for the development of SST, and certainly that was a factor in the development of the modified SST presented here. The problems of BBT were undoubtedly also a factor leading to Danish plasma physicist Hannes Alfven's invention of plasma theory. That theory, that does away with the BB, proposes that electromagnetism rather than gravity is primarily responsible for shaping the universe. But Alfven's theory doesn't seem to qualify as a complete cosmology. It certainly deserves consideration as an alternate or additional explanation for the formation of galaxies and clusters of galaxies, but it fails to take us beyond that.

Another theory that has been considered in recent years is that of multiple small bangs. Rather than one gigantic blast that instantaneously produced all the matter and energy of the cosmos, why not a continuing series of smaller explosions? The discovery of voids and sheets of galaxies could be seen as support for that idea. Certainly many smaller quantum vacuum fluctuations are easier to accept than a single blast that was large enough to produce the entire universe in one instant. (Perhaps it could be combined with Alfven's plasma theory). But this scheme might have some serious flaws. For example, it seems unlikely that energy from explosions distributed in time and space could have produced MBR of the smoothness and the near perfect blackbody spectrum that are observed; and wouldn't we expect to observe blue shifts of radiation from some objects in distant space?

Long ago BB cosmologists ruled out old SST for several reasons. It didn't provide an acceptable explanation for MBR or for the relative abundance of light elements, and it didn't provide for an evolving universe. Because evidence of a greater number of radio sources and quasars at remote distances convinced them of an evolving universe, a SS universe was judged to be impossible. Regardless of the fact that pre-inflation BBT provided no reasonable explanation for the source of the immense mass of the universe or for the enormous force that blew it up, SST's postulated new matter in space and for the continuing expansion of the universe were declared unsound.

But now that quantum theory and cosmic repulsion are used as explanations for inflation, perhaps they can be accepted as rationale for cosmologies such as SST. Now that it has been shown that other sources of energy might have thermalized space, the presence of MBR as proof of the BB is subject to question; now that it is known that light elements may have sources other than a BB; and now that the usual calculations based on red shift have been shown to be questionable, and thus the clumping of quasars as evidence of an evolving BB universe is in doubt, the old proofs of BBT can no longer be evoked.

What had been considered to be important evidence in support of BBT can no longer be relied upon. When the many new problems of BB (such as an Hubble constant indicating the universe to be younger than its stars) are considered, there are few reasons to deny other cosmologies. In fact, the only remaining factor that can be counted against the old rival SST cosmology is its insistence on its Perfect Cosmological Principle, that is, perfect smoothness and perfect constancy of the universe.

A New Steady State theory (NSST) that is proposed here postulates a non-exploding universe that is not steady state, but near steady state. (NSS might stand for near steady state as well as new steady state.) Old SST included large-scale smoothness, similar to that claimed for the BB universe, and also that smoothness is unchanged with time. Under NSST that degree of smoothness, that is contrary to the facts, is not required; and that degree of constancy, that appears to be contrary to the facts, may not be required.

According to old SST the universe is expanding uniformly. Thus its density would be decreasing if it weren't that new matter is continually being created in space. From this new matter, over eons, new stars and galaxies are formed at a rate sufficient to keep the average age of cosmic matter and the average density of the universe constant. Old dying galaxies move further away to become less and less observable, and clumping of distant quasars does not occur.

The average rate of the creation of new matter required for that process was estimated by Bondi in 1960 to be "only one hydrogen atom in the space of an ordinary living room every few million years," which agrees fairly well with Gamow's earlier estimate of about "one hydrogen atom per hour per cubic mile in intergalactic space." (Pagels has more recently estimated one atom per liter per 10^{12} years, which agrees almost exactly with Bondi's number.) The creation of only a minute amount of new matter would thus be required to maintain the density of the universe; and, as SS cosmologist Fred Hoyle said, "It is not at all difficult to understand why the process, if it really occurs, has not been detected in the terrestrial laboratory."

SST proponent Herman Bondi could very well been correct when he said (in 1960) that, although the continual creation of matter in space violates the principles of conservation of mass/energy as it has been observed in laboratories, those observations are subject to a certain measure of inaccuracy. The mean density of the universe is so low that the rate of creation of matter in space does not conflict with the results of any experimental data on which that law was based.

Although almost totally discredited in the minds of BBers, the SST of Bondi, Gold and Hoyle has managed to survive in spite of attacks by a number of eminent BB proponents throughout the years. One of those critics, astrophysicist Dennis Sciama, said (in 1967) that "of all the heretical cosmological theories" SST is the most irritating and "has provoked the most good astrophysicists." Such attacks, perhaps due to some insecurity about the BB position, seem more emotional than scientific. However, another faithful BB proponent, philosophy professor John Leslie was much more charitable in his statement (in 1990), "Continual creation of matter may seem to be a little odd, yet those who are scornful about it while themselves stating that an entire universe appeared all at once might be the pot calling the kettle black."

Science has accepted Einstein's theory on the equivalence of mass and energy. It was long ago demonstrated that mass can be converted to energy. Quantum theory tells us that energy can be converted to matter, supporting Einstein's theory in the reverse direction. The equivalence of matter and energy can be interpreted to mean that energy exists in at least two states; its intrinsic state and its material state. (American physicist Edward Tryon used the term "intrinsic energy" in 1973 and in 1984 University of Adelaide professor of mathematics and physics Paul Davies called matter "locked-up" energy; two apt expressions.)

The term intrinsic energy is used here for the total quantity of energy of space in its non-material state from all possible sources. That energy might be comparable to the energy that quantum cosmologists consider to be that of false vacuum or vacuum fluctuations as derived from their interpretations of quantum theory.

As we have seen, upon general acceptance of quantum theory, BB cosmologists, ignoring the fact that it deals with phenomena only on the scale of fundamental particles, soon put it to work in various attempts to solve the many problems that have long plagued BBT, and especially to provide a source for the mass/energy of the universe in a BB.

That is essentially what is proposed here, but on a microscopic scale. *There is an intrinsic energy of space that provides for the generation of a sufficient amount of matter throughout the universe to maintain its average mass/energy density at or near a constant level while maintaining a fairly uniform and continual distribution of matter, and a degree of randomness that is consistent with the observed randomness of the universe.* The amount of matter required for that process is minute, and on a scale that is consistent with a reasonable application of quantum theory.

Modern BB cosmologists who have incorporated inflation theory into BBT certainly agree that matter can develop spontaneously in the empty space of the universe. Paul Davies, an ardent proponent of inflation, confirms this in his statement, "the spontaneous appearance of matter out of empty space is often referred to as creation out of nothing ... for the physicist, however, empty space is a far cry from nothing." He has assured us that, "The spontaneous production of new subatomic particles out of empty space ... can happen because the energy of motion of space can be converted into matter according to the ideas of quantum theory and relativity ... Calculations show that particles of all types are produced by this mechanism—electrons, neutrinos, protons, neutrons, photons, mesons and even gravitons."

BB inflation theorists readily accept this concept for the conversion of the intrinsic energy of space, which they refer to as quantum vacuum fluctuations or false vacuum, but they apparently prefer to believe in the generation of matter from the vacuum of space only on a scale that can create an entire universe in one fell swoop.

One might think that the idea of matter out of empty space would only be accepted with great difficulty. But it would certainly seem less difficult to accept it on the microscopic level required for the "replenishment" of matter in space, as proposed by NSST, than to accept it as the source of all the mass of the universe in one increment. It was gratifying to learn that BB advocate English astrophysicists Rees and Silk (in 1970) admitted, "that some form of continuous creation of matter may not be ruled out."

There seems to be little doubt that the spectrum of the MBR is that of black-body radiation. At first glance that might appear to present a problem for NSST. BBers maintain that this radiation can only be explained by infrared radiation from the hypothetical BB decoupling that is red shifted by a factor of 1,000 to the microwave region; but there are other possibilities. For example, as mentioned in Chapter 9, Gott and Hawking have suggested that Hawking radiation, resembling black-body radiation from black holes that are scattered throughout the universe, might account for the radiation we receive as MBR.

In answer to the question of how another theory might explain the presence of MBR, BB advocate Dennis Sciama said (in 1967), "It would be reasonable to propose that along with the newly created matter there comes into existence newly created radiation; indeed, some such effect would be expected as a result of the creation process itself." But he went on to say, "But why the observed spectrum should be that of a black body over a wide range of wavelengths is totally obscure." However, others disagree with the second portion of this quotation.

(Peebles, Schramm, Turner and Kron in 1991 said, "it would be reasonable to suppose radiation is created along with the continuous creation of baryons, but absurd to suppose the spectrum of the created radiation is just such that the integrated background ... adds up to a thermal form;" strangely similar to Sciama's comments of 24 years earlier.)

However, a number of BB theorists believe that black-body radiation didn't come to us directly from the decoupling, but that it had been repeatedly absorbed and reradiated by matter in space for billions years since the BB and, as a result, the temperature of the matter of space has been "thermalized;" it produces a black-body spectrum at the present equalized temperature of the surrounding matter in space. (If the MBR comes from black holes as suggested by Gott and Hawking, that would also require thermalization.)

In 1926 Sir Arthur Eddington had suggested that the amount of light from stars was equivalent to a thermal background temperature of 3.2 degrees K, and in 1941 Canadian astronomer Andrew McKellar estimated that temperature to be 2.3 K; temperatures extremely close to what is observed. BBers feel that the prediction of MBR from the BB provides powerful support for BBT. But their predictions of temperature were not accurate, and some of them were made after the fact. Because Eddington's and McKellar's predictions, unlike the retrodictions of BBers, were legitimate predictions, perhaps they can be taken as support for thermalization.

It should not be forgotten that, although the possibility of radiation from the decoupling had been predicted, despite what is repeatedly reported by BBers, the radiation temperature predicted by Gamow and others was quite different than what has been observed.

Some BB cosmologists have attempted to show mathematically that a thermalized background cannot produce a spectrum that closely resembles that of a black-body. But, despite these disagreements, the MBR is most probably photons that have been emitted from relatively nearby space matter, and the thermalization of our surroundings is the result of other sources that happened to provide an average energy level equivalent to a temperature of 2.7 degrees.

Those sources might include Hawking radiation from small black holes scattered throughout space, or a number of other possibilities, but it is most likely to have been produced during the generation of matter in space as suggested by Sciama, and as proposed here by NSST. If BBers can believe that the MBR is due to thermalization of the matter of space by energy from the BB, certainly it must be acceptable to believe that other sources of energy might produce the same result.

According to BBT the uniformity of MBR, recently estimated to be about plus or minus 15 parts per million, provides virtual proof of the BB and of the smoothness of the early universe. But it would seem more reasonable to conclude that such great smoothness provides evidence against BBT. It is difficult to believe that degree of smoothness is consistent with the observed large-scale nonuniformity of the universe, and it is difficult to believe an explosion of the universe could have been sufficiently smooth.

The smoothness of the MBR might more readily be attributed

to the thermalization of energy that may be generated by any number of sources throughout space. It is suggested that throughout the emptiness of space, as the matter of the universe flies apart at a fairly uniform rate of acceleration, the process of the spontaneous conversion of energy to matter takes place; providing the "dust" (particles that make up hydrogen atoms, and perhaps others) from which stars, galaxies, clusters and super-clusters evolve over eons of time; perhaps tens of billions or hundreds of billions of years.

A rather serious problem regarding NSST must be admitted, but it is shared by other cosmologies. According to quantum theory the generation of matter must also produce an equal amount of antimatter. If that is so, why do we see so much more matter than antimatter in our surroundings? If and when quantum theory is ever developed to the point where it can answer that question, it might become a major factor in deciding the validity of any cosmological theory. In the meantime BBT, NSST and other theorists must await an adequate explanation for the excess matter of the universe.

(Several of the explanations for excess matter over antimatter have been offered by BB theorists that involve violation of the conservation of baryon number. But if that law of quantum physics can be violated to provide rationale for BBT, perhaps it might also be violated in support of other cosmologies.)

One might ask why, if it is true that the creation of antimatter must accompany the creation of matter in space, wouldn't a certain amount of it be destroyed by mutual annihilation, possibly producing a strong gamma ray background? If that is a valid question, several factors might provide the answer: The rate of particle generation is extremely low, particles and antiparticles when generated depart from each other, the sites of particle generation are widely separated, and the timing of their generation is random. Thus the probability of particle-antiparticle annihilations in nearby space would be quite low, and the probability of gamma radiation produced that travels toward Earthbound sensors would also be quite low. Only infrequent bursts of gamma radiation might be expected; perhaps not inconsistent with what is observed.

(Gamma ray bursts that are observed uniformly across the sky are thought to originate at great distances and are thus thought to be of extremely high energy. However, it is possible that they are the products of annihilations occurring much closer to us and of much lower energy.)

The NSST conversion of intrinsic energy to matter and radiation, of course, always obeys the law of mass/energy conservation. If matter is generated in space it must be from concentrations of energy of sufficient intensity to fuel that process. That is supported by quantum theory wherein the spontaneous generation of particles is said to result from vacuum fluctuations of the appropriate levels of energy. (The generation of particles from "the intrinsic energy of space" seems a better way to express this phenomenon.)

One can only speculate about the cause or causes of concentrations of energy that might be sufficient for the conversion of intrinsic energy to its material form. Perhaps it is totally due to an inherent energy of space that is the same as, or equivalent to, the energy of vacuum as postulated by quantum theorists; and perhaps it is due (partially or wholly) to other sources, known or unknown.

For example, one possible source of a portion of the energy of space might be the vast amount of energy that has "dissipated" in the universe in the past, and continues to be dissipated, that turns to heat, cools and returns to space. That energy has high entropy, but it doesn't vanish. Maybe it is somehow re-utilized in space.

A suggestion for the formation of magnetic monopoles that has been made by BB theorists is that they might result from solitrons that form in the energetic fields of space, in a manner similar to the way they form in the waves of a water in a channel. But if they can occur on a scale that is sufficient to produce hypothetical magnetic monopoles, as mentioned in Flights of Fantasy, it certainly seems reasonable to suggest that solitrons might develop that have enough energy to produce quantum particles that are known to be real. Of course it is possible that the energy of space might accumulate due to any number of additional unknown or unappreciated processes in space. But it seems unlikely that any satisfactory answers to these mysteries will soon be discovered.

Whatever the source of the energy of space, perhaps due to irregular flow, turbulence or wave action (possibly standing waves), random or otherwise, it piles up in its travels through empty space to produce peaks of sufficient amplitude to cause its conversion to its alternate forms of matter and radiation. Perhaps this occurs within the rules of quantum theory as presently known or modified, or of some theories as yet unknown. These ideas might also apply to BBT, but it seems highly improbable that energy could accumulate to the immensity required to produce a BB.

It's clear that the utilization of dissipated energy implies a decrease of entropy; a violation of the second law of thermodynamics. But it must be realized that much of quantum theory appears to violate that law, and the minute violations proposed by NSST are insignificant compared to the gigantic violation that is proposed by BB inflation.

But perhaps that law isn't inviolate after all. Aren't the heavier elements resulting from fusion more ordered than the lighter ones from which they are formed? Aren't the stars and galaxies more ordered than the dust from which they form. Isn't life, including that of bugs, flowers, fish, trees, elephants, and humans more ordered than the lifeless matter that nourishes them and from which they evolved? Certainly it would seem that the increased organization of matter that happens untold times each day of the year, that of the birth of new life, might be a decrease of entropy. If these are valid ideas, perhaps dissipated energy can be re-utilized in space.

(BBers who believe in a cycling universe—either that the BB followed and resulted from the collapse of a previous universe, or that a future collapse will result in another BB—have, perhaps unwittingly, subscribed to an enormous instantaneous decrease of entropy.)

Recent findings have provided some important evidence of the continuing formation of galaxies in the universe. Cornell astronomers Riccardo Giovanelli and Martha Haynes have reported an immense cloud of hydrogen gas about 65 million light years from us that provides evidence that galaxies could have formed throughout the history of the universe. Lowell Observatory astronomer John A. Holtzman reported finding about 50 globular clusters (in NGC1275) that radiate intense blue light, indicating that they might have been formed only a few hundred million years ago. University of Hawaii astronomer

Lennox Cowie has established the age of a population of small galaxies known as "blue dwarfs" at about two billion years. M.I.T. astronomer Stephen E. Schneider has reported that stars of low surface brightness (LSB) galaxies appear to be very blue, indicating that they are young and deficient in heavy elements.

Regarding such recent findings, Oxford University astronomer George Eftathiou is reported to have said, "People used to think that there was a certain time in the early universe when it (galaxy formation) all happened," but instead, "galaxies have been forming throughout the history of the universe." Recent infrared telescopic observations have discovered clusters of hundreds of new-born stars in hydrogen gas clouds that drift through the universe.

But evidence of young galaxies isn't really news. In a 1970 paper on the origin of galaxies, Rees and Silk wrote, "Other arguments indicate the apparent youthfulness of some galaxies stem from observations of clusters of galaxies ... One seems forced to the conclusion that here are newly formed galaxies born within the past 100 million years." They also stated that astronomers Halton C. Arp of the Hale Observatory and Erik B. Holberg of the University of Uppsala had discovered phenomena that "suggest that violent events, involving perhaps the birth of galaxies, are continually taking place." Although BBT is based on the assumption that all galaxies are about the same age, astronomical observations tend to support the continuing generation of new matter and the formation of new galaxies, as would be expected in a NSS universe.

Having now provided suggestions regarding the source of energy for the formation of matter in space, another failing of the advocates of the old SST, that of not providing a convincing explanation for the continuing expansion of the universe, should be examined.

If the force of gravity alone were at work in space, the universe might be collapsing rather than expanding. If there were not a giant explosion that had long ago provided the expansive impetus for the mass of the universe (and of course there was not) some other explanation for its expansion is required. It follows that, in order for the density of the universe to remain relatively constant as new matter is generated and as old matter is dispersed, it is necessary for some counter-gravitational force or

THE CULT OF THE BIG BANG

"antigravity', to be at work. *Like the generation of the new matter, that expansive force must be fairly continual and uniformly distributed while having a natural degree of randomness that is consistent with the observed randomness of the universe.*

NSST proposes that Einstein's cosmic repulsion provides the necessary force to expand the universe; not as single impulse of a magnitude sufficient to blow it up, but as a relatively minute force throughout the empty space of the universe. As that expansion takes place the intrinsic energy of space is converted to new particles and to radiation. It is suggested that the intrinsic energy of space, that produces new matter and radiation, and cosmic repulsion, that expands the universe, may be different aspects of the same basic force; or, alternatively, that they are separate entities that may bear some unknown physical relationship to one another.

Thus it is proposed that matter is generated in empty space, beyond the gravitational influence of galactic matter, where cosmic repulsion dominates. That is the force that showed up as a term of undefined magnitude in Einstein's gravitational field equations that is called the cosmological constant. Those equations, of course, were written at a time when the universe was still believed to be static. It was therefore logical for Einstein to have assumed that term represented a force, equal and opposite to the force of gravity, that was necessary to hold the universe in static balance. It seemed to solve the philosopher's ancient problem of how the stars were held in space.

Years later, when Hubble and Humason showed distant galaxies to be fleeing each other at a rate proportional to their distance, cosmic repulsion was discarded. George Gamow reported that Einstein confessed to him that "the cosmic repulsion idea was the biggest blunder he made in his entire life." That admission of error instead may someday prove to be Einstein's greatest error.

The implications of cosmic repulsion were not again taken seriously until the early 1980s when it was resurrected to provide the force that fueled the inflation of the Universe. Paul Davies, in 1984, told us that, "the quantum vacuum of inflation theory behaves exactly like the previously hypothetical medium that produces cosmic repulsion" and, "The "antigravity" Einstein threw out the door has come back in through the window."

Both the generation of matter in space and the expansive force in space appear to be consistent with quantum theory.

Although a cosmic repulsive force lasting for an instant of time and having the magnitude necessary to blow up the universe seems beyond reason, it certainly isn't unreasonable to propose that it is of the minute magnitude required to cause continuing expansion through the eons.

Recently cosmic repulsion has gained new credibility among BBers, not only as a source of inflation of the early universe but as a continuing force of its expansion. As mentioned in Chapter 7, Professor Larry Abbott warned against the error of a large cosmological constant that is "dumping too much into the vacuum." At that time (1988) he also indicated that a small positive cosmological constant could cause increased red shifts of remote galaxies to appear more distant than actual, and that it could also cause increasing expansion of the universe.

In April of 1992 University of Chicago physicist Michael Turner confirmed that, because a large cosmological constant would have blown the early universe apart, its true value has to be quite small, and that small a value could provide added expansive force (acceleration) to the BB universe. Harvard professor of astronomy John P. Huchra agreed and added that, in view of the recently confirmed large value of the Hubble constant (about 80 km/sec/mpc), resulting in the paradox of a universe younger than its galactic formations, the extra push of a small cosmological constant is now required to get BBT out of this difficulty. (If expansion was slower in the past the BB could have happened earlier.)

The "ugly" cosmic repulsion, as it has been called by Peebles, may have come to the rescue of BBT. However, now that a number of respected BB cosmologists have given credence to cosmic repulsion (a positive cosmological constant), the world may more readily accept it as the force of expansion of a near SS universe.

As mentioned in earlier chapters, Einstein's work didn't recognize negative curvature of space. To him, if there were no mass, there would be zero gravitational force, and thus zero curvature of space; and if the average mass of the universe were greater than zero, gravity and the curvature of space would be proportionately greater. But, in the absence of knowledge of the expansion of the universe, it seemed quite plausible that there was a negative gravity or its equivalent throughout space, producing the repulsive force necessary to prevent the collapse of a static universe.

(Some writers have stated or implied that Einstein gratuitously added the cosmic repulsion term to his equations. But experts deny that. Silk has said that Einstein's equations "in their most general form contain this term," and Davies has said that Einstein "didn't conjure up cosmic repulsion in an ad hoc way. He found that his gravitational field equations contained an optional term which gave rise to a force with exactly the desired properties.")

Although earlier BBers declared their rejection of the "troublesome cosmic repulsion," logic requires its presence in the FWR cosmology. The concept of negative curvature of space was the result of theorists who rejected Einstein's cosmic repulsion. Instead of only positive curvature as thought by Einstein, they originated the idea of a universe of uncurved (flat) space having a critical density and expanding at escape velocity. The space of a universe of greater density, and thus a lesser rate of expansion, would have positive curvature, and the space of a universe of lesser density, and thus a greater rate of expansion, would have negative curvature.

An aspect of the idea of negatively curved space that seems to be overlooked by BB theorists is that, if the density of the universe is less than critical (which it undoubtedly is) and space were thus negatively curved, with that negative curvature there *must* correspondingly be something akin to negative gravity. There has to be more than a mere equation to describe a physical reaction; the equation must represent a physical cause. BBers thus implicitly subscribe to the "antigravity" of cosmic repulsion.

In BBT it follows that, in the vast expanses of empty space of the universe, negative gravity must prevail. Only in areas of considerable mass, as in the vicinity of galaxies, does the influence of positive gravity exceed that of the negative gravity of empty space. That of course leads us back to Einstein's idea of a minute cosmic repulsion, but of a somewhat greater magnitude than required to balance a static universe. If cosmic repulsion has thus been accepted by BBers, however unintentionally, perhaps it should also be acceptable to other cosmologies.

From what has been said here it is not possible to derive a value for the negative gravity, or cosmic repulsion, of empty space. That shouldn't be too discouraging. Einstein, possessor of what might have been the best brain of the century, was also unable to determine a magnitude for cosmic repulsion. Regardless of that inability, it seems reasonable to suggest a value that is of sufficient magnitude to cause a continual expansion of the universe.

(If Einstein had been able to determine the magnitude of cosmic repulsion he could have shown that the universe was not static; and he might have also been able to determined a value that would define the correct cosmology.)

According to Gamow, based on observed red shifts, it can be calculated that the galaxies are fleeing from each other with a kinetic energy equivalent to about fifty times the gravitational attraction between them. When the infinitesimal weakness of gravitational force between galaxies at distances of millions of light years (billions of billions of miles) is considered, it becomes apparent how minute the required repulsive force might be. When compared to a cosmic repulsive force of 10^{120} times greater than gravity, as estimated by Paul Davies, that was necessary for the explosion of the BB universe, the relative improbability of BB becomes quite obvious.

(Could it be possible that the long suspected "fifth force"— that is, in addition to electromagnetism, the weak force, the strong force, and gravity—that has been suggested due to gravitational anomalies reported to have been detected in mines, is something like cosmic repulsion; or that it provides evidence for the existence yet another other force in the universe?)

It is suggested here that in the vast empty space of the universe, where gravity is negative, that is, where cosmic repulsion prevails and provides the necessary expansive force, the environment is conducive to the spontaneous generation of quantum particles from the intrinsic energy of space. It is also suggested that, during that process, some energy is converted to other forms, including electromagnetic radiation over portions of the spectrum, and perhaps that energy that is ultimately received as MBR.

Because of improved estimates of Hubble expansion that severely limit the age of a BB universe, and the presence of giant galactic formations that would not have had time to develop under any BB scenario, BBers face an enormous problem. CDM appears to be discredited, and they are scrambling to find alternate mechanisms that might explain these formations.

By contrast, the age of vast galactic formations present no problem to NSST. There has been plenty of time for giant structures to have developed from the rather random generation of quantum particles throughout space. Over many billions of years they could have developed due to gravitation alone (ignoring the possibility of electromagnetism as postulated by plasma theory). The presence the giant galactic formations in space discredits standard BBT, but they might add credence to a new near steady state cosmology.

On another topic related to the age of the universe, Henry Olbers, of Olbers' Paradox fame, reasoned that in a universe of vast size and an infinite number of stars, everywhere one looked there would be a star. Therefore the sky would remain bright around the clock. The solution to this paradox, as provided by BB theorists, was that the universe is too young for the light from very distant galaxies to have had time to reach us, meaning that extremely distant stars are departing from us at nearly the speed of light.

But in a NSS universe (or any universe for that matter) that might not be valid. The explanation may merely lie in the fact that smaller, cooler, closer matter can block the radiation from larger, hotter, more distant bodies. That may be verified by viewing areas of our galaxy, and of distant novae and supernovae, where "dust" is believed to hide more distant stars.

The abundance of the light elements helium and lithium in the universe is thought by BB theorists to provide strong evidence in support of standard BBT. However, as discussed in Chapter 10, it has been reported that the ratio of the abundance of beryllium to other elements in early stars is much greater than BBT theory would allow. Observations appear to show that some of it could have been produced by BB nucleosynthesis, but also that at least some of it must have been produced long after that hypothesized era, probably by the action of cosmic rays. (In a non-BB universe, it might have been produced over unknown eons.)

That evidence presents serious problems to BBT. Not only

because cosmic rays can produce beryllium, but because they undoubtedly can also produce lithium. We are told that lithium cannot survive within stars, and therefore all of it must have been produced be BB nucleosynthesis. But if lithium can be produced by cosmic rays that theory is incorrect. It has been suggested by BB cosmologist Joseph Silk that deuterium can be generated by processes other than BB nucleosynthesis.

Furthermore, it is known that helium is produced in stars, albeit at a much lower ratio to hydrogen than BBT predicts for BB nucleosynthesis. But in a NSST universe, that is very much older than of BBT, stellar nucleosynthesis over tens of billions of years might easily account for accumulations of helium to the levels found in the universe today.

In addition, recent measurements have shown the abundance of helium to be less than previously predicted by BBT. However, BBT documentation shows that the ratio of baryons to photons (the baryon number) in the early universe has been selected as needed to "predict" an abundance of helium that agreed with that observed at the time of the prediction. Past events might lead one to believe that these new observations will result in new adjustments to the assumed ratio of baryons to photons. It should by now be apparent that the abundance of helium and other light elements does not provide reliable evidence for BBT, and that they might be accounted for by other cosmologies.

It now seems that was a mistake for proponents of old SST to have postulated a Perfect Cosmological Principle; an exactly steady state, non-evolving and smooth universe.

The universe, of course, has proven to be less than perfectly smooth. Furthermore, SST cosmologists appear to have been led astray by Isaac Newton who reported that, if matter were evenly distributed in a relatively small region of space, that matter would tend to be mutually attracted by gravity but, if it were to be evenly distributed in an infinite universe, there would be no center of gravity toward which it would be attracted.

If the second partition of that statement were correct, the expansion of the universe could not be decelerating due to mutual gravitational attraction, and evolution (clumping of distant bodies) would not occur. However, American mathematician George D. Birkhoff (in 1923) showed that to be incorrect. Regardless of its size, the mutual attraction of the matter of the universe would tend to slow its expansion, further discrediting the Perfect Cosmological Principle.

Reported observational evidence of quasar clumping thus tends to deny the validity of the old SST and, if that clumping is as great as reported, it would also tend to deny NSST. However, due to lack of consideration of gravitational red shift in the determination of their distance, evidence for the clumping of distant quasars is seriously questioned. If evidence for clumping thus proves to be false, it would deny the BBers' claim of evolution and provide support for NSST. On the other hand, if evidence of some clumping of distant quasars were ultimately to be confirmed, it would not necessarily rule out a NSS universe. In a non-exploding, non-smooth, near-SS universe that may be running down, some degree of evolution might be expected.

The range of decelerating expansion of the NSS universe is thought to most probably lie between the balanced and the fixed-rate case, but near to the fixed-rate case. Available data appears to support that situation. That data is dependent on bolometric magnitude and not considered to be very accurate, but neither observation nor theory seem to support an exactly fixed-rate expansion as proposed by old SST.

If plotted on Figure 3, the expansion that is expected of an NSS universe might be illustrated by a slightly downward curved line, just below Line 3 that represents a fixed-rate Hubble expansion. A recent statement by Peebles, Schramm, Turner and Kron tends to support that situation. To wit, "There are observed to be more very distant galaxies ...than would be expected... in the standard model (although the numbers are also roughly in line with the steady state model...). In most cases the observed image parameters are consistent with mild evolution from normal galaxies."

It should be noted that the curves of Figure 3 do not properly represent possible cases of NSST. Under NSST curves for an open, fixed-rate and increasing expansion universe would extend off the chart to the left (as well as to the right). On the left they would extend beyond the terminations shown, that for BBT represent the origin of the universe. A NSST universe having a nearly fixed rate of expansion may have existed for untold eons.

Many BB cosmologists envision a flat BB universe. Like the perfectly fixed-rate universe, that case would require a very special reason; some rationale as to how nature might have provided the necessary precise balance of forces. Inflation theorists believe that their theory provides a rationale for that balance but, under NSST, there is no reason to believe in that unlikely balanced state.

Other BBers believe that the average density of the universe is sufficiently great to cause a collapse of the universe. Observed matter in the universe is only a fraction of that required for collapse, and even the speculations of BB closed universe enthusiasts can account for no more than a few percent of that amount. Under NSST a deceleration sufficient to cause the collapse of the universe is considered impossible within foreseeable billions of years; and there is no need to participate in frantic efforts to find, in fact or in theory, the existence of missing matter.

It might seem reasonable to assume that the total energy, intrinsic and material, of the NSS universe would be a fixed quantity. If the universe were relatively small, perhaps less than a few times the size predicted by standard BBT, one might expect the average mass/energy density of an expanding three-dimensional Euclidean universe to be decreasing (that is, "running down" and "thinning") relatively rapidly, thus allowing some evidence of evolution (quasar clumping) to be observed.

However, if the NSS universe were enormously old and enormously large, resulting in only a very small decreasing rate of generation of new matter (only a very small rate of thinning), confirmation of any appreciable degree of clumping might tend to rule out the possibility of an enormously vast NSS universe.

As in any physical system, frictional losses (or "inefficiency") may cause slowing of the processes of the universe. Thus the generation of new matter in space may be slowing and causing the universe to be running down. Both Bonnor and Carr have suggested that the BB universe may be running down in accordance with the second law of thermodynamics. That might be true of the NSS universe.

A number of prominent physicists, including Dirac, Jordan and Dicke have proposed that the gravitational constant, introduced by Isaac Newton many years ago to quantify the strength of gravitational attraction, is decreasing. (Dirac believed that it might be decreasing inversely as the age of the BB universe; a rate of about one part in 10 billion per year.) Some evidence has been found that it is diminishing, at least in our part of the universe, at a rate of as much as a few parts per billion per century. If that is correct it might also provide evidence for a universe that is running down.

In support of running down, there may be evidence that the formation of quasars and radio galaxies has declined in recent eons. In fact, according to a comprehensive study by Hale Observatory astronomer Maarten Schmidt and *Scientific American* associate editor Francis Bello in 1971, quasars were 100 times more numerous five billion years ago and 1,000 times more numerous 8 or 9 billion years ago. Dennis Sciama tells us there are also far fewer radio sources than there were eons ago. Other astronomers, including Martin Rees, have agreed that is so.

But those opinions are based on an interpretation of red shift that ignores the possibility of gravitational effects on radiation from quasars, thus creating the illusion of severe quasar clumping. If the conclusion presented herein is correct, in a BB universe that has no center of gravity, quasars should be expected to be distributed throughout space. The BBers own theory thus might preclude the possibility of severe clumping, and thus discredit their red shift calculations.

Other astronomers opinions don't support severe clumping. In 1982 Patrick Osmer told us that, "statistical analysis is consistent with quasars being distributed uniformly at random" and "These findings are evidence in favor of an assumption ... that on a large scale the universe is homogeneous." As stated in a previous paragraph, Peebles, Schramm, Turner and Kron have recently said that what is seen is consistent with mild evolution, meaning only slight clumping.

Unbelievably great quasar masses and luminosities, calculated speeds of greater than c, and other inconsistencies that result from the present interpretation of red shift deny its ability to gauge the distance and age of remote massive bodies. Both logic and some observations tend to support only limited clumping of distant quasars; and appreciable clumping tends to deny both BBT and NSST. BBers accept the contrary position that clumping provides evidence of an evolving universe while insisting on a homogeneous universe that is inconsistent with clumping. Appreciable clumping is also inconsistent with a slowly running down, possibly thinning, near SS universe.

(Whether its expansion were slowing, remaining the same or increasing, the NSS universe could be thinning or thickening. It is suggested that both the rate of generation of new matter and the rate of expansion are slowing. If the rate of generation of new matter were slowing more than the rate of expansion, the universe would be thinning; but, if the rate of expansion were slowing more than the rate of generation of new matter, it would be thickening.)

The preceding discussion has presented the attributes of NSST, and compared them to the flaws of old SST as perceived by BBers. Those flaws included inadequate explanations for the generation and the expansion of matter in space, the presence of MBR, the source of light elements, the evolution of the universe, and the Perfect Cosmological Principle. What has been presented regarding those flaws, real or perceived, should be more than sufficient to warrant serious consideration of a near steady state theory that overcomes the problems of old SST, and, except for the common unsolved problem of matter vs. antimatter, and one additional problem if quasar clumping proves to be significant, has none of the many serious problems of BBT.

Chapter 12 provided several different lines of reasoning that showed the age and size of the universe to be much greater than it could be for any of the BB cases. The age of stars and galaxies, and the necessity for more than one star cycle to have occurred in order to provide the heavy elements of our environment, thoroughly discredit BBT. Recent observations of enormous galactic formations would have required as much as 100 billion years to develop. They provide evidence for a very old and very large universe, one that is consistent with NSST, and one that rules out a BB universe of any kind. (The presence of these formations also denies a principle tenet of BBT, that of large-scale smoothness.)

Peebles, Schramm, Turner and Kron were quoted in Chapter 5 as saying that if objects of the universe prove to be more than 17 BYRs old they would be driven to accept a cosmological constant (a universe of increasing expansion). Because the BB universe has clearly been shown to be considerably younger than objects of the universe, they certainly should do that, but it is suggested that they might be driven even further; to abandon BBT altogether.

Many BB proponents, although they may consider the universe to now be flat, so that space may be considered Euclidean, believe that, in earlier times, as the density of the universe was higher, space was increasingly curved. If there had been a BB, the concept of space curvature might be useful in contemplating the gravitational effects of extremely high density but, due to the low density of the universe for at least the most recent billions of years, NSST need not be concerned with such matters.

Although the mathematics of mass (and its equivalent, energy) in the presence of a gravitational field, show it to react in a manner that results in the appearance of "warped space," that concept doesn't seem to be essential. But, even if space truly is curved, that curvature may too low to be of any cosmological consequence in the low average density of a near fixed-rate universe. It could have been ignored in old SST, and can be ignored in the NSS cosmology presented here. NSST is concerned with Euclidean geometry, classical physics, quantum mechanics and other aspects of relativity, but it would seem that the curvature of space might safely be ignored.

If it should be convincingly demonstrated that quasars were more numerous in the distant past, that would support the idea that our galaxy is near the center of the universe. That would of course discredit BBer's belief in homogeneity, which might tend to discredit all of BBT. On the other hand, it might support the fine tuning of the Anthropic Principle, an apparently conflicting idea that is supported by some BBers. NSST avoids involvement in that theory.

The position of NSST regarding fine tuning and the Anthropic Principle can best be stated by quoting physicist Heinz Pagels who said, it's "needless clutter" is "deeply flawed and has no place in physics or cosmology." He asked, "Why do some scientists continue to honor the anthropic principle with their attention?"

Old SST has been criticized for not providing a description of the origin of the universe. The same criticism must also apply to NSST. But BBers who have made that criticism are also subject to it. Regardless of which BB case they happen to support, open, flat or closed, there is an earlier time and universe that is unexplained. As has been pointed out in Chapter 18, the ultimate origin will probably never be known.

(Isn't it odd that BB cosmologists, who accept the possibility of a previously cycling universe without explanation for its origin, criticize SST for the same omission?)

Needless to say, NSST avoids many of the major problems of BBT that include the singularity, flatness, smoothness, missing mass, and age problems, to mention just a few of the more serious of them. NSST may have some problems of its own, but they are relatively few and minor compared to those of BBT.

BB enthusiast Pagels dismissed old SST as a viable competitor of BBT with the comment that "The capacity to rule out well-defined models is the mark of a mature empirical science." Perhaps old BBT should now be dismissed with another comment: The capacity to rule out a discredited old theory is the mark of mature progressive science.

TWENTY

Summary and Comment

Discussions of Einstein's theories of relativity were presented to provide a basis for BBT and cosmology in general. The expansion of the universe from a minutely small sized "atom" of infinite density, pressure and temperature 10 to 15 billion years ago to the universe as we know it today, and the lengthening of the wavelength of radiation from distant departing bodies (shown in Figure 4) are based on relativity.

However, some aspects of relativity are not proven facts. For example, the curvature of space has not been conclusively demonstrated; and certainly relativity has not been tested under the extreme conditions of a BB. Because the evolution of the BB universe is based on relativity operating in that environment it is subject to considerable question.

BBT and, especially, inflationary BBT are based on quantum theory. That theory also is untested under the extreme environment of the BB. What might have occurred in the early stages of hypothetical BB schemes under those conditions might someday be considered pure fantasy. Furthermore, the conflict between relativity's equivalence of gravity/acceleration and quantum theory's graviton mediation of gravity creates doubts about both of these theories.

The particles of the standard model, including those that have been confirmed and those that are purely theoretical, have each been shown, either in the laboratory or by mathematics, to come into existence at a particular level of energy. Because BBT can account for all levels of energy since the BB, the creation of each of the particles has been placed at a point in time since then. But, because any occurrence, requiring any degree of energy from near zero to infinity can be accommodated in that way, that chronology may be totally contrived.

That standard BB chronology (shown in Figure 2), which represents a fixed-rate universe having a Hubble constant of 30 km/sec/MLYs and an age of 10 BYRs is quite different than the universe of most modern BBers. Their universe is often described as flat and 15 BYRs old, quite incompatible with the chronology usually illustrated, i.e., expanding at a fixed rate that starts at a Hubble age of 10 billion years.

BB inflation theory is based on the premise of quantum theory that there is energy in vacuum; enough so that it can cause the generation of fundamental particle pairs. But that has been demonstrated only on a submicroscopic scale. However, according to current BBT, the vacuum of empty space provided the energy for the spontaneous generation of the mass and energy of the entire universe. Inflation theory says that quantum vacuum fluctuations caused a vast expansion of space preceding the BB of the standard theory. It also says that was the result of negative energy; the repulsion that showed up as Einstein's cosmic repulsion.

The Hubble and Humason discovery that nearby galaxies of the universe are departing from us and from each other at speeds proportional to their relative distances (Hubble's law) is haled as important evidence in support of BBT. The universe is expanding as solutions to Einstein's equations might indicate. But the observed expansion of the universe supports the rival SST, and also NSST, equally as well as BBT.

(Various BBers have also cited the limitation of the families of fundamental particles to just three, and the "lensing" of light from distant quasars by closer matter in space, as evidence in support of BBT. Unbiased logic might show that these support rival cosmologies as well as BBT.)

According to standard BBT (the FWR Model) the BB occurred about 10 billion years ago. The universe, starting as an explosion of a point of infinite density and temperature, has expanded ever since. Its size has increased as density and temperature have decreased, until its size is now 10 billion light years and its temperature about 2.7 degrees absolute. At various times since the BB, the original symmetry of the "quantum soup" of the universe has been broken to produce the various fundamental particles. Those remained essentially uncombined until about one second after the BB, when the temperature dropped enough for nuclei of hydrogen to form, and the nuclear fusion of hydrogen produced helium and a few other light elements.

At about 300,000 years after the BB the universe cooled enough for electrons to combine with the nuclei to form complete atoms, and excess energy escaped into space. In that era, called the decoupling, it is said that electromagnetic energy in the form of infrared photons was scattered into the universe and is now received as microwave background radiation. Red shift of about 1,000 from the period of the decoupling to the present accounts for the transformation of infrared wavelengths to those of the microwave region. According to BBT the universe at the time of the decoupling was very smooth, accounting for the extreme uniformity of reception of that energy.

The FWR mathematical model allows a closed universe, an open universe or a flat universe that is on the borderline between the other two. However, observational data put the average density of the universe at a level that is only sufficient to support a BB universe having had a relatively small deceleration of its rate of expansion.

Some BB cosmologists subscribe to an open universe case that decelerates somewhat more than the flat (balanced) case. Some subscribe to the flat case wherein the average density of the universe is at a critical value, and others believe density will be found to be sufficiently high to cause the universe to someday collapse. Those who prefer the flat or closed cases do so in the belief that there is a large quantity of undetected missing matter in the universe. Of those who accept the collapsing universe case, some think it will re-explode, some that it has also done so in the past, and some that it will also continue to do so in the future.

Both the fixed-rate case, favored under old SST, and the flat case require special theory to support their views. The fixed-rate case is not favored by BBers because it would require rates of expansion to always have been as they are now. Observations do not support that position, and it doesn't allow for an evolving universe.

The BB flat case requires a precisely balanced density (the flatness problem), which astronomical observations (the absence of sufficient mass) deny. Any number of explanations have been provided in support of this balanced BB universe case. BB theorists attempted to rescue it by postulating zero total energy in the universe. However, that would require violation of the law of conservation of mass/energy. Inflation theorists attempted to overcome that problem by postulating superluminal expansion, but, even if that were acceptable, the flatness problem and the missing mass problem would remain.

The NSST position is that the flat or closed cases, which might require as much as 99 percent of the mass of the universe to be composed of unknown nonbayronic matter, are extremely unlikely, and observations seem to indicate only a slow deceleration of the expansion of the universe.

In each of the BB cases the expansion of the universe is said to be slowed by gravitational force. However, as mentioned in Chapter 5, because BBers believe that space is expanding (rather than the matter of the universe), there may be an additional problem regarding gravitational deceleration: It has not been explained how gravity might interact with expanding space to cause its deceleration; or is it that matter is decelerating relative to continuously expanding space?

There is considerable confusion among BBers on the shape of the universe. Those who prefer the flat case should understand that General Relativity provides for that case to be Euclidean, and those who prefer the open case should understand that its negatively curved space would have no edge. But both of these groups ascribe positively curved space characteristics to their universe; they use positive curvature for explanations such as "space is expanding" (not merely the distance between objects), the "BB happened everywhere," there is no center of the universe, and black-body radiation comes to us from the decoupling. They ignore the fact that, according to FWR theory, those attributes could only apply to a universe of positively curved space. BBers apparently feel free to chose and intermix various aspects of relativity, quantum theory and classical physics in any manner that supports their beliefs.

Those BB proponents who prefer the flat and closed universe cases have spent great effort to find, in fact and in theory, the missing matter (CDM) required to support those cases. Many suggestions have been made but little evidence or viable rationale has been provided. Those cases suffer from several problems. The density of the universe is too low, the age of stars and galaxies is too great, more than one star cycle would have been required, and newly discovered very-large-scale galaxy formations would have required too long to form. These facts rule out the flat and closed cases, and almost certainly rule out all of BBT.

Until recently BB cosmologists were counting on CDM theory to provide the answer as to how galaxies and clusters formed in the early BB universe. However, because recent developments appear to have destroyed that possibility, some of them have declared BBT to be divorced from CDM theory; BBT is separate and independent of CDM. Los Alamos National Laboratory physicist and cosmologist Anthony L. Peratt, who subscribes to the plasma theory of cosmology, commented regarding that matter, "The Big Bang theorists attempt to decouple themselves from the problem of galaxy formation, but one must ask what kind of cosmology is it that cannot account for the galaxies and stars that we observe?" He is one of the few cosmologists in the world who advocate "scrapping the Big Bang altogether."

Proponents of the cycling BBT aren't as concerned about an initial singularity that might have caused the first cycle of the universe as are proponents of the "one shot" BB. Their concern is the past and future bounces of the universe. That is because there is no theory in physics that can account for the explosion or bounce of a collapsed, universe. The slightest rotation of the universe might result in an enormous black hole rather than another BB. In addition to this spinning universe problem, they should be concerned about "convergence." Upon its collapse, will the mass of the universe simultaneously impact, or will chaos result? In addition to other problems of the non-cycling closed universe case, the cycling case suffers from the bounce problem and the convergence problem.

Some BBers have criticized old SST for deferring an explanation of the origin of the universe (and one would expect NSST to be similarly criticized). It is interesting to note that, although the BB cycling case, a favorite of many BBers, has a similar deficiency, it goes unacknowledged by BB cosmologists.

The singularity of BBT is an enormous violation of the law of conservation of mass/energy; vast quantities of mass and energy suddenly develop out of nothing; and, in mathematics, a singularity denotes a breakdown of theory. The human mind and mathematics have difficulty coping with an infinitesimal space containing all the mass and energy of the universe for an instant of time. Thus the singularity, which might require as much as "an infinity times an infinity of energy," has been a continuing embarrassment to BB cosmologists.

In what seems a desperate attempt to get around that obstacle, the idea that the negative energy of gravity is equal and opposite to all of the positive energy of the universe has been proposed. The net energy of the universe would thus be zero, and energy would not have to be created to produce the universe. Fortunately for practical applications, most Earth-bound scientists don't accept that concept, and NSST avoids that issue by strict adherence to the law of conservation of mass/energy. NSST doesn't have to face a problem as serious as the singularity.

Guth's pre-BB inflation of the universe was an attempt to overcome the magnetic monopoles that are predicted by GUTs. He subsequently discovered that his inflation scheme might also solve some of the other problems of standard BB, including that of the singularity. But Linde wasn't satisfied with Guth's inflation and attempted to improve on it by proposing several changes, including a much more grand inflation.

His new chaotic inflation theory tells us that we live in just one of many domains of the universe. Reactions in our domain "just happened" to have been "broken" into the strong, weak and electromagnetic forces of our domain. Scalar field symmetry breaking accounted for this, and the probability amplitude of quantum theory resulted in each domain having a different set of physical constants, physical laws and numbers of dimensions.

Our domain just happened to be three-dimensional and have the set of physical laws we experience, quantum fluctuations grew in "just the right way" to produce galaxies, and chaotic inflation dispersed troublesome magnetic monopoles and massive domain walls. In addition to solving the singularity problem, new inflation was credited by Linde with solving the horizon problem, the flatness problem and several others.

It was thought that quantum theory might provide an escape from the singularity problem by preceding the BB explosion with an inflation that developed out of a giant vacuum fluctuation. But inflation didn't solve the BB problem of the acceleration of much of the mass of the universe to relativistic speeds that requires infinities of energy. Although Special Relativity tells us that not even communication is possible at speeds greater than c, both Guth's and Linde's inflation schemes involve speeds of expansion far in excess of the speed of light. Relativity's prohibition of faster than light signaling appears to have been ignored.

Inflation theories, that utilize quantum concepts on a grand scale to provide a source for the energy of a BB, and the proposal of cosmic repulsion, also on a grand scale, for its enormous inflation, do not appear to have solved any problems. They only seem to have increased the complexity of BBT beyond reasonable bounds and to introduce some new problems. Regardless of how elaborate these theories have grown, they haven't solved even the most basic BB problem; that of the singularity, an enormous violation of the law of the conservation of mass/energy.

However, if cosmologists can accept the idea that quantum vacuum fluctuations (the intrinsic energy of space) can provide energy on a scale that can produce the entire universe in a single event, it must be conceptually acceptable to them that *quantum vacuum can provide sufficient energy to generate particles of matter throughout space.* It is expected that will prove to be correct and *the cosmological constant will prove to be of sufficient magnitude to provide the minute amount of pressure required for the expansion of the universe* in accordance with NSST.

This offshoot of SST is dependent upon the existence of cosmic repulsion. If that force should be disproven, NSST would be invalidated. But it is of interest to note that, in order for there to be negative curvature in the open BB universe, there must be a repulsive force in space. As previously explained, there must be more than a mathematical formula in support of the idea of negative curvature. Standard BBT theory therefore implicitly accepts the concept of cosmic repulsion, and because inflationary BBT clearly depends on cosmic repulsion, if cosmic repulsion should be disproven, like NSST, both forms of BBT will also be invalidated.

The idea that the generation of minute particles of matter in accordance with quantum theory could be extended to the scale required for the instantaneous creation of all the matter and energy of the universe is a totally unreasonable interpretation of quantum theory. However, the generation of matter on the scale required for NSST is quite compatible with the particle-by-particle processes of that theory; and the extremely low level of cosmic repulsion required for the continuing expansion of the universe, as proposed by NSST, is well within reason.

The smoothness of the universe, the idea that the early universe was just nonuniform enough to cause the formation of galaxies and clusters, and at the same time just uniform enough to result in smoothness on a larger scale, has been a continuing problem to BBers. This concept, which might be superfluous to BBT, is also undoubtedly untrue. Uniformity was not given as a necessary condition for the solution of Einstein's equations, but merely as a simplifying assumption to facilitate their solution.

Newly discovered evidence of very large scale irregularities such as superclusters, enormous voids, sheets of galaxies, and the Great Wall of galaxies have amplified this problem. Despite these findings, many BBers continue to ignore the fact that smoothness originated as a simplifying assumption, and believe that, if observed on a sufficiently large scale, the universe would appear to be smooth.

(When the MBR was found and accepted by BBers as proof of the decoupling, logic forced them to also accept its smoothness as proof of the smoothness of the early BB. As long as they continue to believe that the MBR comes directly from the decoupling, rather from the thermalization of matter of surrounding space, it will be difficult for them to escape this logical trap.)

Closely related to this smoothness problem is the horizon problem; the problem of how matter, that has been blasted apart by a chaotic BB to beyond certain limits of time and space, could mutually interact to cause smoothing. According to relativity, that could not have occurred.

NSST, which proposes some degree of irregularities on all scales, is not troubled by a smoothness problem or by the related horizon problem.

There are many unanswered questions regarding MBR that is alleged to provide virtual proof of the BB. Several factors, such as the length of the period of the decoupling that produced that radiation, the range of temperature during that time, and the irregularities of the universe during and since then that might have distorted the received spectrum, are troublesome. Disagreements of past predictions of the present background temperature, and disagreements among BB proponents as to whether background radiation comes directly to us or whether it has been bouncing around the universe for 10 billion years, cause further concern.

If black-body photons were emitted from the decoupling in a burst, why were they not propagated as a burst? Unless space is positively curved, as ascribed to the closed universe case, which has been shown to be impossible, by what mechanism are black-body photons arriving here from the BB decoupling? If neutrinos left the BB at or near the speed of light in accordance with the normal BB scenario, why are they not also arriving from all directions of the sky?

According to BBT, the matter that became quasars left the early universe at a major fraction of the speed of light. If that is so, why are they receding from us at vast distances when black-body photons, that left in the same era and at only slightly greater speed, are continuously raining on us? Conversely, if photons from the decoupling are raining on us as a result of the curvature of space, why aren't quasars also impinging on us? Also, if the BB happened everywhere in accordance with BBT, why wouldn't one expect quasars to be distributed throughout the BB universe like other stars and galaxies?.

Despite large discrepancies between predictions and observations, because it was predicted by early BBT the presence of microwave radiation is taken as virtual proof of the great decoupling event, and thus proof of the BB. The "most remarkable circumstance" of a gigantic explosion producing uniform radiation, reasons why its spectrum is not "smeared," and an assumed red-shift of about 1,000 all go unchallenged.

How can the extremely uniform arrival of photons from all directions, that came from the early universe be reconciled with galactic formations of enormous sizes; and, if the amplitude of the received microwave signals had been predicted by BB theorists, how would that compare to the received level? According to estimates of the energy of the decoupling in Chapter 9, one might expect the MBR signal strength to be orders of magnitude greater than that received.

NSST proposes that electromagnetic radiation in portions of the spectrum may be generated concurrently with the conversion of intrinsic energy into particles of matter throughout space. That energy results in thermalization of the matter of the space surrounding us at the observed black body temperature, and at an energy level that is compatible with the received signal strength.

The abundance of light elements, such as helium and lithium, in the universe today, as predicted by standard BBT, is considered to be important evidence for the validity of that theory. However, there is considerable question about that evidence. Throughout the history of BBT, estimates of the ratio of helium to hydrogen appear to have been adjusted periodically to agree with new observations, causing doubt about the validity of these "predictions." In making these estimates the ratio of baryons to photons in the early universe has been selected as necessary to be compatible with the observed ratio of helium to hydrogen.

It has recently been found that the abundance of beryllium in ancient stars differs from that predicted by BBT. Evidence has been found that the lithium in the universe might have been produced by processes other that the BB, and that the presently observed ratio of helium to hydrogen in the universe is not in agreement with current BBT. These findings cast further doubt on the validity of the abundances of light elements in the universe as proof of a BB.

As described in Chapter 12, discrepancies concerning the time, speed and distance relationships of the BB, the Earth and quasars, including those that appear to require speeds greater than that of light, raise questions about the current interpretation of red shift upon which measurements in support of BBT are based.

Those discrepancies are explained by BBers to be the result of the curvature of space. However, according their own theory, that can only occur if the curvature of the space of the universe is positive. That explanation is given even by those who profess to believe in the open or flat BB cases that are said to have negative curvature or no curvature.

Red shift calculations of relative velocity and distance of remote bodies in the customary manner may, on the surface, appear to be consistent with BBT. But the manner in which data are applied—as a fraction of an assumed age of the universe—forces agreement with that age. As demonstrated in Chapter 12, the lack of logic of that method results in the calculation of quasar speeds in excess of that of light, and in other serious discrepancies.

The accepted interpretation of red shift presents several severe problems that cry out for a solution. Its validity as a reliable tool for estimating of relative speed and distance of massive remote bodies in space has been questioned by several cosmologists and astronomers. Observational evidence has shown a number of quasars to be close to galaxies having considerably smaller red shifts. There is a lack of correlation between quasar luminosities and their presumed distances. Spectrographs of near and far quasars show little difference. Their perceived enormous masses and luminosities, and high rates of variation of luminosity tend to discredit Doppler red shift as an accurate gauge of their velocity and distance.

The discrepancies and inconsistencies that were described in Chapter 11 concerning the apparent superluminal speeds of quasar flares also causes doubt about an interpretation of red shift that ignores the possibility of gravitational red shift (Einstein Shift) of radiation from massive stellar bodies. (Even Edwin Hubble maintained that velocities inferred from red shifts measurements should be referred to as apparent velocities.)

Theories have been presented in the past that might provide an explanation for these apparent anomalies, but none have held up. A new suggestion that might provide an explanation for this has been presented in this book. It provides a possible rationale for gravitational red shift (in addition to Doppler red shift) that could cause massive remote bodies to appear to be departing at greater than their true velocities.

Others have suggested that a relatively small cosmological constant could add to Doppler red shift. Greater red shift would result in less distant quasars than currently perceived. At lower velocities their distribution would be more linear, reducing the "clumping" that is presently ascribed to them, and discrediting the perceived rapid evolution of the early BB universe.

There is considerable question about the age of a BB universe that started with an explosion about 10 billion years ago, or as much as 15 billion years ago as postulated by some. Recent estimates of the Hubble constant indicate the BB flat universe to be only about 8 billion years old, the open BB universe only somewhat more, and the closed BB universe somewhat less. If that proves to be correct, the BB age problem is more serious than previously thought. BBT can't explain a universe that is younger than its stars.

Furthermore, if some stars of our galaxy are as old as astronomers tell us, the period since the BB could not have provided enough time for them to acquire their heavy elements from other dead and dispersed stars. Perhaps several star cycles, requiring at least tens of billions of years, might have occurred in order to have produced the abundance of elements of our surroundings.

In addition, if estimates of up to 100 billion years required for the formation of giant galactic structures (such as the recently discovered Great Wall) should prove to be correct, BBT would certainly have to be junked. Theorists would at last be forced to consider alternate cosmologies that might account for a much older universe.

BB proponents have used red shift evidence of more quasars and radio galaxies in the distant past (evidence of an evolving universe) to discredit SST, while ignoring the fact that that evidence might also discredit BBT. Fewer new galaxies, quasars and radio galaxies in recent billions of years and the clumping of distant quasars in all directions, could indicate that we are at the center of the BB universe. In that case there may be isotropy (sameness in all directions), but not homogeneity (even scattering.)

The possibility of this "Copernican Problem," which is very much at odds with standard BBT, seems to be ignored by most BB advocates. To some alternate cosmologies such as NSST, whether or not we are at the center of the universe should be of little consequence. Because of the enormity of the NSS universe, consideration of a center would seem irrelevant. Because quasar clumping (as supported by questionable interpretation of red shift data) provided evidence of an evolving universe, a lack of evolution, as postulated by old SST, was said to discredit that theory. If convincing evidence of appreciable quasar clumping should prove to be reliable, NSST might be similarly discredited.

Standard BBT, inflation theory, old and new SST, and other possible cosmological theories, suffer for lack of an explanation for the excess matter over antimatter. The only available theory that addresses the generation of matter in space is quantum theory, and it insists that for every particle generated its antiparticle is also produced. It provides no explanation for why our universe (or our vicinity of the universe) has so much more matter than antimatter. Theoretical physicists have made various attempts to explain how this might have come about, but none of those explanations are satisfactory. (Perhaps there are flaws in quantum theory that haven't been ironed out.)

BB theorists may have created an additional problem for themselves; that of the Anthropic Principle. The Great Coincidences of the Dimensionless Constants led BB theorists to the concept of fine-tuning, and from there to the various forms of the Anthropic Principle, that even went so far as to question the Copernican Principle that is BB dogma. Some cosmologists eventually realized that the border between science and theology had been crossed. That digression really has nothing to do with BBT or science. It certainly has nothing to with NSST.

The BB cosmologists of the world are certainly not cult members. But the "good old boys" of cosmology have many close ties. To the outsider their fraternization could present the appearance of a cult. One of the characteristics of this brotherhood is what has been called "reaching"; special efforts that are made to support BBT. Biased research and investigations have repeatedly been made and are continuing to be made. Often these violations of scientific method are admitted; the perpetrators apparently proud of their special efforts to support the favored theory.

Obviously these violations have been motivated by the quest for answers to questions about origins that drives humans to science, philosophy and religion. Many of us are driven to find those answers. But there aren't any short cuts. The easy path is to continue the search for rationale in support of BBT. But it's time to acknowledge the quantity and magnitude of the flaws of that theory, and to start exploring alternative cosmological possibilities.

Since the beginning of BBT, scenarios of ever increasing complexity have been built on top of the previous inventors' imaginations. Despite that, simplicity has been claimed for the various versions of BBT. Carr said the standard BB universe is "remarkably simple" and Linde told us "Chaotic inflation provides a simple solution to most of the problems of the standard BBT." He said (in 1985) that, in five years, new inflation had solved about 10 major cosmology problems in one simple model. That included solving the problem of the creation of 10^{50} tons of matter of the universe during the enormous exponential expansion that took less than 10^{-30} second. But modern BBT isn't simple, and those problems haven't gone away.

Of science and philosophy it is said that entities are not to be postulated beyond necessity. The following list is presented as an illustration of some concepts of modern BBT that may have been postulated beyond necessity and some of the associated BBT problems (in alphabetical order):

Age Problems, Anthropic Principle, Background Radiation Problems, Big Bang Everywhere, Center of the Universe Problem, Chaotic Inflation, Chronology Problems, Collapsing Universe, Conservation of Mass/Energy, Convergence Problem, Copernican Principle, Copernican Problem, enormous Cosmic Repulsion, Cosmic Strings and Sheets, Cosmological Principle, Curved Space, Cycling Universe Bounce Problem, Deceleration Problem, Domain Walls, Exotic CDM, Expanding Space, Fine-tuning, Flatness Problem (Critical Mass/Density), gigantic Galactic Formations, Grand Unified Theory, Gravitational Red Shift, The Great Coincidences of the Dimensionless Constants, the Great Event (Decoupling), Homogeneity, Horizon Problem, Inflation (Exponential Expansion), Isotropy, Light Element Problems, Magnetic Monopoles, Many Worlds, Missing Mass, Multiple Domains and Universes, Negative Energy of Gravity, New $10^{1,000,000}$ Inflation, Quasar Problems (great mass, size, luminosity and clumping), Red Shift Problems, Singularity (Cycling or One-Shot), Smoothness Problem, Speed-of-Light Problems, Superluminal Flares, Symmetry Breaking, Theory of Everything, gigantic Vacuum Fluctuations, and Zero Net Energy.

If ever a crop was ripe for reaping by William of Occam's razor, this is the time for harvest. It's totally unreasonable for scientists to continue to expend time, energy and expense to generate support for a complex and terribly flawed BBT. In a recent article, commenting on the prevalence of violations of scientific method, cosmologist Robert Oldershaw said, "In the light of all these problems, it is astounding that the big bang hypothesis is the only cosmological model that physicists have taken seriously." It's time for some alternative theories to be developed, presented and examined. Perhaps one of those should be NSST.

Centuries ago Roman philosopher Lucretius warned against "thrusting out reasoning from your mind because of its disconcerting novelty. Weigh it, rather, with a discerning judgement. Then, if it seems to you true, give in. If it is false, gird yourself to oppose it. For the mind wants to discover by reasoning what exists in the infinity of space...."

TWENTY ONE

Conclusion

Ever since the invention of BBT, as its various problems have come to light, they have, one by one, been dismissed or alternate schemes have been devised to circumvent them. None of those attempts have provided simple credible solutions to the problems, and never has the cumulative impact of the problems been addressed. Through the years BBT has become more and more complex and difficult to accept. Nevertheless, it has prevailed.

The object of this book has been to present a description of BBT that does not gloss over and dismiss its many problems, but brings them together in a single document so that their combined impact can be evaluated. In order to provide the reader with the necessary background to make an independent judgment, a considerable amount of material on relativity, quantum theory and "flights of fantasy" has been included.

As BB cosmology is examined more thoroughly, its problems become increasingly apparent and disturbing. The evidence against BBT is now so overwhelming that it is difficult to believe that anyone who is aware of the facts can continue to support such a thoroughly discredited scheme. But if BBT is invalid what is there to replace it? In order to fill that need a couple of possibilities have been mentioned. One possibility that seems to merit further consideration has been presented in some detail.

That theory, for a non-exploding near steady state universe, is similar to old Steady State Theory, but corrects the failure of SS theorists of the past to present a convincing case for the generation of new particles of matter in space in accordance with quantum theory, and for the expansion of the universe as a result of cosmic repulsion. The problems of this new near SST, based on those ideas and on classical physics, including strict adherence to the conservation of mass/energy, seem far fewer and less severe than those of the Big Bang.

Although modern cosmologists have claimed simplicity for their BB scenarios, it is obvious that the complexity of BBT has ever increased. By contrast, NSST is quite simple; and that is as it should be. As Nobelist in quantum electrodynamics Richard Feynman wrote in his down-to-earth, straightforward manner, "You can recognize the truth by its beauty and simplicity ... When you get it right, it is obvious that it is right." Certainly those comments do not apply to BBT.

Cambridge cosmologist Jayant Narlikar, a former proponent of the sadly discredited old SST (now involved in small bang ideas), quoted British astronomer Geoffrey Burbridge as saying, "The views of cosmology in any epoch are largely determined by a few strong individuals, rather than by an objective appraisal of the information available." Narlikar added to that, "Astrophysicists of today who hold the view that the "ultimate cosmological problem" has been more or less solved may well be in for a few surprises before this century runs out." Time my prove him to be correct.

Astronomer and editor of *Star Date* magazine, Jeff Kanipe, recently wrote, "The conflict between differing views of the universe presents a classic example of an established theory undergoing a revolution. Though the Big Bang model may have endured for 75 years, history is replete with erroneous scientific beliefs that survived centuries, as well as some "crack pot" theories that later became accepted."

But apparently such transitions are not easily accomplished. Max Planck is quoted as having said, "Important scientific innovation rarely makes its way by gradually winning over and converting its opponents. What does happen is that its opponents gradually die out and that the growing generation is familiar with the idea from the beginning."

According to Thomas S. Kuhn in his book of 1962, *The Structure of Scientific Revolutions*, as reviewed in *Scientific American* in May 1991, "Scientists are deeply conservative. Once indoctrinated into a paradigm, they generally devote themselves to solving 'puzzles,' problems whose solutions reinforce and extend the scope of the paradigm, rather than challenging it. Kuhn calls this 'mopping up.' But there are always anomalies, phenomena that the paradigm cannot account for or that directly contradict it. Anomalies are often ignored. But if they accumulate, they may trigger a revolution (also called a paradigm shift, although not by Kuhn), in which scientists abandon the old paradigm for a new one.

"Denying the view of science as a continual building process, Kuhn asserts that a revolution is a destructive as well as a creative event. The proposer of a new paradigm stands on the shoulders of giants and bashes them over the head. He or she is often young or new to the field, that is, not fully indoctrinated."

That may describe the present status of cosmology. A revolution may be imminent. Although there's no joy in bashing the heads of the giants of Big Bang cosmology (using the metaphor Kuhn or his reviewer borrowed from Newton), that injustice is probably inevitable; and perhaps it's time for an alternate cosmology to replace the old BBT paradigm, at least for a while.

BIBLIOGRAPHY

Abbott, Larry, *The Mystery of the Cosmological Constant* in *Scientific American*, May 1988

Arp, H. C. et al, *The Extragalactic Universe: an Alternative Viewpoint* in *Nature*, August 30, 1990

Barrow, John D. and Joseph Silk, *The Structure of the Early Universe* in *Scientific American*, April 1980

Bondi, H. and W. B. Bonnor, *Rival Theories of Cosmology* (1960)

Boslough, John, *Stephen Hawking's Universe* (1985)

Bowyer, Stuart, *Extreme Ultraviolet Astronomy* in *Scientific American* August 1994

Carr, Bernard J., *On the Origin, Evolution and Purpose of the Physical Universe* in *The Irish Astronomical Journal* March 1982

Carter, Brandon, *Large Number Coincidences and the Anthropic Principle* in *Cosmology in Confrontation of Cosmological Theories with Observational Data*, edited by M.S. Longair (1974)

Chaikin, Andrew, *Great Wall of the Cosmos* in *OMNI*, August 1991

Cornell, James, Editor, *Bubbles, Voids and Bumps in Time: The New Cosmology* (1989)

Courvoisier, Thierry and E. Ian Robson, *The Quasar 3C 273*, in *Scientific American* June 1991

Davies, Paul, *Other Worlds* (1980)

Davies, Paul, *The Edge of Infinity* (1981)

Davies, Paul, *Superforce* (1984)

Dicke, R. H., *Dirac's Cosmology and Mach's Principle*, in *Nature* November 1961

Dicus, Duane A., John R. Letaw, Doris C. Teplitz and Vigor L. Teplitz, *The Future of the Universe* in *Scientific American* March 1983

Dressler Alan, *The Large-Scale Streaming of Galaxies* in *Scientific American* September 1987

Einstein, Albert, *Relativity—The Special and General Theories* (1961)

Ellis, G. F. R, *Cosmology and Verifiability* in *Quarterly Journal of The Royal Astronomical Society* No. 3 1975

Feynman, Richard, *The Character of Physical Law* (1965)

Flam, Faye, *In Search of a New Cosmic Blueprint* in *Science* November 1991

Freedman, David H., *The Theory of Everything* in *Discover* August 1991

Freedman, Wendy L., *The Expansion Rate and Size of the Universe* in *Scientific American* November 1992

Friedman, Herbert, *The Amazing Universe* (1985)

Gale, George, *Cosmological Fecundity: Theories of Multiple Universes* (1989)

Gamow, George, *Modern Cosmology* in *Scientific American* March 1954

Gamow, George, *The Evolutionary Universe* in *Scientific American* September 1956

Gamow, George, *Biography of Physics* (1961)

Gehrels, Neil et al, *The Compton Gamma Ray Observatory* in *Scientific American* December 1993

Gibbons, Ann, I*n the Beginning, Let There Be Beryllium* in *Science* January 1992

Goldberg, Stanley, *Understanding Relativity* (1984)

Gott, J. Richard III, James E. Gunn, David N. Schramm & Beatrice M. Tinsley, *Will the Universe Expand Forever?* in *Scientific American* March 1976

Gregory, Stephen A. and Laird A. Thompson, *Superclusters and Voids in the Distribution of Galaxies* in *Scientific American* March 1982

Groth, Edward J., P. James E. Peebles, Michael Seldner and Raymond M. Soneira, *The Clustering of Galaxies* in *Scientific American* November 1977

Gulkis, Samuel, Philip M. Lubin, Stephan S. Meyer and Robert F. Silverberg, *The Cosmic Background Explorer* in *Scientific American* January 1990

Guth, Alan H. and Paul J. Steinhardt, *The Inflationary Universe* in *Scientific American* May 1984

Halliwell, Jonathan J., *Quantum Cosmology and the Creation of the Universe* in *Scientific American* December 1991

Hart, Michael H. and Ben Zuckerman, Editors. *Extraterrestrials; Where Are They?* (1982)

Hawking, Stephen W., *The Quantum Mechanics of Black Holes* in *Scientific American* January 1977

Hawking, Stephen W., *A Brief History of Time* (1982)

Hoyle, Fred, *Astronomy* (1962)

Hoyle, Fred, *The Nature of the Universe* (1960)

Huchra, John P., *The Hubble Constant* in *Science* 17 April 1992

Jayawardhana, Ray, *The Age Paradox* in *Astronomy* June 1993

Kanipe, Jeff, *Beyond the Big Bang* in *Astronomy* April 1992

Kaufmann, William J.,III, *Relativity and Cosmology* (1973)

Krauss, Lawrence M, *Dark Matter in the Universe* in *Scientific American* December 1986

Kuhn, Thomas S, *The Structure of Scientific Revolutions* as reviewed in *Scientific American* May 1991

Leslie, John, *Physical Cosmology and Philosophy* (1990)

Linde, Andrei, T*he Universe: Inflation Out of Chaos* in *New Scientist* March 1985

Margon, Bruce, *The Origin of the Cosmic X-Ray Background* in *Scientific American* January 1983

McGraw-Hill Encyclopedia of Science and Technology 7th Edition 1992

McMullin, Ernan, *Is Philosophy Relevant to Cosmology?* in *American Philosophical Quarterly* July 1981

Muller, Richard A., *The Cosmic Background Radiation and the New Aether Drift* in *Scientific American* May 1978

Narlikar, Jayant, *Was There a Big Bang?* in New Scientist July 1981

Oldershaw, Robert, *What's wrong with the new physics* in *New Scientist* December 22, 29, 1990

Osmer, Patrick, *Quasars as Probes of the Distant and Early Universe* in *Scientific American* February 1982

Pagels, Heinz R., *Perfect Symmetry* (1985)

Pagels, Heinz R., *A Cozy Cosmology* in *The Sciences* March 1985

Peebles, P. J. E. and David T. Wilkinson, *The Primeval Fireball* in *Scientific American* June 1967

Peebles, Schramm, Turner and Kron, *The case for the relativistic hot Big Bang cosmology* in *Nature* 29 August 1991

Rees, Martin, *The 13,000,000,000 Year Bang* in *New Scientist* December 1976

Rees, Martin and Joseph Silk, *The Origin of Galaxies* in *Scientific American* June 1970

Rowan-Robinson, Micheal, *Cosmology* (1977)

Rubin, Vera C., *Dark Matter in Spiral Galaxies* in *Scientific American* June 1983

Sagan, Carl and Frank Drake, *The search for Extraterrestrial Intelligence* in *Scientific American* May 1975

Sandage, Allen R., *The Red Shift* in *Scientific American* September 1956

Schmidt, Maarten and Francis Bello, *The Evolution of Quasars* in *Scientific American* May 1971

Schramm, David N. and Gary Steigman, *Particle Accelerators Test Cosmological Theory* in *Scientific American* June 1988

Sciama, Dennis, *Cosmology before and after Quasars* in *Scentific American* September 1967

Shapley, Harlow, Editor, *The Source Book on Astronomy* (1960)

Shapiro, Robert and Gerald Feinberg, *Life Beyond Earth* (1980)

Silk, Joseph, *The Big Bang* (1980, revised 1989)

Sobel, Dava, *George Smoot Interview* in *OMNI* March 1994

Swinburne, Richard, *Argument from the Fine-Tuning of the Universe* in *Physical Cosmology and Philosophy* edited by John Leslie (1990)

Thorne, Kip S, *The Search for Black Holes* in *Scientific American* December 1974

Trefil, James S., *The Moment of Creation* (1983)

Tryon, Edward P., *Is the Universe a Vacuum Fluctuation?* in *Nature* December 1973

Velinkin, Alaxander, *Cosmic Strings* in *Scientific American* December 1987

Veltman, Martinus J. G., *The Higgs Boson* in *Scientific American* November 1986

Webster, Adrian, *The Cosmic Background Radiation* in *Scientific American* August 1974

Weinerg, Steven, *The First Three Minutes* (1977)

Wheeler, John Archibald, *Beyond the End of Time* in *Gravitation* by Charles W. Misner et al, (1971)

Wilczek, Frank, *The Cosmic Asymmetry between Matter and Antimatter* in *Scientific American* December 1980

Wilkes, Belinda, *The Emerging Picture of Quasars* in *Astronomy*, December 1991

Name Index

(See also: SUBJECT INDEX)

G

Galois, Everiste, 26
Gamow, George, 22, 45-46, 58, 89-
90, 97-100, 106, 112, 135, 160,
163-164, 185, 189, 194, 197
Gell-Mann, Murray 27, 40, 77, 161,
164
Geller, Margaret, 91, 164
Gide, Andre, 150
Giovanelli, Riccardo, 192
Glashow, Sheldon, 43, 163-164
Gold, Thomas, 62, 163-164, 183,
186
Goldberg, Stanley, 22
Gott, J. Richard, 48, 58, 60, 92, 108,
136, 164, 188
Gulkis, Samuel, 137
Gunn, James E., 48, 58, 60, 92, 136-
137, 163-164
Guth, Alan H., 83-87, 91, 93, 138,
142, 161, 164, 170, 175, 212-213

H

Hawking, S. W., 59, 64, 78-79, 108,
142, 149, 159, 163-164, 173, 188-
189
Haynes, Martha, 192
Heisenberg, Werner, 37-38, 41, 43,
150, 160
Herman, Robert, 62, 98, 186
Higgs, Peter, 38, 43
Holberg, Erik B., 193
Holtzman, John, 192
Hoyle, Fred, 46, 62, 112, 115, 164,
183, 185-186
Hubble, Edwin, 19, 45-46, 49, 59-60,
111, 117, 119, 135, 160, 194, 197,
200, 208, 217
Huchra, John, 91, 117, 164, 195
Humason, Milton, 45-46, 117, 160,
194, 208

J

Jordan, Pascual, 37-38, 201
Joyce, James, 27

K

Kanipe, Jeff 115, 224
Kron, R. G., 49, 61, 114, 188, 200,
202-203
Kuhn, Thomas S., 171, 225

L

Lebedev, P. N., 17
Lemaitre, Georges, 45-46, 61, 160
Leslie, John, 186
Letaw 149
Linde, Andrei, 59, 62, 74, 85-87, 93,
138, 142, 161, 164, 168-169, 175,
212-213, 220
Lorentz, H. A., 15, 18
Lovell, Bernard, 182
Lubin, Philip M., 137
Lynden-Bell, Donald, 163-164

M

Mach, Ernst, 21, 70
Margon, Bruce, 109
Maxwell, 17, 19
McKellar, Andrew, 189
McMullin, Ernan, 90, 171, 180
Meyer, Stephen S., 137
Michelson, Albert A., 14-15
Mills, Robert, 43
Misner, Charles, 164
Morley, Edwards W., 14-15
Morrison, Philip, 164
Muller, Richard A., 100

N

Narlikar, Jayant, V. 180, 224
Newton, Isaac, 15, 19, 119, 161, 199,
201, 225
Nostradamus, 99

O

Olbers, Henry, 198
Oldershaw, Robert, 165, 175, 221
Oppenheimer, J. Robert, 37

Subject Index

(See also: NAME INDEX)

equivalence of gravity and acceleration 74-75, 201, 207
equivalence of mass and energy 15, 17-18, 38, 74, 86, 186, 204
escape velocity 57-58, 77, 196
ether 13-15, 17, 42
Euclidean geometry 19, 47, 58, 141-142, 201, 203-204, 210
event horizon 77-78, 108, 125-126, 130, 142
evolving universe 50, 53, 55, 94-95, 128, 130, 168, 178, 183-184, 200, 202, 207, 210, 218
ex nihilo (See out-of-nothing)
excess matter, excess matter problem 87, 147-151, 171, 181, 190, 203, 219
European Laboratory for Particle Physics (CERN) 28
exchange force 36
exclusion principle 36
expanding space 48, 66-67, 84, 143, 161, 177-178, 210, 220
extra-terrestrial life 156

F

false vacuum 69, 83, 85, 186-187
families of particles 27, 112
faster than light signaling 48, 86, 213
Fermilab 28, 51, 157
fermions 26-27, 30, 36, 41
fifth force 197
fine-tuning 90, 93, 154-157, 204, 219, 220
fission 113
Fitzgerald contraction 14
fixed-rate universe 54, 59-61, 102, 118-120, 134-135, 140, 142, 199, 200, 204, 208-210
flares 122-124, 127-128, 130, 141, 217, 220
flat space, flat universe, balanced universe x, 46,-47, 54, 57-59, 61-63, 65-67, 78, 83, 86, 102, 106-107, 118, 120, 124, 134-136, 140, 142-143, 145, 155, 170, 175, 181, 196, 200, 203-204, 208-211, 215-216, 218
flatness problem 59, 62, 84-87, 205, 210, 213, 220

flavors of quarks 29, 40
fossil stars 113
fractals 41
fusion 31, 49, 113-115, 178, 192, 209
FWR cosmology, FWR model 46, 61, 196, 208-210

G

galactic drift, motion, speed, orbit 64, 107, 139
GALLEX 103
gallium-71 103
gamma radiation 26, 38, 79, 109-110, 190
Gamma Ray Observatory satellite 79, 110
gauge theory 25, 32, 41, 43-44, 72, 85
generations of stars (See stellar cycles)
geodesics 22
germanium-71 103
globular clusters 136, 192
gluons 30-32, 38-39, 51-52, 71-72
Grand Unified Theory (GUT) 32, 44, 50-52, 70-73, 75, 85, 87, 148-149, 181, 212, 220
graphite 137
gravitation, gravitational fields, gravity (throughout)
gravitational constant 124, 153, 155, 201
gravitational red shift 19, 124, 126-131, 143-144, 200, 202, 217, 220
gravitational waves 63, 170
gravitinos 63, 170
gravitons 25, 30, 32, 38, 50-51, 75, 187, 207
Great Attractor 91, 107, 144
Great Coincidences of Dimensionless Constants 154, 157, 219, 220
great event (See decoupling)
Great Wall 66, 90-91, 138, 174, 176-177, 214, 218
group theory 25, 40-41, 43

H

hadrons 26-27, 29-31, 39-40, 51-52
Hale Observatory 60, 129, 137, 164, 193, 202
Hawking radiation 64, 78-79, 108, 188-189
heavy elements 113-115, 136-137, 154, 192, 203, 218
heavy hydrogen 112
helium 53, 97, 112, 113, 115, 137, 198, 199, 209, 216
Higgs boson 25, 30, 32, 43-44, 72, 85
Higgs field, force 32, 38, 50-51, 71, 74
homogeneity xi-xii, 47, 49, 89, 91, 94, 121, 131, 144, 155, 161, 168, 174, 202, 204, 218, 220
Hopkins Ultraviolet Telescope 170
horizon problem 48, 62, 64, 84-87, 93, 213-214, 220
hot dark matter 170
Hubble constant 19, 54, 59, 65, 84, 86, 117-118, 120-121, 133-137, 154, 175, 185, 195, 208, 218
Hubble expansion xii, 49, 59, 110, 118, 197, 200
Hubble Space Telescope 113
Hubble time, Hubble age 59-60, 65, 118, 120, 133-134, 136, 153, 208
Hubble's law 46, 49, 117-118, 194, 208
hydrogen 38, 53, 97, 112-113, 136, 185, 190, 192-193, 199, 209, 216

I

index of refraction 14, 18
inflation 81-87 and throughout
infrared radiation 100, 109-110, 127, 138, 188
Institute of Theoretical Physics (See Copenhagen Institute)
intelligent life 156
interference patterns 13-14
intermediate vector bosons 31, 44
interstellar gas 109
intrinsic angular momentum 26
intrinsic energy 186-187, 191, 194, 197, 201, 213, 216

iron 113, 136
isotopes 112, 136
isotropy xi-xii, 47, 64, 89, 90-91, 94, 121, 131, 155, 161, 168, 174, 218, 220

L

lamdas 30
Large Electron-Proton (LEP) Collider 28
Large Magellanic Cloud 65
laser beam 22
lensing 208
leptons 26-28, 31, 36, 51-52, 71, 103
lepton era 103
light elements 49, 53, 111-116, 160, 184, 192, 198-199, 203, 209, 216, 220
light supersymmetrical particles (LSPs) 75
lithium 53, 112, 114-115, 198-199, 216
Look back 119-120
Lorentz transformations 15, 19, 23, 40, 119, 130
Los Alamos National Laboratory 211
low surface brightness (LSB) galaxies 193
Lowell Observatory 192

M

MACHOS 63, 170
Mach's principle 21
magnetic monopoles 63, 71-74, 85-87, 154, 170, 191, 212, 220
main sequence 125
many-worlds, multiple domains, universes 73-74, 81, 154-155, 220
Markarian 129
mass width 31
matrix mathematics 37
Max Planck Institute of Astrophysics 129
Maxwell's equations 17, 19
MBR amplitude, energy, signal strength 105-106, 215-216
mediators, mediation 26, 30-32, 36, 51, 75, 207
Mercury 21

mesons 27-30, 39, 52, 148-149, 187
meteorites 102, 136-137
Michelson-Morley experiment 14-15
microwave background radiation
(MBR) 97-110 and throughout
mirror image symmetry 148
missing mass, missing matter, missing
mass problem 47, 52, 58-59, 62-
63, 71-72, 87, 138, 143, 169-170,
201, 205, 209-211, 220
mixmaster universe 164
Mount Wilson Observatory 117
muons, mu mesons 27-28, 51-52
muon neutrinos 52
mutuality of Special Relativity 16,
23

N

negative gravity 67, 69, 84, 196-197,
212, 220
negatively curved space x, 22-23, 46,
58, 66-67, 103, 107, 124, 178,
195-196, 210, 213, 216
neutralinos 63, 170
neutrinos 27-29, 39, 51-52, 63, 103-
104, 110, 169-170, 187, 215
neutron stars 77-78, 109, 125-127
New General Catalog (NGC) 128-
129
new inflation 62, 74, 85-87, 93,
213, 220
new steady state theory 183-205,
208-214, 216, 218-219, 221, 224
nonbaryonic matter (See cold dark
matter)
novae 115, 137, 198
nuclear reactions 18, 31, 38, 53, 97-
98, 103, 113, 125, 135
nucleons 30

O

observer participation 37, 73, 150-
151
Occam's razor 220
Olber's paradox 198
one-shot singularity 61, 182, 211,
220
opaque universe 53, 98

open space, open universe x, 46-47,
54, 57-59, 61, 63, 65-67, 78, 94,
102-103, 118, 124, 134-136, 142-
143, 178, 181, 200, 204, 209-210,
213, 216, 218
out-of-nothing (ex nihilo) 61, 81,
187, 212
oxygen 113, 137

P

particle pairs 31, 51, 70, 73, 78,
171, 208
Perfect Cosmological Principle 185,
199, 203
periodic table 114
photino 63, 170
photomultiplier tube 26
pilot-wave model 150
pions, pi mesons 27, 30, 39, 71
Planck's constant 27, 35-36, 39, 153
Planck's length 82
Planck's time 50
planetary nebulae 133-134
plasma 53, 73, 97, 115
plasma theory 184, 198, 211
plutonium 136
point particles 40-41
polarization 26, 37, 139
positrons 28, 31, 38, 52, 70-71, 84,
109-110, 147
probability amplitude, probability
distribution 38, 43, 73-74, 81-83,
150, 174, 212
Project Cyclops 156
proton decay 27, 71, 148-149
pulsars 109, 127

Q

quantum chromodynamics (QCD)
31, 39, 70, 77
quantum electrodynamics (QED)
31, 39, 41, 43, 70, 73, 84, 224
quantum fluctuation (See vacuum
fluctuation)
quantum gravity 82, 86, 90, 180
quantum theory, mechanics, physics
35-44 and throughout
quantum vacuum 81-82, 84, 184,
187, 194, 208, 213